John Celona
The Power Chef®

Turkey goes here.

Here's the table *almost* all laid out for our annual
Holiday Party. Hungry people coming soon!

REACH OUT!

- Email me at ThePowerChef@gmail.com. Priority
  given to folks who buy a book!

- Go to www.ThePowerChef.com for tips, recipes, and
  my blog.

- Follow me on Twitter @ThePowerChef.

- Check out ThePowerChef channel on YouTube for video episodes.

DEDICATION

This book is dedicated to my spouse and partner, Sing Gong, without whose inspiration, support (and recipe testing!) it would never have come to fruition. Also to our furry babies Pawlina Paraskova CG (now departed) and CoCo Giselle for putting it all in perspective by sitting on my lap at critical junctures to temporarily stop all progress.

WHAT PEOPLE ARE SAYING ABOUT "THE POWER CHEF":

"Truly, the Food of the Gods." —*Zeus*

"I agree." —*H.G. Wells*

"If I had this cookbook before leaving Elba, the army would have been well-fed and victorious." —*Napoleon Buonaparte*

"This may well be the most important cookbook ever written. Then again, it may not. Actually, I have no idea. I did not even author this quote." —*Craig Clairborne*

"John *who*?" —*Martha Stewart*

"Hahahahaha. Next question." —*Paula Deen*

"I really love John's cooking, and am so appreciative when he makes me something. I must confess, though, that I do not understand his sense of humor." —*Magen Gong, John's mother-in-law*

"Please buy my honey's cookbook. He does a remarkable job of tricking me into eating healthy food that tastes good." —*Sing Gong, John's spouse*

"This cookbook is meant to be entertaining, but actually has real recipes in it you can make. I hope you enjoy reading it and trying them out." —*John Celona*

"Meow."[1] —*CoCo Giselle, John's cat*[1]

---

[1] "Where's my fat free turkey breast?":

Just back from chasing turtles and fish in Hawaii.
None of the turtles were enthusiastic about the soup idea.

CONTENTS

Finishing the swim on my way to the bike leg. I'm going to be hungry!

THE POWER OF FOOD, FITNESS & FUN

Everybody loves to eat. Nobody likes to count portions or worry about their weight. That includes me. I love to eat.

This book is a comprehensive, lifestyle self-help approach to eating as much as you want and looking great. The secret is changing what you eat, and balancing what you take in with what you put out. Bite it and burn it is my motto. Seconds are always allowed. The power part is making this fun, great tasting, and easy. It works whether you're eating in or out. This book covers both.

The Power of Food, Fitness & Fun. That's what can make you a Power Chef.
I started off as a fat kid. It was not a lot of fun. My parents had to buy me large-waisted pants and get them shortened. Gym class was an embarrassing ordeal. I spent a lot of time staring in the mirror and wishing.

Then I started cooking and exercising. Cooking I started really young. Nothing special at first; just trying to make what Mom made.

Exercising I started the day after my fifteenth birthday. I was one of the world's slowest joggers. Still am. I just look like I must be fast. Nope! It was the power of good food and good fitness and having fun doing both that made the difference for me. It can for you, too.

This is not a diet. This is a long term, permanent change to how one eats which, combined with some exercise, permanently reduces body fat. It has worked for me for thirty years—despite my own and my family's history of weight issues.

This approach has taking me a long way. In forty-plus years of cooking, I've made great, healthier versions of everything from fried chicken to fettucini for folks ranging from small dinner parties to pool parties for 150 guests. I use unique and time-saving methods and every powered device I can muster. Hence The Power Chef: awesome results for your dinner plate and body with minimal time or effort wasted. Having fun along the way is key to sticking with it.

In this book, you'll find simple recipes and ones fit for an emperor—all following this approach. It even has a recipe for the fastest, simplest, and best tasting cup of coffee you'll ever drink. Plus a section on how to follow this approach when eating out—especially valuable if you're on the road and eating out a lot (like I used to do!).

There are three, simple secrets to having Power Food at each and every one of your meals. Allow me to explain.

POWER FOOD

THE THREE SECRETS OF POWER FOOD

Watch The Fat	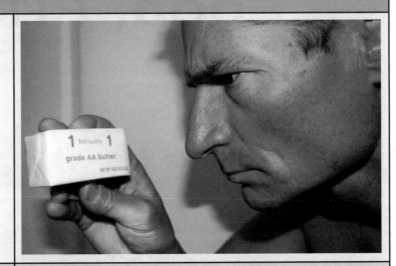
Balance Higher Fat Foods with Low-Fat, High-Fiber Foods	
Load up on Good Carbs and Cut Bad Carbs	

Watch The Fat

This doesn't mean eliminating the fat. Fat is a huge part of what makes food taste good and satisfying. Most entirely fat-free foods I've tasted—from salad dressings to desserts—I find just dreadful. I don't even like the taste of low-fat milk. I wouldn't want to live eating food like this.

But there's a huge difference between having a little fat for flavor and the amount of fat one finds in most foods. Take popcorn, for example. The variety you get at the movies (even if you ask them to skip the extra butter at the end) has enough fat that you might as well just plop it directly on your waistline instead of eating it.

As you'll see in my Perfect Popcorn recipe, instead I start with air-popped popcorn and drizzle just a little bit (a few tablespoons) of real melted butter over it, preferably French or European-style butter. This infuses the whole batch with a wonderful real butter aroma and taste and keeps popcorn in the healthy, whole-grain category. This kind of popcorn you can eat as much of as you like—and I do!

I follow this approach in all my recipes: a little fat for great flavor, but no more than you need for flavor. It's a big part of why people (including me!) love my cooking, and why I can stick with eating and looking this way for decade after decade.

Balance Higher Fat Foods with Low-Fat, High-Fiber Foods

Some foods are just high in fat and there's no way getting around it. If someone actually managed to make a fat-free bacon I shudder to think what it might taste like.

But you can still include high-fat foods with their big flavor punch as part of a healthy meal—if you balance them out with low-fat, high-fiber foods. Then the overall balance of the meal comes out okay.

For example, I include bacon in my somewhat untraditional Pasta Carbonara recipe. First (as I always do with bacon), I cook it until crisp and drain off most of the fat. This is part of watching the fat. Then, it's combined with generous portions of low-fat, high-fiber foods: in this case, whole wheat pasta and lots of steamed cauliflower. Sometimes I'll also throw in pieces of skinless chicken to pump up the protein content. The result is a dish that tastes great, is satisfying and filling to eat, and won't add pounds on the spot.

Awwwrrright! Now we wants some *good* food what we can EAT!

Sometimes, as with the Carbonara, the balancing happens in a single dish. Other times, as with my 60 Minute Barbecued Steak Dinner, the balancing comes from other things you have at the meal, such as a tossed salad or a big helping of a steamed vegetable.

When in doubt, have a can of corn or some tossed salad with a little oil and vinegar. It's that simple. The third secret also helps out.

Load Up on Good Carbs and Cut Bad Carbs

Like people, all carbs are created equal. The issue comes with what happens to them after that!

Good carbs are the ones that stay close to the way they grew, otherwise known as whole foods. This includes whole grains, vegetables, and fruits. These I load up on and don't count quantities. More is better. Whole grains include whole wheat, brown rice, barley, oats, polenta—all the stuff you know you love!

And with good reason, I might add. Good carbs pack a considerable nutritional punch. They are loaded with vitamins, minerals, antioxidants, fiber, some protein, and, indeed, are the basic energy source your body is designed to run on.

As an added bonus, the fiber in good carbs helps keep things moving along and reduces absorption of calories from the food you eat. "Regularity" is a beautiful thing.

Then there's the matter of Bad Carbs. This is what happens to good carbs when they're refined to remove most of what's really good for you (the vitamins, fiber, protein, etc.) until what's left is basically just the starch or sugar that used to be part of a whole food. Think white flour and white sugar.

These have gotten a bad rap, and with good reason. Shorn of their natural accompaniments, these carbs are absorbed quickly and lead to rapid rises in blood sugar level (the "sugar rush."). Then, your body reacts to this onslaught by pumping out insulin, which crashes your blood sugar level—leaving you feeling tired, hungry, and wanting to eat something and start the whole process over again.

It's a viscous cycle that quite readily takes you to a more "prosperous" looking physique. This is one cycle I don't want to get on!

So I avoid bad carbs, trying to cut them to the absolute minimum in my diet. These days, it's surprisingly easy to stick with whole grains, vegetables, and fruits. They are now found in every grocery store. Even some Chinese restaurants offer brown rice instead of the usual refined white variety.

I load up on the good carbs (whole grains, fruits and vegetables), and strictly limit the bad carbs (white flour and refined sugars). I always include generous portions of good carbs in a meal to balance out the fatty things (meats, cheese, nuts, oils, etc.) For me, that always includes a generous helping of vegetables (including salads) and usually some whole grains, too.

Like cooking bacon until crisp and draining off the fat, many recipes in this book reduce unnecessary fat. My Easy Oven Roasted Chicken gets a lot of the fat melted off with high temperature roasting on a vertical rack but, even then, I'll often have some of the crisp skin and meat on a slice of whole wheat toast.

Brown rice is pretty easy to find in the store, but whole wheat bread much less so than what you might think. Lots of breads look brown and have names like "9 Grain" or "Oats and Grains." But, unless the bread actually says "Whole Wheat Bread," the first and largest ingredient listed is usually white flour. Even this gets gussied up with a description like "Enriched flour"—which means white flour to which some vitamins have been added.

And, to make it more difficult, sleuthing this out in the store requires reading teeny weeny listings of ingredients when you may not have your reading glasses with you. Easiest just to look for "Whole Wheat" in the name.

Call me an unreformed Carb Lover: I'll confess. I just stick to the good carb varieties. For me, they're an important part of how I put everything together and balance everything out to keep the same trousers (more or less!) fitting year after year.

Watch the fats, balance high fat with low-fat, high-fiber, load the good carbs and cut the bad carbs. Those are my Power Food secrets. The recipes in this book can help get you started on making Power Food a part of your healthy life.

But let's not forget the "burn it" part of "Bite it and Burn It." Power Fitness is part of the picture.

POWER FITNESS

We've all heard it: "you need to work out more." Could be from family members, a spouse, or even a close friend. If you hear it from a doctor, chances are the doctor is overweight (and needs to work out more or eat less!).

Getting the right balance between intake and output is not easy, but being out of balance usually sends the scale heading north. I, for one, don't like squeezing into the pants that used to fit so well, and don't like the thought of going out to buy bigger ones. That's like an admission of defeat. And it's not especially healthy, for a list of reasons that seems to be growing longer by the day.

Hence my motto:

Bite It and Burn It

If I work out less, I eat less. But, generally, I love to eat. So one way of keeping the poundage steady is to eat great tasting, but more healthy (lower fat!) food, as in the recipes in this book. It's a lot easier to add two less pats of butter than to spend an additional 20 minutes on the treadmill.

Another way is to add enough exercise to burn off the calories you're taking in. This gets us to the dreaded "workout."

Personally, I'm against "working out." I get more than enough work at work. Add a little yard work, housework, working on my taxes, and working on the "honey do" list and there seems to me more than enough work to go around. I see little reason to add to the list.

So my suggestion is to do something you find enjoyable and gets you moving and sweaty, and is maybe even relaxing. The last is the main motivator for me. I go for a run or a swim not to work more, but to get away from work and the phone and the email and relax for a bit. Nothing leaves me feel more tight, sore, and cranky than a day without a movement break away from all the work.

A brisk walk is also a great way to get some cardio in. Take your favorite route and enjoy being outdoors. Some of my friends love to go for a walk by the neighbors' houses and see what they're up to.

Different types of movement do this for different people. My spouse only dances. Sound silly? You wouldn't think so after attending a real 90-minute dance class.

For other people, it's doing something social, like a group exercise class in one of the innumerable varieties (aerobics, boot camp, body pump, dance class, water aerobics, etc.) or even a masters' swim workout. (Some might argue that, with all the time spent with your head in the water and little time for conversation, masters' swimming is distinctly antisocial, but that's another matter!)

The variety is nearly endless. There must be some kind of movement you would find enjoyable.

I do believe everyone can get there. We were all born with a lot more body than is needed to work a fork and the remote control. Getting more enjoyment out of it than our mostly sedentary, mechanically-assisted lifestyles requires is within everyone's grasps.

Not all movement activities are created equally. Some are better at building cardiovascular fitness, others at building strength and bone density (very important for women!), and others flexibility or coordination. For example, a brisk walk or exercise class are great for cardiovascular fitness, while resistance movement (weights, kettle balls, etc.) are good for strength training. Yoga builds flexibility and strength at the same time.

Seemed to me that a good movement "stew" would hit all the points, just like the FDA's food pyramid covers all the food groups.

Not wanting to recreate the wheel, I looked around for an analogous fitness pyramid. Turns out there are lots—but they all are aimed at progressing to competition, and left some stuff out. Nothing wrong with racing, of course, but I don't see why one needs to race to stay in shape. (Disclaimer: I did do a lot of racing, but presently don't. My excuse is that I already have enough t-shirts!)

So I made up my own pyramid, which included the various things emphasized by different types of movement: cardiovascular fitness, strength, flexibility, and coordination. Here it is.

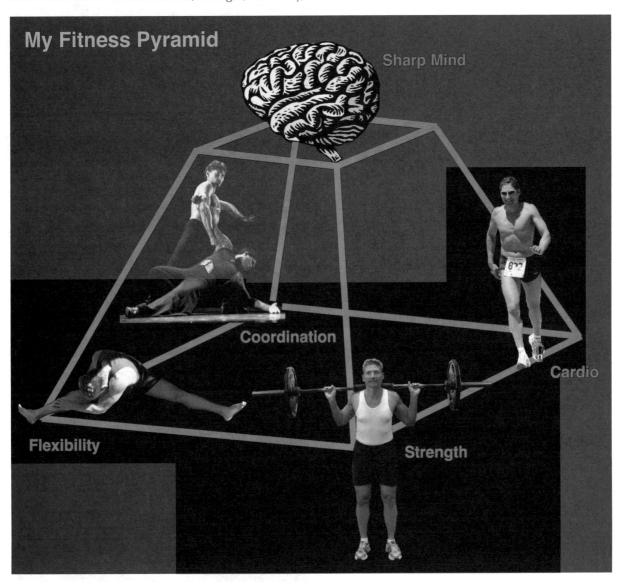

Yes, there is a top of the pyramid: sharp mind. It's there because of a brilliant theory I have which will be a shoo-in for a Nobel prize in medicine as soon as I get more experimental data: Your Brain Is Connected To Your Body. Novel, huh? I'll spare you the details of the studies on senior citizens to improve their mental acuity and memory. I already feel quite "senior" enough to be in need of mental challenges and conditioning. I'll summarize this as my Three (Not-So!) Secrets of Power Fitness:

The Three Secrets of Power Fitness

Have Fun

Stick With It

Work the Whole Pyramid

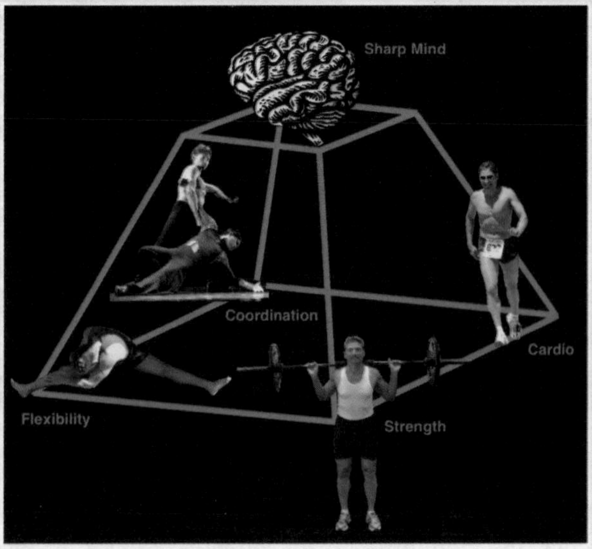

Follow these and you'll get a whole lot more out of your fitness program, and there's a lot better chance you'll stick with it! And you'll avoid suffering the fate of uncountably many friends of mine who focus on one or two activities until The Injury hits. Unfortunately, the conversation often goes like this:

"How's the biking going?"

"Oh, I can't bike right now."

"I'm sorry to hear that. How come?"

"My back is bothering me."

Of course, I had on previous occasions politely inquired about stretching ("Don't do it.") or some strength training ("I only need cardio for the health benefits.") to no avail.

Fitness pyramids missing legs fall over, just like food pyramids do!

A headless pyramid I don't even want to think about.

POWER FUN

I'll be the last one to suggest I can tell people how to have fun. Some folks, for example, actually enjoy shopping. For me, it's more a matter of identifying and acquiring the target with the least time, effort, and cost. And I've been told that some people enjoy watching bridge played on television. Go figure.

I can, however, offer a few thoughts on getting more fun out of two activities that many people don't enjoy: cooking and exercising. I enjoy these a lot and do both almost every day. They're key contributors to my enjoyment of one activity everybody likes: eating! And if you think you already enjoy eating, just think how much more you'll enjoy it when the food tastes great and you don't have to worry about its effect on your body!

Allow me to offer my three secrets of power fun at least insofar as they pertain to cooking (the main topic of this book) and to exercising.

The Three Secrets of Power Fun

Make Abundant Use of Power Tools

Enjoy the Time; Don't Waste It

Give Yourself a Break

Make Abundant Use of Power Tools

This doesn't mean just using electrically or gas powered tools, it also means using the right tool for the job. And why a picture of my Porsche? Well, not only is it the right tool for racing, it's also the perfect catering car. With its mid-engine layout, the back trunk is warmed by the engine while the front trunk stays cool. Every Thanksgiving when I'm heading off to the family gathering, the just-cooked turkey goes into the back trunk to stay warm while salads and relishes go into the front trunk. What could be more perfect?

Okay, so one can be a very fine cook without a Porsche. But other tools in your kitchen are fairly critical. A good, sharp set of knives is crucial, as are good pots and a hot stove. I like the all-aluminum pots because they conduct the heat so much better than ones with any stainless steel in them. There are many makes of these, a lot of them anodized so you don't have to worry about acidic foods (such as tomatoes or fruit) leaching the metals, and even Costco has their own set now.

Copper pots I've never cooked with so I can't say if that makes a difference, but stainless steel pots are to be avoided. Likewise, I don't care for heavy, enameled cast iron pots, though I do have a cast iron skillet for certain uses (such as Cajun blackened fish).

A very hot stove is also key, and here the clear choice is gas. There are now lots of choices for commercial-type stoves with space for large pots and very hot flames. Look for a burner rating of 12,000 btu or more. Electric cooktops are simply dreadful to cook on and infrared even worse.

Good, all-aluminum pots and a hot, gas cooktop alone will revolutionize your cooking, making short work of searing and sautéing.

As for ovens, I like a gas oven for all roasting and baking breads and pizzas, and a convection electric oven for cakes, cookies, and the like. If you can only have one oven, go for the gas oven. For example, a gas oven heated to 450°F is a key element of my roast chicken.

Probably the only other critical power tools for cooking are a food processor, a spice grinder, a good mixer, and a blender. My KitchenAid mixer does a great job on all sorts of jobs, including kneading pizza dough. A small, inexpensive coffee mill works great for grinding spices. I'd suggest using one just for spices so you don't end up with cumin-flavored coffee or coffee-flavored chile!

Don't forget the hot air popcorn popper! I couldn't rent a movie without one. I also have a meat grinder and a chinese steaming pot set, but these one can make do without.

Having the right tools makes cooking a lot easier and more enjoyable. I can't describe the frustrations at having to do without them once you've gotten used to them. An investment in these will bring you years of enjoyment in the kitchen.

For exercising, I'll be brief. Join a well-equipped health club. Almost all I've been in have enough for what you need. On the other hand, I've never seen facilities in a hotel, resort, or apartment complex which I would even rate as "adequate." It used to be good equipment meant Nautilus, but now the brands are too numerous to mention.

I like to swim, and that means a pool of at least 25 yards in length (the standard, non-Olympic length). I've swim in 50 meter-long Olympic pools with wide-lanes and gutters to keep the waves down and they are truly wonderful. My club's pool is only 25 yards, but the rest of the facility is great, so I make do. Likewise, I've never encountered an apartment, hotel, or resort pool which did the trick. Always so short that after a few strokes you're at the wall again. No fun.

Enjoy the Time; Don't Waste It

I get a lot of enjoyment out of cooking with the right tools, as I've mentioned. I also strive to keep the effort down to a minimum by only doing the things that make a real difference in how the food turns out and skipping the rest.

These time- and effort-saving tips are throughout the book (often in boxes like the one at right), but let me give a few examples so you get the idea.

> Power Food tips appear in boxes like this throughout the book. They could be about saving time and effort, about finding the right ingredients, keeping the fat in balance, etc.

For example, I use fresh garlic all the time, but never peel it myself. Too much time and trouble. Instead, I buy the plastic containers of peeled garlic cloves and pop them in the freezer. When I need garlic, 30 seconds in the microwave and they're ready to go.

Similarly, I rarely make chicken stock, and usually only when I have bones left over for some reason. Chicken stock base, which is a paste and comes in plastic or glass containers, does the job wonderfully. A few tablespoons flavors a whole pot. The opened container goes in the fridge and is ready when you need it. Dry chicken bullion cubes I find simply awful. Canned chicken stock can be good (depending on the brand), but it's a lot of trouble to keep buying cans and reducing it down when you need more concentrated flavor. The stock base tastes just as good to me and is much easier.

Good tools and using shortcuts whenever they're good enough will get you a long way to enjoying cooking more. I'll offer another suggestion: don't cook any more than you're inclined to.

That's right: this is a cookbook advising against cooking all the time.

Sometimes, I haven't the time to cook or just don't feel like it. Sound familiar? Then I don't cook, either. Many of the recipes in this book freeze quite well, and I'll often make extra so I can freeze some. The recipes usually say when they freeze well. In general, well-cooked and soupy foods freeze very well, while dishes with raw or crisp-cooked vegetables do not. Leftover stew can be frozen very successfully; not so for a stir-fried dish. Frozen leftovers thaw expeditiously in the microwave or leisurely in cold water while you do something else.

If I don't have a lot of time or only feel like cooking a little, then I'll make something simple. My easy oven roast chicken is one of my short of time go-to recipes. The recipes in each section are arranged from fastest and easiest to more involved to help you choose.

How you go about doing your cooking also makes a big difference in enjoyment. Trying to turn everything out at the same time in short order is a recipe for high stress and low enjoyment. I used to have one thing sautéing while I chopped something else, but no more. Now I get everything ready to go before I light up the big fire. It's a lot more fun this way. The French have a term for this: Mis en Place. It means having everything in its place and ready to go before you start cooking. Get all your bowls of cut meats, chopped vegetables, ground spices, broth ingredients, etc. ready first and you'll find the process much more enjoyable, perhaps even contemplative.

Lastly, I'll offer my super-secret method for enjoying cooking: Don't Measure.

Like the cooks you see on TV, skip measuring unless you really need to. Sure, measuring is a good way to ensure a recipe comes out right when you're not familiar with how it comes together. But measuring everything makes cooking too much like chemistry class. The faster you move away from it, the more you'll enjoy cooking. For this book, I just made stuff and noted along the way about what I did. Feel free to do the same and adjust to suit your taste.

And when it's all done and you're ready to eat? Do set the table. You put a lot of yourself into the meal and it deserves a nice setting. These days, much fine china and glassware can go into the dishwasher. Gotta love it.

For exercising, as mentioned, find something you like to do and work at it while you're at it. I can't tell you how many people I see at the club sort of going through the motions. Is there a fitness benefit from what they're doing? Minimal, at best. You've invested in the membership and gotten yourself there, you might as well get some benefit from doing so. In the process, you'll avoid the frustration of starting a program and not seeing any results. Personal trainers and exercise classes can help with this.

Make the fitness component of your life fun—an expression joy with the wonderful body you've been born with. The benefits will spread to all aspects of your life: mood, productivity at work, sound sleeping—and fun at the beach!

Give Yourself a Break

This last secret is about recognizing that, unless you're Superman, you're not Superman! (or Wonder Woman!). So give yourself a break. If turning out great-tasting, healthy meals and getting into great shape was so easy, you'd have done it already. (Maybe you already have! Good for you. Hopefully, there's something in this book to help you with those. :)

I would advise against tackling too much too quickly and getting frustrated. It took me a number of attempts and modifications to perfect the Szechuan Turkey (particularly the smoking), so don't expect perfection right off. Things may not come out quite the way you were hoping the first time, but not to worry. It's part of the process of discovery. I've made a few bombs along the way. We're all still here!

Have confidence and you will get there. These recipes have been tested both by me and by lots of other people, so they do work. If you're a little apprehensive, start with the simpler ones, savor the enjoyment of excellent results, and move on from there.

Cooking should be a fun way of expressing your creativity—and then eating it! These recipes are just a starting point. Feel free to modify, adapt, improvise, and even to make up your own! Suit your own personal taste in how you like your food: more or less spicy, at least. Few things are as much fun as creating your own personal culinary masterpiece and then sharing it with other people.

Food is edible art and nourishment for the body and soul, as it should be. Enjoy the journey without rushing for the destination (there isn't one!). (That I know of, anyway.) Healthy, satisfying, delicious, and nourishing food that maintains or improves your figure is within your reach. Trust me on that one.

Starting out slow is helpful for cooking, but critical with exercising. With cooking, unless you start a fire (Hint: don't do that.), the worst that can result with cooking is something that didn't turn out the way you hoped. This has happened to me many times, so don't worry about it. You'll do better next time. The first time I tried a Thai curry resulted in the worst meal I've ever made. Looking for a way to save time (and cooking in a rush, as I no longer do!), I thought that, rather than adding lime juice and grated lime rind to the curry paste, I would just add the whole lime.

Big mistake. It turns out that the white membrane of a lime is incredibly bitter, and the resulting curry was pretty much inedible. My poor dinner guests were polite enough to pick at it nonetheless. (Note to self:

make big new cooking adventures for yourself, first!).

However, with an exercise program, the results can be more dire: extreme soreness or even injury. One woman friend of mine who had never run before started with a group that was training her for a half-marathon. Within weeks, she was so sore she was barely able to walk. She had to drop running entirely.

There's nothing wrong with taking a day off from cooking or exercising. I took the day off from exercising today to write this chapter. (Okay, okay. I will be just itching to hit the pool tomorrow!)

Lastly, do tell yourself that who you are and what body you have is just great. Few of us are or would want to be underwear models. You need to accept, love, and nurture who and what you are. You are wonderful just as is. Respect your body, appreciate what it does for you each day, and do take care of it. Exercising it is part of respecting and valuing yourself.

The table's set and the food's mostly ready. Time for a breather!

So do give yourself a break, both with cooking and with exercising. Try a little at a time and, as you get the hang of it and get into better shape, try a little more. Your progress will be more steady and you'll enjoy the journey.

Here's wishing you the best of success on your journey to becoming a Power Chef.

THREE MEALS TO SAVE YOUR LIFE

**For a really fast fish dinner, just sprinkle some fish food on top of the water.
They don't seem to care that you didn't make it fresh.**

The rest of this book has recipes: the building blocks of a meal (or, in some cases, an all-in-one meal). They give you the pieces for putting together meals to suit you and your family's tastes. They're starting point for your own culinary creativity and expression.

This chapter gives three examples of how to put meals together following The Three Secrets of Power Food:

1.   **Watch the Fat**

2.   **Balance Higher Fat Foods with Low-Fat, High-Fiber Foods**

3.   **Load up on the Good Carbs and Cut the Bad Carbs**

Putting meals together like this for most of your meals (barring the occasional splurge) can Save Your Life. How?

By making it easier to take weight off and keep it off. By giving you food choices you can stick with for the long haul, getting off the on-a-diet/off-a-diet merry-go-round. By giving you more of all the stuff that's good for you (complex carbohydrates, vitamins, minerals, fiber) and less of the stuff that's not good for you (artery-clogging fats, blood sugar-spiking white sugar and flour).

Over the long haul, eating lots more of the good stuff and lots less of the bad stuff can save your life—and put a lot more life, health, and vitality into the years along the way.

We're talking about avoiding the dreaded Metabolic Syndrome. That's science-speak for when the diabolical duo of too much weight and not enough exercise lead to heart disease, stroke, diabetes, and other such nasty stuff.

We're all about avoiding that. Following the Three Secrets of Power Food can help with that a lot. And in The Three Secrets of Power Fitness & Fun and you've got a complete package.

At least that's the idea.

Granted, some potential threats to life and limb are a little harder to respond to with just the The Three Secrets of Power Food. For example, if an assorted idiot is proceeding through the red light and straight for your car, you may not have handy a high-fiber, low-fat food like a whole head of cauliflower to heave in his or her direction. (Wouldn't it be great if you did?). In such cases, you'll have to rely on sharper reflexes (the coordination leg of the Fitness Pyramid) for leaning on the horn and getting the heck out of the way.

My spouse, who has lightning-quick reflexes and outstanding balance from regular and intense dancing and is not otherwise the greatest driver, has avoided many collisions this way. I like to think regular and abundant helpings of vegetables for all those vitamins helps, too.

And now on to the meals. I've chosen three of the fastest and simplest to get you started. Take them as a launching point for your own food adventures.

THE MEALS

These three meals are just examples of fast, easy, delicious—and healthy!—meals you can make. The recipes throughout this book are building blocks for many more. Then make up your own!

60-MINUTES BARBECUE STEAK DINNER

From scratch, this meal is ready in about an hour—with plenty of time along the way to read the paper! And you'll save yourself the $30 or more per person it would have cost to go out.

Wait! you protest. How can a steak dinner be healthy? Aren't steaks just loaded with fat and cholesterol?

Well, yes, and if that's all you ate for dinner that's what you'd have. But we're combining it with a big helping of steamed broccoli and a baked potato. That's part of the magic is in applying the Three Secrets of Power Food. Here's how they apply to this meal:

1. **Watch the Fat.** For the steak, this means picking the leanest steaks you can and trimming off excess fat around the edges (either before or after cooking). This is fairly easy to do with New York Sirloin, for example, and much harder with ribeye steaks because there's so much fat throughout. Top sirloin is much leaner, but not as tender. It also means having the broccoli and potato with just a little added butter or olive oil.

2. **Balance Higher-Fat Foods with Low-Fat, High Fiber Foods.** Here, this means balancing the steak with a big helping of broccoli and the baked potato. Both are fat-free (until you add the butter!).

3. **Load Up on the Good Carbs and Cut the Bad Carbs.** This meal has only good carbs in it: broccoli and the baked potato! That was easy.

Ready to go! Although, truth be told, I usually have the broccoli first while the steak is resting after coming off the grill.

The objective is not to have the kind of extreme fat-free diet meal you and I have come to dread. I, for one, would not want to give up steaks in favor of boneless skinless chicken breast for the rest of my life (though I do have a fantastic recipe for poached chicken breasts!).

Rather, the idea is to apply The Three Secrets of Power Food to arrive at a healthy, satisfying, and delicious dinner—the kind you can keep on eating. This meal isn't no-fat, but it's low enough and very healthy overall. And you'll enjoy eating it over and over.

Here's how you make it.

The Gist

Marinate and grill some steaks. Bake some potatoes. Steam some broccoli. Eat!

Ingredients

Steaks

1/2 tsp. salt, 2 tsp. fresh ground black pepper, and 2 tsp. vodka per steak (multiply by the number of steaks)

A bag of broccoli florets for steaming

However many potatoes you would like to bake

Method

Start your oven heating to 450ºF. A toaster oven would also work. Wash the potatoes and place them in the oven.

Combine the salt, pepper and vodka in a bowl or baking dish to make the marinade. Toss the steaks thoroughly in it.

Rinse the broccoli and place it in a pot with about 1/4-inch of water in the bottom.

Start your barbecue heating.

Take a break until the potatoes have been in the oven about 45 minutes. Turn over the marinating steaks.

Turn the broccoli on high to steam it. Cook the steaks. Turn off the broccoli. Take the potatoes out of the oven. Salt, pepper, and butter on the side for the potatoes and broccoli.

Enjoy!

> Though I get my coffee ground at the store (because home grinders can't do Turkish), I do keep a small propellor-style grinder around just for black pepper. It's very easy for doing larger quantities, and you can grind as finely as you need. I keep a second one around for grinding other spices. At around $15 each, what's not to like about them?

Notes

This is one of my regular, almost instant dinners. I'll stop at the store on the way home, grab 3 ingredients, then buzz out through the quick check lane. It's done in about the time it would take to order pizza and have it delivered.

In the summer, I'll take 5 extra minutes in the store to husk a dozen ears of corn, then have steamed corn on the cob instead of the year-round staple of steamed broccoli. Yummy!

Variations

For extra nutritional punch and a little sweetness, bake some yams or sweet potatoes instead of or along with your regular potatoes. They pack a real wallop of nutrition and fiber.

ROAST CHICKEN DINNER

Oven-roasted chicken is a real regular at our house: one of those of-so-easy meals to make. I always do two to have one left over. Pieces reheat really well under the broiler.

I'll make a roast chicken with all sorts of different things, depending on what I'm in the mood for. You could have it along with the baked potatoes and steamed broccoli from the steak dinner and cook the potatoes in the oven with your chicken.

For this meal, though, I'm adding just a little more preparation with polenta instead of the potato and a tossed salad instead of the steamed broccoli. It's all still done in the time it takes to cook the chicken! And you have a meal which would pass muster with the most discriminating dinner guests.

Here's how The Three Secrets of Power Food apply to this meal:

1. **Watch the Fat**. Most of the fat from the chicken is in the skin. By cooking it with high heat on a vertical roasting rack, the fat melts and drains off from all sides while it cooks. This drastically reduces the fat content of the chicken. I also remove any excess fat while washing the chickens.

For the polenta, I add just a bit of butter and cheese to give it a rich flavor but low overall fat content. The salad gets just a drizzle of (heart healthy!) olive oil.

2. **Balance Higher-Fat Foods with Low-Fat, High Fiber Foods**. The chicken is combined with a polenta (corn) and a tossed salad.

3. **Load Up on the Good Carbs and Cut the Bad Carbs**. This meal has only good carbs in it: polenta and the tossed salad. (Beginning to see a trend?)

Here's how to make it.

Looks good enough to eat, if I do say so myself.
Yes, I did have a second piece of chicken!

The Gist

The chickens get rubbed inside and out with a combination of salt, pepper, and granulated garlic, then roasted on vertical racks. Dry polenta is poured into boiling, salted water, simmered, then finished with a little butter and cheese. A tossed salad (your choice of greens and extras) is lightly dressed with extra virgin olive oil, balsamic vinegar, salt and pepper.

Ingredients

For the chickens:

2 chickens

2 Tb. salt

1 Tb. granulated garlic

1 Tb. fresh ground pepper

For the polenta:

5 cups water

1 tsp. salt

1-1/2 cups polenta (course cornmeal)

1 Tb. butter

1/3 cup grated parmesan-romano cheese mix

For the salad:

Your choice of greens

Your choice of add-ins, such as: red onions, tomatoes, avocados, black olives, green olives, garbonzo beans, etc.

a little drizzle each of extra virgin olive oil and balsamic vinegar

a little sprinkle of salt and fresh ground black pepper

> A little organization helps greatly in getting dinner on the table and making cooking more enjoyable. Get all your ingredients out so you don't forget anything. Start the stuff that takes longest first. Have all your vegetables chopped and your mixes ready before your start cooking or combining. Then have fun with it! What could be better than creating edible art?

Method

Start your oven preheating to 450ºF. Wash the chickens thoroughly in cool water, removing any excess fat from the neck or cavity openings. Pat dry with paper towels.

Combine the salt, garlic, and pepper and rub thoroughly inside and outside the chickens. Start the water and salt heating to a boil for the polenta.

Place the chickens on the vertical racks and set them in one or two separate shallow pans. I find two separate pans easier to handle without the chickens tipping over. I also put a little ball of aluminum foil inside the chicken cavity so they sit higher on the racks and I can entertain myself by watching the fat drip off them as they cook. Add about 1/4 inch of water in the bottom of the pan(s) and set them in the oven.

By now, the polenta water ought to be close to boiling. Add the polenta in a slow steam while whisking constantly so no lumps form. Once the mixture is thickened, turn your burner down to its lowest setting and simmer till thick and the corn is soft, about 30 minutes, stirring every few minutes along the way.

While the chicken and polenta are cooking, wash and chop your salad ingredients.

The chickens will take 45-60 minutes to cook depending on how hot your oven is. When done, remove them from the oven and let them rest a few minutes. Shut the heat off under your polenta, then add the butter and cheese to finish it.

Drizzle just a little (a few tablespoons at most) olive oil over your salad fixings. Toss to distribute the oil. Then drizzle the balsamic vinegar, salt and pepper over it and toss again.

You're ready to eat!

Notes

The chickens need to set 10-20 minutes after they come out of the oven so the juices stay in them when you carve them. I generally have the salad course while this is happening. The polenta will stay warm on the stove for a good 30 minutes or more until you're ready.

Variations

See my recipe for No-Rotisserie Rotisserie Chicken for a tasty variation on simple oven-roasted chicken. It has more flavorings and you do have to watch and flip it on the grill. The oven version has the great virtue of proceeding on chicken autopilot until it's done.

ALMOST-INSTANT WHOLE WHEAT PASTA

My "add-ins: for this one were frozen Italian flat beans, canned garbonzo beans, sliced black olives, and sliced fresh garlic. Yum!

A great, homemade pasta meal is so easy and fast it just has to be part of your repertoire. An easy, fast, nutritious and good meal is only 30 minutes away. The basic version works for vegetarians. Try some of the variations if you'd like something a little more.

Here's how The Three Secrets of Power Food apply to this meal:

1. **Watch the Fat**. There's almost no fat in the basic version! Just a little from any olive oil you may have added and from the cheese. Even adding chicken pieces or sausages still results in a very modest fat content. And it still tastes great. In contrast, many other pastas are loaded with oil, cream, cheese, or all of the above.

2. **Balance Higher-Fat Foods with Low-Fat, High Fiber Foods**. There are no high fat foods! (Unless you've added the sausages, in which case they're balanced by the low fat pasta, tomatoes, and vegetables.) Who'd a thunk low fat could taste so good!

3. **Load Up on the Good Carbs and Cut the Bad Carbs**. This meal has only good carbs in it: whole wheat pasta, tomatoes, and vegetables (plus the non-carb meat, if you've added any). Okay, I will confess: about the only place simple carbs make it into my cooking is desserts. And, even then, I use whole wheat white flour! All tastes great. Gotta love it.

Here's how to make it.

The Gist

Buy pasta in the store and cook it according to package directions. Heat a jar of your favorite tomato sauce, a can of tomatoes, some add-ins, then add to the pasta.

Ingredients

1 lb. (dry) of whole wheat pasta

a big pot of boiling salted water

your choice of add-in frozen vegetable, such as green beans, italian flat green beans, or even frozen peas (really!)

1 jar of your favorite pasta tomato sauce

1 26-oz. can of diced tomatoes in juice

your choice of add-in spices: such as dried oregano, parsley or basil, black or red pepper, granulated garlic, onion powder, crushed red pepper, or even a few fennel seeds. A little bit of extra virgin olive oil is also good.

> I used to have to visit a health food store to find whole wheat pasta, but now my local grocery store has a good variety. Be sure only to cook it until it's still a little tough because, when overcooked, it tends to fall apart more easily than white pasta.

Method

Bring a big pot of salted water to a brisk boil. I use about a gallon of water for 1 pound of dry pasta. You can have too little water, but it's impossible to have too much.

While the water is coming to a boil, start heating your favorite pasta sauce in a separate saucepan. Add the can of tomatoes and your choice of spice add-ins.

When the water is boiling hard, add the pasta all at once and stir for a minute or two as it softens so the noodles don't stick together. Turn the heat down to medium high (the water should still just be boiling), and stir every minute or two to prevent sticking.

The pasta is done when it's no longer hard but still a little tough ("al dente"). It should be slightly underdone when you drain it so that it finishes cooking with your sauce. If in doubt, a little underdone is better than a little over (it will soften more in the sauce).

When the pasta is ready, add the frozen vegetables and stir for a minute. Drain the pasta and vegetables in a colander, return to the cooking pot (burner off!) and immediately add the warmed sauce. Toss thoroughly and let it sit for a minute or two. Serve with grated paremesan-romano cheese mix. Then, as my Nona would say, "manga!"

Notes

I find most all varieties of ready-made sauce bland and curiously thick. A can of diced tomatoes in juice and some add-in spices seems the perfect and easy remedy.

Whole wheat pasta has much fuller flavor than the white varieties and is immensely better for you. You get all the germ and bran otherwise milled out to make white flour. Once you try it, you'll think (as I do) that white pasta is bland.

Beware of the "spinach pastas." They are usually white pasta with just enough spinach added to make them green. You may have to read the label to make sure the pasta you're getting is whole wheat. "Whole wheat flour" should be the first ingredient on the label.

Variations

Instant cacciatore: while you're at the store, pick up one of those ready-to-go roasted chickens. Cut or pull apart the chicken (depending on how neat you want to be), and drop the pieces in the sauce as it heats. Raw chicken pieces would also work, but would need to simmer in the sauce about 20 minutes.

Instant primavera: use a packaged medley of frozen vegetables instead of a single variety. I like the vegetable medleys with kidney beans in them.

Instant la pasta con le salsicce: drop some italian sausages into the sauce as it heats. If raw, these will likewise need to simmer for 15-20 minutes.

Instant bolognese: drop some raw lean, ground beef (or pork) (or both!) in the sauce as it heats. This will be cooked as soon as the sauce comes to a simmer.

I'M LOVIN' LEFTOVERS

Leftovers have gotten a bad rap, but it's really a matter of what and how. Here's what and how to have as "leftovers" so good the don't deserve the name. Maybe, "Ready Gourmet Meals"? These are good enough to serve to company (I have!) and they never suspect.

> A key to better frozen leftovers is buying a "frost" freezer—not a "frost free" one. The defrost cycle (a blast of warm air) is what causes freezer burn. No defrost cycle means no freezer burn. These freezers are very cheap, and can go a year or more before you need to defrost them manually.

The Gist

When you are set to make something, make extra and freeze the rest in containers you can quickly defrost and reheat.

Method

Many recipes (and many in this book), make a one-course, all-in-one meal. These are ideal for making extra and freezing at least some of the remainder in containers for later. For the most part, soups come out of the freezer as good as new and are far better than anything from a can. Saucy dishes (like pastas) also do really well. Anything that's fairly well-cooked and has a medium to high liquid content is a candidate for a later meal. This includes things like hummus, for example.

> Defrosting leftovers on your microwave's defrost cycle is very slow and especially not necessary if your microwave has a turntable. Just nuke it on high for a few minutes, then remove as much of the thawed food as you want to eat and finish heating it in a dish. The rest can go in the fridge to finish defrosting slowly.

What doesn't work well are dishes with lots of still-crisp fresh vegetables (stir frys for example), or meals in multiple courses. The latter gets you into the TV dinner problem of everything overdone and goopy when it's all hot. And I would never freeze and reheat a grilled meat of any sort; the results are simply dreadful. Leftover roast turkey: no; leftover turkey made into turkey barley mushroom soup: just great.

The beauty of this is that when you want something great and don't feel like cooking, you don't have to! Just pop something from the freezer into the microwave to defrost while you take a shower, read the paper—whatever. You'll get a better meal than take-out without having to run an errand or wait for the delivery. And, if you timed it, it's even faster. I'll often get something defrosting to "start dinner" while finishing something else.

One last note: for special soups and such that I've frozen, I actually will defrost and serve them to guests on occasion. For a great soup, it's just as good. I just make sure the containers are washed and put away before they arrive so they don't know they're getting dreaded "leftovers!"

OUT TO DINNER

I would absolutely advise that, on a special occasions like a holiday family gathering, there's nothing wrong with just enjoying yourself and not worrying about what you do or don't eat. "Give yourself a break" (the third secret of Power Fun) applies to eating as well as exercising. If I'm having the tasting menu at an exceptional restaurant where my meal will cost what I used to make in a week, I'll be relishing the food and the company rather than sweating just how much butter and cream went into that sauce. Indulging once and a while won't put you off your program, but it will keep you in a much better frame of mind!

Of course, for some people, indulging "once in a while" can become a daily event. This can be a waist-buster. The minutes on a cardio machine equivalent to one "small" piece of cheesecake every evening is some large multiple of TOO MANY.

Help is on the way. Restaurants will soon be required to start providing nutritional information on what they serve. Great if you eat out a lot—though for special occasions I'd probably rather not know!

Then there's the matter of folks who need to eat out frequently, as I did when traveling for business. If every meal on the expense account becomes a special indulgence, then one joins many of my former colleagues whose extensive travel schedules had them looking steadily more "prosperous."

Fortunately, there is no necessity of throwing prudence and your hard-earned progress to the wind every time you walk through the doors of a restaurant. You already know how to avoid that trap: by applying The Three Secrets of Power Food. Here they are again:

1. **Watch the Fat**

2. **Balance Higher Fat Foods with Low-Fat, High-Fiber Foods**

3. **Load Up on Good Carbs and Cut Bad Carbs**

They apply just as well to eating out as to cooking at home, and doing so is so simple you already know what I mean.

Take Watch the Fat, for example. Who would be surprised to learn that anything deep fried is likely high in fat, especially if it's batter-dipped? Or that a cream sauce consists mostly of cream and butter, both of which are mostly fat? These are easy to spot.

39

Here's our table for dessert at home after an Easter Brunch out.

There are a few places where food in a restaurant can be surprisingly fatty. Typical potato salads, for example, are usually loaded in mayonnaise (see my recipe for one with just a bit of olive oil!). Tomato pasta sauces sometimes bear a heavy load of olive or other oil. Salad dressings are often extremely fatty. Order yours on the side. A cheese and sausage pizza—well, we won't even go there.

This is where the second secret of Power Food comes in: Balance Higher Fat Foods with Low-Fat, High-Fiber Foods. If you're just dying for that deep fried calamari, go for it. Just make the rest of the meal balance it out. A large side order of steamed vegetables (no butter) or an entrée-sized salad (dressing on the side) will do the trick. Maybe even consider ordering some fresh fruit for dessert. Probably the restaurant can bring you some even if it's not on the menu.

The third secret of Power Foods, Load Up on Good Carbs and Cut Bad Carbs, also applies when eating out. We've already mentioned making sure you get a good helping of vegetables or of salad (or both!). Those are definitely good carbs which pretty much every restaurant has.

The other varieties of good carbs—whole grains—are easy to find at breakfast and a little tougher later in the day. If there's any variety of oatmeal (old fashioned, quick oats, or even instant), it's a good carb regardless of which type it is. The only difference is how small the oats are milled, but they're all whole grains. Most restaurants also have whole wheat bread which you can have as toast or in sandwiches throughout the day.

Other grains get considerably more dicey. It's a rare restaurant where the basket of warmed bread, the pasta, or the pizza crust is made with whole wheat flour. Likewise, Asian restaurants (Chinese, Thai, Japanese, Indian, etc.) which offer brown rice are pretty few and far between. I'm famous at my favorite local Chinese restaurant for arriving with my own pot of brown rice. The staff, thankfully, is fascinated by this rather than indignant. Maybe because we always order so much food! All in all, best to avoid the many things white flour finds its way into at restaurants and indulge your pasta cravings at home where, of course, all you have in the pantry is whole wheat pasta!

Likewise, healthy desserts in restaurants generally stop at the fruit cup. I've yet to find an equivalent of my Low Fat Ricotta Cheesecake when eating out. You might try deciding at the outset whether to go for the fried calamari at the beginning or the cheesecake at the end—hopefully not both!

Above all, just be sensible in your choices. A little off what you might have at home is just fine so long as, overall, you maintain the balance in your diet. When I'm on business and the offerings look particularly suspect, I'll just order two of the entrée-sized salads and call it dinner! And, once in a while, I'll get really lucky like once in Vancouver when the restaurant was offering as a featured entrée grilled salmon on a bed of lentils and carrots. It was utterly wonderful and the inspiration for my Black Bean Steamed Salmon with lentils, carrots, and whole wheat linguine with fresh sage.

After all, a truly great and healthy meal can provide fond and savory memories for years to come. They're worth looking for and restaurants are, more and more, providing healthier offerings than they used to.

If all else fails, I'll order the burger on wheat toast instead of a bun, a big salad to go along with it, and call it a day. Enjoy all your meals, and make them good for you, too!

DRINK ME

A cocktail before dinner has a checkered history. Once de rigeur, it fell out of favor for a time and now seems to be making a comeback with increasing evidence of the health benefits of light drinking. Too much is definitely still bad for you and always has been. But, if there's no history of alcoholism in your family, a little seems better than tee-totaling. Perhaps there is some justice in the world, after all.

Gourmet traditions notwithstanding, I must confess that I am not a fan of wine or any other alcoholic drink during or after dinner at all. It's too easy to drink way too much as you continue eating and end up dangerously inebriated. Drinking and then driving is worst of all. I'll have my cocktail before eating, then switch to water from then on.

Of course, starting one's day usually is better with coffee, so that first. Then, in the spirit of a little before dinner á santé, my favorite cocktails.

TRULY GREAT, FAST, AND EASY COFFEE

Simply the best, easiest, fastest coffee you will ever drink! Use less grounds if you like it less *fortissimo*.

The Gist

Put 2 tbs. of turkish grind coffee in a mug with boiling water. Stir vigorously, let settle for a few minutes, then enjoy—but don't sip the last half-inch, which has the settled grounds.

Ingredients

Truly great, dark roasted coffee ground for Turkish

Boiling water

Method

Put some water on to boil. Place two tablespoons of ground coffee in a mug. Add boiling water, stir thoroughly, and let settle for a minute or two. Add cream if you like.

Here's my "everyday" cup of coffee—complete with foam just like from an espresso machine. Except the only cleanup is the mug and spoon go in the dishwasher!

Sip and don't drink the last half-inch worth (unless you want all the extra fiber from the grounds!).

Notes

If you're in a hurry, add one ice cube and the grounds will settle out almost instantly.

This makes the best-flavored cup of coffee out of all the methods I've tried—better even than a french press. You get the espresso-like brown foam on the top without the bother of an espresso machine. And—better yet—when you're done, just rinse out the mug and put it in the dishwasher. What could be simpler.

It is critical to get really good coffee for best results. Lots of places now offer this. In a pinch, Starbucks will do. Just make sure they can actually grind it for Turkish. With coarser grinds, the coffee will float on the top rather than settling to the bottom. And, no, unfortunately, I've never come across a home coffee grinder that can get it this fine —regardless of what the settings on the machine claim.

By the way, this is the way professional coffee tasters do their coffee. Try it and you'll know why.

> Please be sure to have your coffee ground for turkish at your local coffee shop. This is the #1 setting on many commercial grinders. Even though good quality home grinders have a turkish setting, I've yet to find one which actually grinds it finely enough.

A CAFÉ MOCHA AT HOME

I must confess that, after so many years of having a Starbucks at the airport, I developed a fondness for an occasional café mocha. Here's my version; no espresso machine required!

The Gist

Mix some cocoa powder and brown sugar with the turkish grind coffee, then add the boiling water. Stir, add half-and-half to taste, then let settle for a minute or two.

Ingredients

2 tbs. turkish grind coffee

2 tbs. cocoa powder

1 tbs. dark brown sugar

boiling water

half-and-half

Method

Mix the coffee, cocoa, and sugar together in a mug. Add boiling water and stir thoroughly. Add half-and-half to taste, then let settle a few minutes before drinking. If not hot enough, nuke for 30 seconds in the microwave. Remember not to drink the last half-inch!

Looks like I saved $6—again! Tastes better, too.

Notes

Microwaving the finished drink not only warms it up, it also seems to help the grounds settle better. Must have something to do with fluid dynamics.

To me, this drink is better flavored than what Starbucks makes—and it doesn't require a trip, an espresso maker, or steamed milk! Use a big mug, more water, and less coffee is you like it less strong.

I have great results with good old Hershey or Nestlé cocoa. If you have a decent chocolate syrup around, you can add that with the cream and skip the sugar. I prefer more chocolate flavor and less sweetness than most syrups. Regular sugar would also work instead of brown sugar, with a slight loss of flavor.

I've not experimented with using other flavoring syrups (I think Starbucks even sells them by the bottle), but I see no reason why they wouldn't work (if they're not too loaded with sugar!)

TRIPLE CITRUS PUNCH

A wonderfully sweet-tart combination, this juice stands on its own or turns into a great adult cocktail.

The Gist

Combine equal parts grapefruit and orange juice with a splash of lime juice.

Ingredients

1 part grapefruit juice

1 part orange juice

1 Tbs. each of lemon juice and lime juice per cup of the other juices

Method

Mix. Chill. Drink!

Notes

Although orange and grapefruit juices mixed from frozen concentrates will do, the fresh ones (not from concentrate) have much better flavor. For safety, most of these will still have been pasteurized, but this doesn't seem to have too much effect on the flavor. For the lime juice, I just use the bottled lime juice. But feel free to buy and juice some limes if it suits you!

Great for the kids and the adults—but don't mix them up!

Variations

To zip it up for the kids without boosting the sugar, add some diet ginger ale for a little fizz. I'll usually do about a 1/5 ginger ale proportion.

For a totally delicious adult cocktail, add a little vodka or tequila, a splash of triple sec, and a bit of sparkling water. Serve over ice with a garnish of an orange slice and mint leaves and you have a $12 cocktail sure to impress.

THE TURBO CARRERA

I created this cocktail for the 50th anniversary celebration of the Golden Gate Region Porsche Club of America. It definitely has a very fast 0 to 60 time!

The Gist

Mix together, shake over ice, pour into your favorite martini glass and enjoy!

Ingredients

2 parts vodka

2 parts pink grapefruit juice

1 part Grand Marnier or Triple Sec

1/2 part lime juice or Rose's Lime Juice

Method

Mix all ingredients together, shake over ice, and strain into a martini glass.

Notes

Use fresh lime juice to make it more tart, or Rose's Lime Juice if you like it sweeter.

Get ready to rev up your engines!
(Suggest keeping traction control ON!)

TENNESSEE LEMONADE

On hot summer days in the south before air conditioning was developed, a glass of lemonade could spoil within minutes of being poured. Luckily, the inventive people of Tennessee discovered that adding a "tiny" amount of Jack Daniels would make the lemonade safe to sip in a more leisurely fashion. Thank goodness for frontier resourcefulness!

The Gist

Fill a glass with ice, add half full of Jack Daniels and the remainder with Italian lemon soda. Enjoy!

Ingredients

ice cubes

Jack Daniels

Italian lemon soda

Method

'Bout the same.

Variations

Top with crushed mint leaves for a "Julep-y" lemonade.

If you like it a little more tart, add a spritz of fresh or bottled lemon juice. Costco has a bottled "Italian Volcano Lemon Juice" which is just too good to come from a bottle!

Add hydrangeas on the table for a real southern touch!

I suspect this would fare much better at corner lemonade stands.

THE COOL CLOUD MARTINI

It's said that a good martini is like "a cool cloud passing briefly through your mouth." This recipe definitely fits the bill.

The Gist

Combine 4 parts gin from the freezer with 1 part dry vermouth over ice in a chilled container. Shake, strain into a chilled glass, add an olive and enjoy.

Ingredients

4 parts Bombay Sapphire gin

1 part Noilly Prat dry vermouth

ice

1 big green olive per serving

Method

Put the bottle of gin in the freezer to chill several hours ahead of time. The mixing container and glasses could go in later because they take less time to chill, but if you put them in now you won't forget them!

Combine the gin and vermouth in the mixing container. Swirl together briefly. Add around 3 or 4 ice cubes per serving. Cover and shake. Strain into martini glasses from the freezer and add 1 big green olive per glass. If there's more in the container, return it to the fridge to stay cold.

Enjoy!

One is nice, two is too many, and three is not nearly enough. Oh, dear.

Notes

The secrets to this recipe are top-shelf ingredients and the pre-chilling. Gin in the freezer won't freeze solid (because of the alcohol content), but it will get cold. You could also put the vermouth in the fridge (not the freezer—it would freeze solid!), but there seems to be enough cooling power from freezing the gin, the container, and the glasses. The ice, of course, is also frozen!

The pre-chilling does two things for this cocktail. First, it means that your martini is actually still very cold when you drink it. This is critical. Also, the freezer means that the ice cubes only melt just a little and add only a slight dilution to the cocktail. A warm, watery martini is barely palatable with top shelf ingredients, and cheaper ingredients make it utterly undrinkable.

> Of all the gins, Bombay Sapphire seems the best to me. It claims to have more flavoring ingredients than other gins. Tanqueray or Beefeater would also do. Lesser gins taste cheaper to me. Likewise with Noilly Prat for a good vermouth. Cheap vermouth will also spoil the flavor.

You'll notice that I don't specify amounts, only proportions. Anything from a single serving up to about a quart in volume will work (enough to serve perhaps 10 folks at once!). Larger amounts are hard to handle and tend to get watery.

Beware: this produces a potent brew. One may be enough for you. You know the old saying about martinis: "one is enough, two is too many, and three is not nearly enough!"

I realize the fashion today is for all manner of sweet, fruity cocktails labeled "martinis," the most famous of which is perhaps the Cosmopolitan. The purity of a real one is like the cold breeze off an alpine glacier. Save the sweet ones for the wine cooler crowd!

> For the garnish, I like to use a large green olive. Many fancy varieties are available in most grocery stores. Pick one in brine rather than oil (so you don't get an oily drink!). Bottled is fine, as is a pimento in the middle. I don't like the ones stuffed with garlic, onions, chili peppers, etc., because they overpower the flavor of the drink. The result should be deliciously cold, complex, and subtle.

INSTANT HEAVEN

A little bit of heaven?

One would expect heavenly things from Isle of Skye!

The Gist

Pour some single-malt scotch in a suitable glass. Smell and sip to your heart's delight!

Ingredients

Any variety of single-malt scotch

A suitable glass

Method

I think The Gist rather covers this one.

Notes

Allow me to add a caveat on the varieties of single-malt scotch. I like many varieties, but, as it turns out, I do not like the ones most commonly available: Glenlivet and Glenfiddich. My apologies to the respective distilleries. In a pinch, I find them tolerable over ice.

The many I do like the best include: Talisker, Oban, Laphroag, Glenmorangie, The Balvenie, The Macallan, and so on. There are many varieties, so feel free to sample and find the ones you like best.

Cost likely won't determine your favorite. 10-year-old Laphroag at around $30/bottle is one of my favorites—more so than some costing $60 and up per bottle. Do expect to spend somewhere north of $30/bottle, though. There are some varieties costing less, but most seem harsh and unpalatable to me.

Flavors vary hugely. Some are "peatier," some are smokier, some are lighter and some are fuller flavored. Let your palate be your guide. Some scotches pass their final aging in either sherry or madera casks, which rounds out the flavor and adds a hint of sweetness. These I also like.

Blended scotches don't do it for me. I'm not sure what they do, but it doesn't taste like scotch to me at all.

Some folks like a good single malt scotch over ice. But, then again, some folks also put ketchup on their steak!

For a glass, I like a good, short, clear, lead crystal tumbler. Let's me enjoy the color and shows respect for the scotch. I've never tried a snifter glass, but I suppose you could. I'm not sure what a Scotsman would think of that.

VINO MADE SIMPLE

The Gist

If I like the wine, I'll drink it. Otherwise, not. Inexpensive red wines tend to be more drinkable than inexpensive whites, which I find mostly awful.

Method

Wines come in a staggering variety of types, vintages, and wineries. Even for a given grape and winery, quality varies by the year grown and by the age of the wine. Many people devote a lot of time and effort to tracking exactly what is how good, and it is often specific to the variety, vineyard, and year.

> There are lots of fancy gizmos for keeping leftover wine "fresh," but I just cork it, put it in the fridge, and use it for cooking or sangria . Why worry?

I invite you to peruse these many guides if that interests you. For me, it is too much trouble.

Even worse: price is often not a predictor of how much you will like a given wine. And opinions vary by the person.

My simple solution is to drink a wine if I like it, not if I don't, and not worry about the particulars. Please consult one of the many authoritative guides if this approach doesn't suit you.

Wines you don't like can be corked and refrigerated and make an elegant addition to a soup or sauce. Red wines are also good in sangria.

THE PERFECT MANHATTAN

This is definitely an old-school cocktail, one your grandparents may have enjoyed. I like it with lots of ice and add a generous amount of fresh lemon juice to balance the sweetness of the bourbon and vermouth. I once read that "if martinis are the drink of James Bond, then Manhattans are Bruce Wayne." Works for me!

The Gist

Four parts good bourbon, one part sweet vermouth, juice of half a lemon, lots of ice, and a toast to Bennie Goodman.

Ingredients

4 parts good quality bourbon, such as Jack Daniels or Wild Turkey

1 part good quality sweet vermouth, such as Martini & Rossi

1/2 fresh lemon

ice

a suitable glass

Worthy of a night near you!

Method

Fill the glass with ice. Add the bourbon and sweet vermouth. Squeeze the half lemon into the glass, then add the lemon half (or perch on the rim of the glass).

Relax and enjoy. Do not operate heavy machinery!

Notes

With these sorts of undisguised cocktails, good quality liquors are key. To my taste, only Jack Daniels or Wild Turkey will do for the bourbon, and only Martini & Rossi or Noilly Prat for the vermouth.

LA MIA SANGRIA

Great for a crowd, and great for using leftover red wine. The fruit and triple sec provide all the sweetness needed. This recipe is easily doubled, tripled. etc.

The Gist

Red wine, triple sec, brandy, orange or grapefruit juice, lemon juice, and fruit slices are mixed together and chilled before serving.

Ingredients

1 bottle red wine

1/4 cup triple sec

1/4 cup brandy

1 cup orange or grapefruit juice

if using orange juice, also add 2 tbs. lemon juice

sliced lemons or oranges or both

> This is a great recipe for using left over red wine. If you're buying the wine, an inexpensive , full bodied wine like a cabernet, zinfandel, or merlot in the 750 ml or 1.5 liter bottle is fine. A really great red wine would be lost, as would using Grand Marnier instead of Triple Sec. An inexpensive brandy is also fine No cognac for this recipe!

Method

Combine all ingredients and chill thoroughly before serving. Serve over ice, hopefully with a fruit slice or two in each glass. If you're in a hurry, skip the chilling and just serve it over ice.

Notes

This recipe is a lot fruitier than traditional sangria recipes. I like it that way, but feel free to alter the proportions to suit your taste. Using orange juice will make it sweeter, grapefruit juice will make it tarter.

Skip the extra lemon juice if you're using the grapefruit juice unless you like it really tart. On the other hand, adding more triple sec will make it sweeter and more potent.

A traditional presentation would also serve sangria chilled, but not over ice. I think the ice makes it a perfect drink for hot summer days.

NIBBLERS

Appetizers, for sure! Because some people are just so hungry when they walk in the door and you don't want them chewing on the furniture. That's what dogs are for. So here are my best appetizer recipes, plus my home recipe for great tasting popcorn which you can eat in unlimited quantities. At my house, de rigeur for rented movies—unless it's edged out by the guacamole!

CREW D'ÉTAT

Here's the Crew we had at our holiday open house: lots of veggies on the right, flanked by a cheese platter and smoked salmon tray on the left. It didn't look like this later!

A quick appetizer for government employees. No relation whatsoever to crudités. (Kidding!)

The Gist

Make some very fancy, tasty, and unusual Szechuan peanut sauce (see Recipe), then serve it with ready-to-go raw vegetables from the store so people wonder just how much you did yourself.

Ingredients

Szechuan peanut sauce (see Recipe)

your favorite ready-to-go raw vegetables from the store.

> Lots of stores these days have cut raw vegetables ready to go, but I find many of them (carrot sticks, for example) seem to lose a lot of flavor and texture in the process. Try different ones to find which are good store-prepared and which are better washed and cut at home.

Methods

Arrange the vegetables on a platter. Put some of the peanut sauce in a fancy bowl (a rice dish would do nicely) and plop it in the center. Serve.

Notes

To take this over the top, make some of the Amazing Asparagus (see Recipe), and serve this with blanched fresh snow peas, blanched carrot sticks, blanched broccoli florets, and strips of fresh jicama and red bell peppers. Round it out with raw radishes (stems and roots cut off) for extra crunch and spiciness. Garnish with radishes or tomatoes cut into flowers.

Yes, I did say over the top. But just think how impressed your in-laws will be.

PERFECT POPCORN

A little butter is all it takes to make the whole batch taste buttery without a lot of unneeded fat.

A potentially healthy and tasty snack, poor popcorn typically is buried in fat and salt. Here's a great version much lower in both. I make a whole lot when renting a movie. Did you know? Popcorn counts as part of your daily whole grains. How wonderful!

The Gist

Add a little melted butter and salt to hot air-popped popcorn

Ingredients

Unpopped popcorn, preferably Orville Reddenbacker's

1-2 tbs. butter per batch, preferably French or "European style"

salt

> I've tried many varieties of popcorn and Orville's does seem the best. It pops up lighter and fluffier and has fewer unpopped kernels ("old maids" in industry parlance). Big plastic jugs of it are available at Costco for cheap. I buy two at a time.

Method

Start with a hot air popper. Any will do, though, after much experimentation, I've settled on Toastmaster products.

Put as much corn as your popper calls for in it (they typically come with their own measuring cup), then start it. Set a metal bowl under the spout to catch it. The metal bowl heats up with the hot air and helps keep the popcorn warm.

> "European style" butter has now appeared in my local grocery store. It seems to have a lower moisture content than "regular" butter. I buy it just to use on this popcorn. The flavor difference is subtle but wonderful!.

While that's running, put 2 tbs. of butter per batch in a coffee mug and set it in the microwave to melt. 20 seconds should do it. For 3 or 4 batches (4-1/2 or 6 tbs. butter), more like a minute.

When the popcorn is all popped, shut off the popper and use the coffee mug to drizzle the butter over the entire top layer. Give it a good toss with something. I use the butter knife I cut the butter pats with.

Sprinkle the salt over the top and give it a final toss. Start the movie!

Notes

The key to the recipe is using real butter for maximum flavor, and only having enough to flavor the corn rather than bathing it. It's also enough to help the salt stick to the corn. The result is a snack with hugely better flavor than plain air popped, but much less fat and salt content than microwave varieties. Move theater popcorn is almost inedible in my opinion with its thick sauce of butter-flavored oil. Yech. My popcorn you can eat as much of as you like.

I've tried other toppings (such as grated cheese, herbs), but they really don't stick well to the corn and just seem to confuse the flavor. I now stick to real butter.

Time for a movie!

CUATRO FRESCA DE SALSA DE CHILI (FOUR CHILI SALSA)

Worthy of any chip in the land.

This four-chili fresh salsa livens up any dish or chips and keeps well in the fridge. It can be made year-round with either fresh or canned tomatoes.

The Gist

Combine chopped tomatoes, red onions, and chiles with a little chinese chili garlic sauce, canned chili sauce, cider vinegar, and maybe a dash of sugar.

Ingredients

2 cups chopped tomatoes

1/2 red onion, chopped

1 7-oz. can diced mild green chiles

1/2 cup red chili sauce

1 Tb. chinese chili garlic paste

1 Tb. chili powder

1 tsp. salt

2 tsp. cider vinegar

maybe a dash of sugar

> Good tomatoes are key for this salsa. If good vine-ripened ones aren't available, cherry or grape tomatoes are a good year-round choice. Diced canned tomatoes in juice also work great.

Method

Chop the tomatoes and red onion. If using canned tomatoes, drain some of the juice (or leave it for a more liquid salsa). Combine with remaining ingredients. Add a dash of sugar if the salsa seems too tart.

Variations

Substitute chopped fresh jalapeño chiles for the canned variety. For a less fiery salsa, have the chiles lengthwise and scoop out the seeds before chopping them. For more heat, leave some or all of the seeds in. (Warning! With all the seeds, this salsa will be south-of-the-border incendiary.)

Another option would be to use roasted fresh chiles instead. These would need to be roasted, peeled, seeded, and chopped. Roasted poblano chiles would be delicious.

Notes

Canned red chili sauce and chinese chili garlic sauce (in jars) may be found in many regular grocery stores, or try a specialty store. In a pinch, substitute red chili flakes and granulated garlic for the chinese chili garlic sauce and just omit the red chili sauce. The salsa will still be delicious.

GUACAMOLE DE LA CASA

Here's some guacamole topped with my Four Chile Salsa—my favorite way to have it!

This is my usual guacamole recipe. The fresh, clean flavor highlights the avocados.

The Gist

Mash two ripe, Haas avocados with minced jalapeños, cilantro, and red onion. Add a dash of salt and one of lime juice.

Ingredients

2 ripe Haas avocados

1/4 minced red onion

1/4 cup minced fresh cilantro

2 fresh jalapeño chiles, seeded and chopped

1/2 tsp. salt

1/4 tsp. lime juice

> Haas avocados are my favorites because of their nutty, oily flavor. When ripe, they should be just a little bit soft. With other varieties (such as Pinkerton avocados), add a teaspoon of mayonnaise to help fill out the flavor.

Method

Chop the red onions, cilantro, and jalapeños and place in a bowl. Cut the avocados in half lengthwise, remove the pit, then scoop out the fruit onto the chopped vegetables. Sprinkle over the salt and lime juice. Mash the avocados roughly with a fork (leaving some chunks), and mix in the vegetables.

Serve with corn chips, over taco salad or enchiladas, or—unorthodox but very good—spread on bread instead of mayonnaise to make a sandwich. Yum!

Notes

Guacamole is best eaten soon after you make it because the flavor of the avocados changes. I've read all sorts of tips supposed to prevent this (such as leaving the pit in or omitting the salt until right before serving), but have not had good luck with any of these. Perhaps you'll find something that works!

WINTER GUACAMOLE

I like having guacamole year-round, but the avocados in the winter don't seem to have the rich, creamy flavor of summer avocados. This recipe fixes that. Feel free to try it in the summer, too!

The Gist

Make a guacamole with avocados, fresh garlic mashed with salt, and a little chili powder, mayonnaise, and lemon juice.

Ingredients

2 ripe avocados

4 cloves of garlic, minced

1/2 tsp. salt

1 tsp. chili powder

1 tsp. mayonnaise

Method

Halve the avocados lengthwise, remove the pits, and scoop out the fruit. Mash together the minced garlic and salt until well-combined. Add to the avocados along with the chili powder and mayonnaise. Roughly mash and mix the avocados with everything else, leaving some chunks.

Variations

A little minced red onion, seeded jalapeño, and cilantro are good in this version, too. And feel free to top it with some salsa if you're so inclined.

PÂTÉ PRONTO

Pork liver pâté on the left and chicken on the right. Good, but so rich!

Fast, easy, and good, but very fatty. Buy it in the store and serve with vegetables, whole grain crackers or fruit to lower the overall fat content.

The Gist

Serve some decent store-bought pâté on a nice platter with some good crackers or bread, preferably whole wheat

Ingredients

a package of your favorite store-bought pâté

some crackers or bread, preferably whole grain

In my experience, the Marcel et Henri line of pâtés have been consistently good across their many flavors. You'll need to see what's available locally and decide which ones you like best.

Method

Place the pâté on a serving platter and arrange crackers or bread slices around it. Plunge a butter knife into the pâté and leave it there so people don't feel shy about starting. Serve.

Notes

An elegant appetizer which you don't need to feel reticent about serving because no one expects you to make your own pâté. Try the next recipe if you really want to surprise them!

PÂTÉ MAISON

My own pâté recipe. Very good, much lower in fat than commercial varieties, and easier to make than you would think. This recipe makes 1 loaf of pâté, which can then be cut into slices for serving.

The Gist

Onions are sautéed with butter and madera, then liver. This mix goes into the food processor along with ground pork, ground veal, eggs, cream cheese, salt, pepper, allspice and thyme. It all then gets baked in a tray of water.

Ingredients

1/2 cup finely minced onions

2 tbs. butter

1 lb. (2 cups) liver

1/2 cup port

3/4 lb. (1-1/2 cups) finely ground pork

3/4 lb. (1-1/2 cups) finely ground veal

8 oz. cream cheese

2 beaten eggs

1-1/2 tsp. salt

1/2 tsp. fresh ground black pepper

1 tsp. thyme

a big pinch of allspice

> As I go through chickens and turkeys, I accumulate the livers in Ziploc bags in the freezer for eventual inclusion in pâté. You can buy these separately if you haven't saved any. Goose livers would be really good, but I've not seen these sold separately.

> The Cuisinart does a great job of finely grinding meat. I just buy pieces of pork and veal for this and then grind them myself. Ground veal is hard to find in the store, though your meat department might be able to grind some for you.

Method

Preheat the oven to 350°F.

Sauté the onions in butter until translucent. Add the livers and sauté them just long enough to lightly brown the outsides (still very pink inside). Remove these to a bowl to cool a bit.

Add the port to the skillet and cook over high heat until it has boiled down to about half its original volume. All alcohol smell should be gone. Take the pan off the heat.

Set a kettle of water on the stove to boil. When it boils, turn it down to simmer to stay hot.

Put the cooled liver and onions in a food processor and process until very finely ground (almost a paste). Scrape this into into the mixing bowl of a heavy duty mixer (like a Kitchenaid).

Add the reduced port and remaining ingredients to the mixing bowl. Beat with the paddle attachment until the mixture is thoroughly blended and almost whipped in texture.

Grease a loaf pan with either bacon fat (preferred) or butter. Pour the mixture into the loaf pan then cover it with aluminum foil, being sure to tightly crimp the edges.

Set the loaf pan in a roasting dish, then place the roasting dish on a rack in the lower third of your oven. Pour in enough of the boiling water from the kettle to come halfway up the sides of the loaf pan.

Bake the pâté for 1-1/2 hours. Let the pâté cool completely before cutting slices to serve.

Better yet, refrigerate it overnight before serving. This gives the juices time to form a delicious aspic around the pâté.

Notes

The secret ingredient in this recipe is the cream cheese. It substitutes for the pork fat in a traditional recipe, giving it the smooth consistency and creamy taste with far fewer calories.

The pâté will still appear distinctly pink in the middle when you slice it. This is fine; it really is done enough. If you cook it until it's brown all the way through, it will be dry and the texture not nearly as good.

Traditionally, after cooking a pâté is refrigerated with some sort of weight on top to force out any air spaces in the meat. Try this if you like, but I generally don't bother. The flavor is still great.

Leftovers may be frozen at the risk of some texture loss. Fresh or thawed, the leftovers make great sandwiches with tomato, lettuce, and some thin sliced red onions.

HUMMUS

Hummus is very easy to make: it just takes a little time to cook the dried garbonzo beans. And you can make it as spicy (or not) as you like!

The Gist

Soak and cook some dried garbonzo beans, then add as much tahini, garlic, salt, lemon juice, and cayenne pepper as suits you.

Ingredients

2 lbs. dry garbonzo beans

1/2 cup tahini

1 Tb. salt

8 cloves fresh garlic, mashed and minced

4 Tb. lemon juice

1/2 tsp. cayenne pepper

1/2 cup fresh parsley, minced

2 Tb. extra virgin olive oil

> Tahini is ground sesame seeds, so you may find it labeled as "sesame butter" instead. It's the same thing. Most stores carry it but, if you can't find it, a little sesame oil instead will give you much the same flavor as the ground seeds.

whole wheat pita breads, cut in wedges

Method

If you have time, you can soak the garbonzo beans for a few hours, then discard the water (for easier "digestion.") Otherwise, just rinse them and then start cooking them.

Place the beans in a pot with enough water to cover (more if not soaked) and bring to a simmer. Cook until the beans are very soft, which will take about one hour for soaked beans and longer for unsoaked. Drain and mash.

Add the tahini, salt, garlic, lemon juice, and cayenne pepper. Add more of any or all if it suits you. Mix well.

To serve, place in a bowl and drizzle the olive oil over the top, then sprinkle with parsley. Serve with wedges of whole wheat pita bread for dunking. You may need a knife to help out if your hummus is really thick, as I usually make it.

Notes

To expedite the process, you can start with canned garbonzo beans instead of fresh ones. I like to start with the dried beans because they have more flavor. You will likely still need to cook the garbonzo beans a little longer to soften them.

Variations

My Greek neighbor Anastasia is an excellent cook and likes to make her hummus with just lemon, salt, garlic, and olive oil. It's very good, but I like the extra complexity the tahini gives. And she likes mine, too!

I've also been known on occasion to add a little soy sauce.

I can make it, but, according to my Jewish friends, I can't pronounce it properly! Oh, well.

EYE OPENERS

Breakfast is an important start to your day. Don't skip it! I used to have my coffee and just go. I'd be dragging by noontime and then ravenous later in the day. And the worst way to end your day is with a really huge dinner, then going to sleep. Much better to spread those calories throughout your day when you can use and burn them—instead of directing them to "storage" while you sleep!

Here's a few suggestions for fast and easy ways to get your day going. The key is to get some carbs in you for energy and some protein so you don't feel hungry. Or just have a huge bowl of oatmeal! One can never eat too much oatmeal.

Time for breakfast. Hope you're hungry!

THE 4-MINUTE EGG

Eggs with a consistency like butter!
Almost makes me want to own some chickens...

This was the result of an experiment: what if one cooked an egg longer than a runny, soft-boiled egg, but short of hard cooked? The result is an egg with a delicious, thick-custard consistency yolk—wonderful even just by itself. Try this with some wheat toast for a different, very easy breakfast.

The Gist

Boil an egg for 4 minutes. Enjoy!

Ingredients

Eggs

Water

Method

Place the eggs in a sauce pan with enough cold water to cover. Set over high heat. Once it starts to boil, turn the heat down to medium high and boil for about 4 minutes. Shut the heat off and dump out the boiling water. The eggs can sit a few minutes if you're not quite ready to eat, or give them a brief rinse with cold water if you'd like to eat them right away.

Delicious with just a little salt and pepper, or spread them on a piece of wheat toast.

Notes

If you serve the eggs right when you take them off, the entire yolk with have a beautiful, thick and creamy consistency. After about 20 minutes, the yolk will set slightly, but still be creamy in the center. These eggs can even be refrigerated for lunches later in the week.

Variations

You can toast your wheat toast (or whole wheat english muffins) in the toaster oven, then put a slice of ham on top and leave them in the toaster oven to warm while you watch the eggs. Place a cooked egg on top of the ham and voilá! An easy breakfast sandwich.

A slice of cheese on top of the ham would be really good too, but then I'd want some fruit with breakfast to balance out the extra fat!

SUPER CEREAL

This day I added lots of fresh blueberries and raspberries. Why skimp? Bananas are also great to mix in for a little extra sweetness.

I love shredded wheat, but—although very healthy—it's a little too stark for me to have on its own. Combining it with a sweeter variety of whole grain cereal plus fresh fruit turns it into a brunch-worthy breakfast that's ready in moments.

The Gist

Mix some shredded wheat with a sweeter, whole grain cereal and add fresh fruit and milk.

Ingredients

Shredded wheat (either spoon size, or the whole biscuits crumbled)

A sweeter whole grain cereal, such a Kashi

> I generally use whole milk for my cereal and everything else. The flavor is so much better than skim milk and the fat difference in your daily diet is—in my opinion—negligible!

Your choice of fresh fruit

Milk

Method

Mix everything together in your favorite cereal bowl and eat with your favorite spoon. Read the paper and eat!

Notes

This method of mixing a less- and more-sweet cereal works will all sorts of pairings. For example, I also like Cheerios (less sweet) mixed with a corn bran cereal (usually sweeter). Or you could try Grape Nuts with granola. Let your imagination run wild!

Bananas are fine if berries aren't handy.

BAGEL MORNING

Deliciously fast and easy! Vary the cheese and meat to suit your moods and what's in the fridge!

This is what I have for breakfast on mornings when I'm planning on working out an hour or two later. It's fast, easy, and gets you some complex carbs and protein to get you through the most intense gym workout. A piece of fresh fruit to go along would also be great.

The Gist

Toast half a bagel, spread it with a little cheese, and top with a piece of low-fat turkey or chicken breast. Done in about the time it takes to make a cup of coffee!

Ingredients

1 whole wheat bagel

a little cheese (sliced or spreadable)

2 slices of turkey or chicken breast sandwich meat

Method

Toast the bagel halves in a toaster or toaster oven. Spread a little cheese or use a slice of cheese, and top with the turkey or chicken. Read the paper and watch the sun rise (optional!).

Notes

I like to use a toaster oven for toasting because then I can pop the finished bagel back in for a minute or two to melt the cheese and heat the turkey. With the whole wheat bagel and low-fat turkey, the overall package is quite acceptable from a fat standpoint and much lower in fat than a typical breakfast sandwich.

My favorite cheese for this is Cambozola: a spreadable, brie-type soft cheese with bleu cheese flavors. Any of your favorite cheeses would do!

MORNING OATS MEAL

I love oatmeal in the morning—I just don't care for the gooey, institutional variety, or for washing the sticky pot! This method gets you delicious, almost-instant oatmeal for one.

The Gist

Add boiling water to oatmeal in a bowl. Cover and microwave for another minute or so. Enjoy with your favorite oatmeal add-ins.

Ingredients

1 part oatmeal

2 parts water

dash salt

Method

Add one part oatmeal to a large, high-sided bowl. Add a dash of salt. Bring around 2 parts of water to boil in a kettle on the stove (proportions only have to be approximate—I never measure!). Pour enough boiling water in the bowl to cover the oatmeal by about 1/2-inch, and be sure to leave at least 1-inch space to the top of the bowl so it won't boil over in the microwave.

Loosely cover the bowl with plastic wrap and place it in the microwave. Turn the microwave on high and watch the bowl. Turn off the microwave as soon as the oatmeal starts to bubble up. Let sit for a minute, then enjoy with your favorite oatmeal add-ins. I like a little brown sugar and a little milk. Other possibilities include raisins, fresh fruit, homemade jam—whatever you're in the mood for. Finnish folks like their oatmeal with a little pat of butter.

Notes

This recipe works great when you only want a single bowl of oatmeal for yourself. For larger quantities, I'll use a saucepan with the traditional stovetop method.

Some people like their oatmeal thick and soupy, while others like the grains more chewy and not so thick. For thick, soupy oatmeal, add the oats to the cold water, bring the whole mixture to a simmer, and cook longer.

For less thick, boil the water first, then add the oatmeal, and cook for just a few minutes.

Me, I have it either way depending on what I'm in the mood for!

> The only difference between "regular" oats and "quick" oats is the oat grains have been milled finer so they cook faster. Both are just as nutritious, although I like the texture of regular oats better. Steel-cut oats leave the oats in bigger pieces instead of milling them flat. Although some people swear by them, I don't find the flavor enough different to justify the much higher price. Good ol' Quaker Oats will do it for me!

So good it almost seems it shouldn't be so good for you! But I like it anyway...

SUPER CRISP BACON

The golden brown color and bowl of melted fat tell the story. Have one!

A little extra time makes the bacon super-crisp and tasty—and gives you a chance to drain off a lot of the fat!

The Gist

Cook bacon slowly over medium heat until very crisp, then drain on paper towels.

Ingredients

1 lb. bacon

Method

Add about a 1/4 cup of water to a large fry pan with a cover. Turn the heat on high. When the water is bubbling, spread the bacon out across the whole bottom of the pan. Cover, leave the heat on high for another minute or two, then turn the heat down to medium. Every five minutes or so, arrange and flip the pieces of bacon so they crisp evenly.

When the bacon is really crisp, remove from the pan and drain on paper towels. If needed, you can keep it warm in a low oven. Save the melted fat in a jar in the fridge for frying other things (like oatmeal pancakes!—see Recipe).

Notes

Starting with a little water in the pan helps speed up the process of melting off the fat and helps the bacon not to stick. If your slices do stick, add a little more during the cooking process to help deglaze the pan.

HAMINATED EGGS

Three if you're really hungry. Almost seems to call out for some grits to go along, don't you think?

This takes just about as long to make as it takes to fry some eggs. It is utterly exceptional when my friends with chickens pass along fresh eggs! (No, I don't just mooch; I trade them for fresh lemons. If only the chickens would eat the lemons...)

The Gist

Toast some bread, fry some ham, fry some eggs, then layer these on the toast. I like to finish this with a dash of Tabasco.

Ingredients

> As eggs get older, they spread out more in the pan when you fry them and break easier. Fresher eggs work better for making fried eggs.

1 slice of whole wheat bread for each Hamination

1 egg for each

1 slice of ham for each

salt and fresh ground black pepper

dash of Tabasco (optional)

Method

Put the bread in a toaster or toaster oven to toast. Heat a frying pan and grease the bottom with just a little bacon fat or butter. Briefly fry the slices of ham on each side, then deposit each slice on a piece of toast. Fry the eggs (sunny-side up or easy-over, as you like them!), then put each egg on a ham/toast. Very lightly salt the eggs, give each a good grind of black pepper, then top with a dash of Tabasco if desired.

Serve!

Notes

I like to serve these still warm, so if you're not making and serving everything all at once (as I usually do!), or perhaps keep the slices of toast warm on plates in a warm oven.

GOOD MORNING FRITTATA

Good enough for a fancy brunch or a quick supper. A few eggs, some cheese, and whatever's leftover in the fridge will do the trick!

The Gist

Sauté some fresh or leftover vegetables (onions, red peppers, and potatoes in this case), add some lightly scrambled eggs and cheese, and serve with whole wheat toast. That's it!

> To make a frittata for a crowd, sauté the vegetables on the stove, put them in a large baking dish, pour the eggs and cheese on top, then pop them into a 400°F oven . When the eggs are starting to cook, shut the oven off and the whole thing can wait in the warm oven until you're ready to serve.

Ingredients

1 yellow onion, chopped

1 red bell pepper, chopped

1 leftover baked potato, sliced

2 Tb. butter

4 eggs, lightly scrambled

1/4 tsp. salt

1/4 tsp. fresh ground black pepper

1/2 cup grated cheese, such as cheddar or swiss

Method

Lightly scramble the eggs with the salt and pepper, I like the white and yolk still a little distinct, but mix more if you like.

Heat the butter over high heat in a large skillet, preferably one with a cover. Add the onions, red peppers, and potatoes, and sauté for 2-3 minutes until the onions are wilted. Turn the heat down to medium, pour the eggs over, sprinkle the cheese on top, and cook on low until barely heated through (3-4 minutes).

Serve hot with whole wheat toast.

Good morning to you! Where's the whole wheat toast?

Notes

If your skillet doesn't have a cover, just use a large plate on top. The covered cooking time avoids the need to stir or flip, and should be just enough time to almost set the eggs. I like my eggs still a little runny, but do cook longer if you like your eggs thoroughly.

Please don't cook so long that the eggs get tough!

Variations

The variations to this are as wide as your imagination. Green onions? Crumbled bacon? A little bleu cheese? How about artichokes and jack cheese?

The egg and cheese base will accommodate almost anything you'd like to throw together. Have fun with this one.

PETER'S FRY-TATTA

Eggs cooked to easy-over consistency—just the way I like them!

My friend Peter has a number of chickens (he calls them "the girls") who lay the most fantastic eggs—much more flavorful than what you can buy in the store. I came up with this version of a fry-tatta with it's easy-over consistency to highlight these eggs. It's great with store-bought eggs, too!

The Gist

Sauté whatever you have on hand for vegetables, add cheese, then eggs on top, and cook covered over medium heat until the eggs are just barely set. Serve an egg and stuff on top of dry whole wheat toast.

Ingredients

2 Tb. butter or leftover bacon fat

1 yellow onion, diced

2 leftover baked potatoes, diced

2 jalapeño peppers, seeded and diced

2 tsp. salt

1 tsp. fresh ground black pepper

1 cup diced ham or smoked turkey

1/2 cup grated robust cheese (such as swiss or Gruyere)

a few eggs (your choice on the number)

dry whole wheat toast

Method

Heat the butter or bacon fat in a sauté pan with a tight-fitting lid. Over high heat, sauté the onions until crisped and brown. Add the potatoes, jalapeño peppers, salt, and pepper, turn the heat down to medium, and continue cooking and tossing until the potatoes are warmed and browned. When you're not actually tossing, cover the pan to help warm the potatoes and the cover.

Add the ham or smoked turkey, toss, cover and let cook for a minute or two. Make the whole wheat toast while things are cooking.

Add the cheese, place the eggs on top of everything, and cover. Cook covered for 1-2 minutes until the eggs are just set but the yolks are stil soft.

Serve an egg and stuff on top of a slice of whole wheat toast.

Notes

One of the eggs in the photo broke. Oh, well.

The dry whole wheat toast adds fiber, crunch, and keeps the overall fat content and calories in balance.

WHOLE WHEAT OATMEAL PANCAKES

Great by themselves, and also great to pair with a little bacon. The combination gets the fat content down and packs in a lot of nutrition.

The Gist

Soak oatmeal in milk, then add eggs, flour, baking powder, baking soda, a little sugar and a little salt. Fry away.

Ingredients

3 cups oatmeal

3 cups milk

3 eggs

1-1/2 cup whole wheat flour

1-1/2 tsp. baking powder

1 tsp. baking soda

1 tsp. sugar

1/2 tsp. salt

fruit or fruit jam to top

maple syrup

> If you can find it, try the Grade B maple syrup instead of the Grade A more commonly found. It has more maple flavor. Just make sure it's 100% real maple syrup for best flavor.

Method

Put the oatmeal and milk in a bowl and let soak for 5-10 minutes. While they're soaking, combine the flour, baking powder, baking soda, sugar and salt in another bowl and whisk together to blend thoroughly. Start heating a griddle or large fry pan. If your pan has a cover, even better—it helps the pancakes cook faster and more evenly.

Beat the eggs into the oatmeal and milk, then blend in the dry ingredients, mixing just enough to blend thoroughly. Lightly grease the pan with oil, butter, or saved bacon fat. Use about 1/3 cup of batter per pancake, and make as many as can fit in your pan with room for the batter to spread. Cook until golden brown on the bottom, then flip and finish cooking.

Serve with fruit or low-sugar fruit jam on top, then top with a little maple syrup.

Notes

Fresh fruit or low-sugar fruit jam (such as the recipes in this book), add more nutrition and enough sweetness that you only need just a touch of maple syrup. The result is a delicious holiday breakfast with all the good stuff that you don't have to feel guilty about!

Whole wheat oatmeal pancakes topped with blueberry-plum jam and a little of maple syrup, plus a side of super crisp bacon. A perfect weekend breakfast after a big workout!

WENCHY SAUCES

Some foods are just so embarrassed at being served naked. So here's a selection of sauces to dress them up and make them presentable in front of proper company. They range from a Szechuan peanut sauce for vegetables to a giblet gravy to die for (and extras keep great in the freezer!) You'll never want to open a gravy package or can again.

GRATED CHEESE FOR PASTA ET AL.

Although not a sauce, but I use it like one on top of all sorts of things. I always keep some around to make life more pleasant.

The Gist

Separately grate equal amounts of romano and parmesan cheese, then mix together. Serve over pasta.

Ingredients

Pecorino romano cheese (hunk)

Reggianno parmesan cheese (hunk)

Method

For small amounts, you could get buy with a hand grater. However, that's a fair amount of work. I do large amounts with a Cuisinart, keep some in the fridge in a sealed plastic container, then store the rest in the freezer in Ziplok bags.

I love the combination of nutty Parmesan with the salty sharpness of Romano. The best pasta topping ever!

To grate the cheese in a Cuisinart, use the blade attachment. Cut the cheese into cubes and process it a little at a time (1-2 cups worth). The romano goes very easily. The parmesan you'll have to make the cubes dice-sized and do small amounts because it's hard enough to jam the blade.

About 2 minutes of time per batch seems to do the trick. The process does make a lot of noise, so I try not to do it when people are sleeping. I usually do 5 lbs. each of romano and parmesan. The whole process takes me about an hour and yields a 6-month supply of cheese.

Varieties of romano and parmesan cheese vary greatly. Make sure you buy the "pecorino" romano and the "reggianno" parmesan. These are made with sheep's milk rather than cow's milk and are aged longer. The flavor is world's better.

Notes

The grated cheese produced by this recipe is so much more

flavorful than any kind of grated variety you can buy in the store that, once you try it, you'll never go back. The difference is huge.

I like combining the two cheeses because you get the saltiness of the romano and the nuttiness of the parmesan. Call me unorthodox.

These cheeses may be pricey in your local grocery store. Try Costco or Trader Joe's for the real thing at a lower price. I've also had Argentine parmesan which is not "reggianno" but still quite good. If you're really lucky, your local cheese store may have or be able to order for you shaved parmesan in 5-pound bags. It's almost indistinguishable from reggianno and you don't have to grate it: just mix the shaved parmesan with the grated romano.

A little of this cheese is also very good sprinkled over a tossed salad, over sliced avocados, over your loved one... oops. Ahem.

CHIPOTLE CHILE PURÉE

Here's what you start and end up with. The purée stays good in a glass jar in the fridge for months.

This wonderful seasoning takes just a few minutes to make in the blender, then goes in a jar in the fridge to offer magical taste by the spoonful to whatever you think needs it!

The Gist

Buy a can of Chipotle chiles in adobe sauce and purée them in a blender.

Ingredients

1 can of Chile Chipotle en Adobe

Method

Open the can and purée the contents in a blender. Store in a glass jar in the fridge to use by the spoonful as you need it.

Notes

I use this in everything from chile to stews to marinades (such as my Yucatan Style Pork). Use whenever you need a good shot of smoky chile flavor and some of heat.

BARBECUE MEGASAUCE

**Here's the sauce on baby back ribs that have been marinated and then grilled.
Also great on beef or chicken.**

This sauce has intense flavorings for marinating meat before it is barbecued. If you'd also like to use some as a dipping sauce at the table, add a little water to thin it out and simmer it for a bit beforehand.

The Gist

Mix together the sauce ingredients and use the sauce to marinate meats before they are grilled. Overnight in the fridge would be ideal.

Ingredients

1/2 cup ketchup

1/4 cup molasses

2 tsp. salt

1 Tb. granulated garlic

1 Tb. onion powder

3 tsp. Chipotle Chile Purée (preceding Recipe)

1 Tb. fresh ground black pepper

2 tsp. paprika

Method

Mix all ingredients together thoroughly. Use generously to coat an marinate meat before grilling. Works great for pork, chicken, or beef.

Notes

This sauce keeps quite well in the fridge, so feel free to make extra and store the rest in the fridge. If there's extra sauce in the bottom of the marinating pan, though, do bring it to a simmer before serving or discard.

EASY BEEF & MUSHROOM GRAVY

This is a great, fast gravy to make when you'd like beef gravy, but don't want to make or wait for suitable drippings. Great on mashed potatoes!

The Gist

Onions, garlic, and mushrooms are sautéed in a little butter, then water, beef stock base, salt and pepper finish it off.

Ingredients

2 Tb. butter

1 yellow onion, minced

4 cloves garlic, minced

1 lb. fresh mushrooms, sliced

2 cups water

4 Tb. beef stock base

1 tsp. salt

Got the gravy. Where's the beef?

2 tsp. fresh ground black pepper

4 Tb. fresh parsley, minced

3 Tb. flour

Method

Heat the butter in a sauce pan. Sauté the onions over high heat until browned and crisp. Add the garlic, toss for a bit, then add the mushrooms. Sauté just until the mushrooms start to give up their juice. Add the water, beef stock base, parsley, salt and pepper and bring to a simmer.

Mix the flour with just enough water to make a thin paste. Whisk the paste into the gravy, then heat till smooth, thickened and bubbling. Keep warm until ready to use.

Notes

This gravy can simmer for a bit if you'd like to blend the flavors a bit more, but is basically ready to go when thickened.

RED-N-READY CHILI SAUCE

It's just crying out to have something dipped in it. Quick—grab a chip!

I experimented a long time with red chile sauces to find the combination of spice and body I was looking for. This version finally did it for me. Great on enchiladas, burritos, in one of the baked recipes, and even just with chips.

This Gist

Sauté onions, garlic, cumin, and oregano in a little oil. Add a can of red chile sauce and a can of ground tomatoes in heavy purée. Simmer a bit and salt to taste.

Ingredients

2 Tb. peanut oil

1 white onion, chopped

6 cloves garlic, minced

1 tsp. ground cumin

2 tsp. mexican oregano (or the regular variety)

1 28-oz. can red chile sauce

1 28-oz. can ground tomatoes in heavy purée

1 tsp. salt

Method

Heat the peanut oil in a sauce pan over high heat. When hot, add the chopped white onions and cook until golden brown, stirring frequently. Add the minced garlic, cumin, and oregano and toss together for a minute. Turn down the heat, add the red chile sauce, tomatoes, and salt. Bring to a simmer and cook for at least 20-30 minutes.

Serve with anything needing a red chile sauce.

Variations

For a delicious and easy way to intensify the flavor, use cumin seeds instead of the ground cumin. Roast the seeds in a dry skillet over medium heat until fragrant and browned. Turn the heat off, add the oregano, and toss together for a minute. Let the two cool for a bit, then grind them together in a small coffee or spice mill. Add the ground spices to the sauce.

ROASTED BELL PEPPER PURÉE

This recipe works for both red and yellow bell peppers. I've not tried it with green bell peppers, because they lack the sweetness that makes this sauce so good. Orange bell peppers would also work. This sauce goes well with roasted vegetables or with roasted chicken or pork.

The Gist

Bell peppers are rubbed with extra virgin olive, then roasted, seeded and peeled, then puréed with a little salt and choice of herb.

Ingredients

6 red or yellow bell peppers

extra virgin olive oil

1 tsp. salt

1 tsp. minced fresh herb, such as savory or thyme

Method

Start your oven preheating to 400°F. Wash the peppers, rub them with olive oil, place them in a baking dish, then cover the dish tightly with tin foil.

Bake until the peppers are thoroughly soft, about 45 minutes. Let cool, then remove the stems, seeds, and peels. Don't worry about keeping the peppers whole or even in large pieces; anyway you get there is fine.

Place the pieces of roasted peppers in a food processor with the salt and herb. Add another splash of extra virgin olive oil. Purée until smooth.

All done and just ready to pair up with something.

Notes

Free free to turn your oven up to 450°F and cook longer if the peppers don't seem done enough. I've used some ovens where 350°F worked fine and others where 450°F was required. The photo at right shows the right degree of doneness.

These peppers are ready to peel and purée—although you may be tempted to eat them right off!

SZECHUAN PEANUT SAUCE

Very good as a dipping sauce for any kind of blanched or raw vegetables. A surprisingly spicy and delicious combination of flavors.

The Gist

Peanut butter goes into the food processor along with cilantro, garlic, soy sauce, sugar, sherry, and hot chili oil.

Ingredients

1/2 cup *real* peanut butter (see hint to the right)

1/2 cup soy sauce

5 cloves fresh garlic

1 bunch fresh cilantro

5 tbs. sugar

1 tsp. sherry

1 tsp. hot chili oil or chinese chili sauce

Chances are, there is real peanut butter in your grocery store: you just need to check labels. Real peanut butter contains peanuts and maybe salt. That's it. If there's more than that, please keep looking. Real peanut butter will have oil on the top that separated out, so you'll need to give a good stir and store it in the fridge. Such a small price to pay for true nectar of the goober.

Method

Roughly chop the cilantro and garlic. Add to a food processor along with the remaining ingredients. Process on low speed until smooth, stopping once or twice to scrape down the sides.

Place in a sealed container (like a glass jar) and let sit at least overnight in the fridge to the flavors have a chance to mingle.

Notes

This sauce has a rather unusual nutty, aromatic, spicy flavor which goes well with almost any raw or blanched vegetables. Leftovers keep well in the fridge, so it's handy to make extra and keep on hand.

Here's the sauce ready to go with blanched asparagus and carrot sticks. Ready for a dip?

SPICY SZECHUAN OIL

Here's some oil ready to go with poached chicken and blanched vegetables. Yum!

This oil is great whenever you'd like to add a little zip, such as over Easy Poach Chicken. Or use it to stir-fry vegetables.

The Gist

Minced scallions, ginger and red and black pepper are seared in hot sesame and peanut oil, then a little soy sauce finishes it.

Ingredients

1/4 cup sesame oil

1/4 peanut oil

4 Tb. minced fresh ginger

4 Tb. minced green onion

1 tsp. fresh ground black pepper

1/2 tsp. red pepper flakes

3 tsp. soy sauce

Method

Combine the minced ginger, green onions, black and red peppers in a small bowl so it's ready to go. Heat the sesame and peanut oil together in a small sauce pan until very hot (shimmery, but not yet burning). Turn the heat off and dump in the ginger/onion bowl contents. Swirl these for about 30 seconds as they sizzle. Add the soy sauce.

The oil can be used immediately or stored in a jar in the fridge until you need it.

Notes

The flavors in this oil get better as it sits, and it keeps well in the fridge. I make up more than I need so I can keep some on hand.

For a little cross-cultural excitement, this oil also works well as a dipping oil for bread in lieu of olive oil and balsamic vinegar.

GUSTO GIBLET GRAVY

This gravy is on the lookout for a gang of mashed potatoes and turkey riding together.

This gravy has enough flavor to stand on its own—far superior to ready-made products. Extra keeps well in the freezer for a quick accent to mashed or baked potatoes.

The Gist

The giblets are simmered for at least several hours with the onions and parsley, then chopped and bones removed before going back into the stock. Add the chicken and beef stock concentrates, adjust salt and pepper, then thicken with a mixture of flour, corn starch, and water.

Ingredients

2-3 lbs. Poultry giblets (hearts, necks, and gizzards)

1 small onion

1 bunch fresh parsley

2 Tbs. chicken stock concentrate

1 Tbs. beef stock concentrate

salt and pepper

2 tbs. flour

2 tbs. corn starch

> If you would like a richer flavor and don't have a cache of frozen giblets, you can always buy extra giblets at the store. Hearts, gizzards, and necks from any type of bird would do. No, I haven't tried an ostrich neck, but that just may be a little much.

Method

Start at least with the heart, gizzard, and neck from a turkey or several chickens. I recommend not using liver because boiled liver imparts a bitter taste to the stock.

Place the giblets in a stock pot big enough to hold them and leave space for boiling, then add water to cover. Peel and chop the onion, wash and mince the parsley, then add these to the pot. Simmer until the necks come apart easily.

Remove all the giblets from the stock and set them in a bowl to cool. Then remove the meat from the necks and chop the gizzards and hearts. Don't bother being too fussy about removing neck meat because it's easy to end up with teeny weeny neck bones in your gravy. Return the meat to the stock.

Bring the mixture back to a simmer as you get close to serving time. If you wish, you can add the drippings from the turkey pan at this point. You may need to skim off excess fat because a lot tends to drip off the turkey as it's cooking.

Add the stock concentrates, pepper, and test for salt. Since most stock concentrates are so salty, you will likely need little to no extra salt.

> Although I generally only use whole wheat flour, for thickening white flour is fine. Feel free to use whole wheat flour if that's all you have on hand (as is often the case for me), but you may need slightly more of it to get the desired thickening.

Combine the flour and corn starch in a coffee mug with just enough water to make make a thick-ish liquid (about the consistency of paint). Stir with a sturdy fork. Make sure your gravy mixture is simmering, then add the flour/starch mixture in a thin stream directly into the gravy as you stir it in with the fork. You'll need vigorous fork action to keep the gravy smooth. Bring the gravy to a convincing simmer, stir thoroughly to make sure all the flour mixture is mixed in, then give it a final tasting. There should be no uncooked flour taste, and it should have just enough salt and pepper. Adjust if not.

The gravy is ready and can be kept warm on a very low burner.

Notes

Canned stock can be used instead of stock concentrates. Leave the lid off while simmering to reduce it down and concentrate the flavor.

Here is my present stock of frozen giblets ready to be made into gravy. I guess I've been cooking a lot of chickens and turkeys. Heck, they are cheaper than gas!

Variations

There are three ways to make this gravy extra special.

> I use a 50/50 mixture of corn starch and flour to thicken. The corn starch avoids lumps in the gravy, while the flour keeps it thick. Corn starch alone seems to go thin on too much heating or with reheating.

For the first way, when you've done everything except thicken it, set a colander over a bowl or pot large enough to hold all of the gravy mixture. Then, purée the stock (including simmered onions and parsley) and the boned and chopped giblets in two or three batches in the blender. Make sure you have a roughly even amount of solids and liquids in each batch so the blender can work, and that you leave about two inches of space in the top of the blender container so the mixture doesn't spurt out when you press the button (very messy if this happens).

After each batch is puréed, pour it into the colander and allow it to drain into the bowl underneath. This process extracts the last bits of flavor from the simmering ingredients and leaves you with a completely smooth and intensely flavored gravy. I used to purée and not strain the mixture, but found that the simmered and puréed meat has a somewhat pasty and unappealing texture.

The second way is thicken it like a french sauce. This method can be done in addition to the first. If you're inclined to do both, your guests will enjoy a giblet gravy of such sublime flavor and consistency it seems to deserve a french name. *La sauce d'abat de dinde*, perhaps?

To do this, you would skim the turkey fat from the turkey drippings and place 4 tablespoons of the fat in a small saucepan. Heat the fat over low heat, then add 4 tbs. of flour only (no corn starch). Stir this mixture with a whisk until it's bubbling away and makes a paste. This is a french-style roux, but made with the turkey fat instead of butter. Slowly add and beat in about two cups of boiling hot broth. The paste will initially be very thick, but then thin out as you add more broth. It should be perfectly smooth and velvety.

Return the thickened fat, flour, and broth mixture to the rest of the broth and beat it in with the whisk. The sauce should be thick, smooth, and have a sheen to it from the emulsified turkey fat. Although this sauce has a much higher fat content than the skimmed version (my usual version), the flavor is so rich and wonderful that, for special occasions, it's worth it. Just have extra of the steamed vegetables to balance it all out.

Third, you can add a little half-and-half or heavy cream for a truly rich flavor. Just a few tablespoons will do the trick.

BACON-ONION GIBLET GRAVY

Bubbling hot and ready!

The crisped bacon and caramelized onions give this gravy a slightly smoke and sweet flavor—perfect to with an Orange-Ginger Hickory Smoked Turkey (see Recipe).

The Gist

Chopped bacon is fried until crisp, then used to caramelize minced onions. A deglazing with port wine, a little flour, and chicken or turkey giblet stock finishes the gravy.

Ingredients

2 lbs. chicken or turkey giblets (or mixed)

2 Tb. chicken stock base

1 Tb. beef stock base

water to cover

1/4 bacon, chopped

1 yellow onion, minced

4 Tb. flour

1/4 cup port or madera wine

2 tsp. fresh ground black pepper.

Method

Place the giblets, chicken and beef stock bases in a sauce pan and add enough water to cover. Bring to a simmer, then cook until the giblets are tender (about 2 hours).

Remove the giblets from the stock and let cool until you can handle them. Finely chop the gizzards and hearts, bone out the necks, and return all to the stock. Keep the stock warm.

Cook the chopped bacon in a sauce pan over medium high heat until crisp and most of the fat has melted off. Add the minced onions and sauté until the onions are golden brown and caramelized. As the onions are browned and start to stick to the pan, add the port or madera a little at a time to deglaze the pan. Scrape the bottom well.

Add the flour to the bacon and onions, Stir thoroughly for a minute or two. A cup at a time, drizzle the warm stock into the pan, mixing thoroughly as you do so. Let the mixture come to a simmer before adding the next cup. This will form a thick paste at first, then progressively thin out as you add more stock. Adding a little at a time and mixing constantly ensures you end up with a completely smooth and lump-free gravy.

When all the stock and giblets have been added in, add the pepper and bring the mixture to a simmer. Check for seasoning. Likely the stock bases will have added enough salt, but feel free to adjust. Keep warm until ready to serve.

Notes

This gravy may be prepared a day or two ahead, then reheated. Unlike corn starch, the flour thickening stays thick with reheating.

THAI RED CURRY PASTE

Not really a sauce, this curry paste is for simmering with coconut milk before you add whatever else you'd like in your Thai curry. Shrimp? Chicken? Eggplant? It all would work. I probably wouldn't use this curry with beef, but—if you like it—go for it!

This Gist

All the ingredients are processed in a food processor until you have a fairly fine and uniform mixture.

Ingredients

15 small red dried hot chiles, soaked in hot water then deseeded

2 tsp. cumin seed

1 Tb. coriander seed

1 Tb. pepper corns

4 shallots, peeled and cut in hunks

8 garlic cloves, cut in hunks

4 slices fresh ginger, either young ginger (galangal) or the regular variety

1 stalk lemon grass, chopped (discard the tough part at the green end)

2 heaping Tb. cilantro

1 tsp. shrimp paste (optional)

Method

Soak the dried red chiles in hot water for about 10 minutes, then drain the water and remove the seeds and stems from the chiles.

While the chiles are soaking, heat the cumin and coriander seeds and peppercorns in a small skillet over medium heat until they smell roasted (the coriander seeds may start to pop). Remove from the heat, let cool for a few minutes, then ground to a powder.

Prepare the chopped fresh ingredients (shallots, garlic, ginger, lemon grass, and cilantro).

Combine the chiles, ground spices, and chopped fresh spices in a food processor. Process until you have a fine mixture. It will be somewhat dry and more like a finely ground mix than a paste.

Use with coconut milk to make the curry of your choice.

Notes

It took a number of attempts to arrive at an authentically Thai curry paste I could make at home with ingredients I could find in the store. Most Thai curries call for the young, pink ginger roots ("galangal") which I can sometimes find in my local asian market, but regular ginger seems to work pretty well. Many grocery stores carry lemon grass these days. Coriander root I have only ever found frozen in Thai grocery stores in San Francisco, so I just use cilantro instead. Seems to work for me!

I usually make a triple or quadruple quantity of the paste and store the rest in a jar in the fridge. It stays good in the fridge for weeks.

Shrimp paste can also be found in asian grocery stores. Be sure to buy the Thai variety because there are chinese varieties, too. It can be omitted if the pungent smell is a little too much for you. As an alternative to shrimp paste, much the same flavor balance can be achieved by adding the fish sauce to your curry.

I've found one can vary the proportion of the ingredients quite a lot and still achieve a delicious result, so feel free to use more or less of each according to your tastes.

Variations

To obtain a green curry sauce, use fresh green chiles (either thai chiles or serranos) instead of the dried red chiles, plus the grated rind of either a kaffir lime or standard lime. You may also want remove some of the seeds from some or all of the chiles to tone down the heat.

SOUPER FOR SURE

What do you do if global warming missed you this winter and, instead, the snow just keeps on falling? Why, make soup, of course. Here's a selection of recipes to tide you over until the next dog sled is due in. And, if you're lucky enough to have frozen the remainder of a prior batch, you just need to defrost! These recipes will even warm you in San Francisco's frigid summer fog.

MISO SOUP

Miso soup is so simple and fast to make there's simply no excuse not to have it all the time. Sorry, Campbell's!

An instant and elegant soup you make up fresh! What could be better.

The Gist

Water is heated almost to boiling, then mix in instant dashi and miso. Shut off heat and add tofu and seaweed (wakamé) garnish.

Ingredients

4 cups water

4 tsp. instant dashi

4 tbs. miso

1 cup soft tofu, cubed

1/2 cup seaweed squares

> My regular grocery store sells miso and seaweed (wakamé), but you may need to look around. The sheets of seaweed sold for sushi can be crumpled into pieces and used. Miso comes in different varieties. Try them and see which ones you like. Any variety can be used in this soup.

Method

Heat the water and dashi until almost boiling. Taste and adjust according to whether the flavor is full enough for you. I prefer more dashi than most recipes call for.

Whisk in the miso. Shut off the heat and add tofu cubes and sea weed squares. Traditionally served in small bowls and often without a spoon! (But they're allowed all the same.)

Notes

This soup is so easy to make and so good you'll wonder why you only got it in Japanese restaurants. Not substantial enough for a meal unless you add lots of garnishes, it is a perfect first course.

Variations

This soup is usually served this way in restaurants, but Japanese use a variety of different vegetable or meat garnishes. Possible vegetable garnishes include: spinach, onion, cabbage, turnips, daikon, asparagus, carrots, string beans, snow peas, green onions—you get the idea. Possible meat additions include crab meat, chicken pieces, and pork.

Basically, you could pick almost any vegetable and/or meat and see if you like it as an addition. I would probably do this on top of the sea weed and tofu. Enough garnishes and it becomes a quick meal in itself!

I would probably add a meat raw in the almost boiling broth before the tofu and sea weed so the heat can cook the meat and the meat can flavor the broth.

Japanese stores also see dried bonito flakes and a variety of seaweed and hot red pepper mixes you can add to pump up the flavor even more. Toasted sesame seeds are also a popular topper.

SPLIT PEA VEGETABLE SOUP

Great by itself, and great with whole wheat bread dunked in it.

So much better than the canned varieties, and easy to make in quantities with extra to freeze. I usually use an entire ham in a 20-quart pot—though this recipe makes a quantity that will fit more easily in your kitchen! This soup is rich in flavor and light in calories.

The Gist

Dry split peas are simmered with parsley, thyme and a ham bone (if you have one!). Ham chunks, onions, carrots, cabbage, and frozen green peas finish the soup.

Ingredients

2 lbs. cubed ham

2 lbs. dry split peas

(optional) ham bone

2 tsp. fresh ground black pepper

1/2 cup chopped fresh parsley

2 Tb. minced fresh thyme

2 yellow onions, chopped

1-1/2 lbs. carrots, sliced

1 head cabbage, chopped

2 Tb. butter

2 lbs. frozen peas

Method

Rinse the split peas in a colander, then place in a large stock pot. Add 2 quarts of water and optional ham bone and bring to a boil. Turn the heat down to low and add the pepper, parsley, and thyme. Cook until the peas are falling apart, about 20 minutes. Add more water if you like the soup less thick.

Add the onions and cook about 10 minutes. Adjust your burner to keep the soup simmering, and be sure to stir well because the split peas have a tendency to stick to the bottom as they cook. Add the carrots and cook for 5 more minutes. Add the cabbage and butter, then turn the heat off. Let sit for 5 minutes, then stir in the frozen peas. They just need to heat through, and then soup will be the perfect temperature for serving.

Notes

Adding the carrots first, then the cabbage produces the textures I love best: crisp but cooked carrots and cabbage. Feel free to cook the soup longer if you like your vegetables all soft.

Variations

For an exotic flavor accent, add 2 tsp. of curry powder. Personally, I like the soup even better this way.

TURKEY BARLEY MUSHROOM SOUP

Worth making a turkey just to end up with this—and sometimes I do!

The turkey bones, carcass, and other leftover bits need not meet an early grave in the trash. They can receive a new life as turkey barley soup, then an afterlife as frozen leftovers. Here's to a second (or third) coming!

The Gist

Simmer the turkey bits in water, then remove to bone out and add barley, mushrooms, leeks, and cabbage. Simmer until done.

Ingredients

All the leftover bits from the turkey, especially bones and carcass

2 cups dry barley

2 pounds sliced mushrooms

2 leeks, washed and sliced

1 head cabbage

2 Tb. chick stock base

2 Tb. beef stock base

fresh ground pepper

> Equal parts chicken and beef stock base seem to me a pretty fair approximation for turkey bullion. I use the pastes, which come in plastic containers and go in the fridge once you open them. I find them at Costco. If you can't find them, use concentrated stock instead. Bullion cubes seem to me mostly MSG and salt.

Method

Amount here are approximate, depending on how much turkey bits you have left over. Please adjust if you have a lot or a little.

Place the turkey bits in a large stock pot and add just enough water to cover. Bring to a boil, then simmer for an hour or two. With a slotted spoon, remove all the bits to a bowl to cool. Best not to simmer too long because, once everything starts to fall apart, it's a mite tedious to fish all the little bones out of the broth.

Add the barley to the stock along the parts chicken and beef stock bases, then taste the stock. Add a little more if the flavor seems weak. Bring the stock back to a boil, then lower to a simmer. Add the sliced mushrooms.

Cut the root ends off of the leeks, slice in half lengthwise, then rinse thoroughly under cold water, partly peeling back the leaves to find pockets of dirt. Leeks always seem to be hiding some. Slice them, then add them to the broth.

The turkey bits should now be cool enough to remove the bones without burning yourself. Accumulate the meat in a bowl as you pick through it. I mainly go for the big chunks so I'm not pulling apart teeny weeny bones.

Add the meat back to the broth. The barley should be almost done. If not, let it simmer a little while longer while you chop the cabbage.

When the barley is done, add the chopped cabbage, bring the soup back to a boil, then shut off the heat. There will be enough heat in the soup to leave the barley cooked but still crisp.

Add fresh ground pepper to taste, 2-3 tsp. for me. Check for salt. There will probably be enough salt from the bullion that you don't need more.

Serve hot for a one-dish dinner, and freeze the leftovers for later. (In may case, the leftovers never make it to the freezer because the in-laws come knocking for them!).

Notes

If you have drippings left from cooking the turkey or extra giblet gravy you don't want to freeze, they make a great addition to the simmering water at the beginning. You may need to skim extra fat off if all the melted fat from the turkey makes a layer.

If I have big chunks of meat leftover that I want to add (such as big pieces of breast meat or whole thighs), I'll cut the meat into chunks and save it to add at the end. That way, you get some reasonably intact pieces of turkey along with the well-simmered meat.

For a very elegant soup, substitute fresh shitake or portabella mushrooms for some or all of the mushrooms, and add 2 cans of sliced water chestnuts at the end.

Alternatively, you could omit the barley and cook dumplings in the broth.

CHICKEN NOODLE SOUP

Not quite as fast as a can, but so much better. Done in the time it takes to read the paper!

A staple of everyone growing up, this is my improved version with extra flavor and whole wheat noodles. Mmm, mmm, good!

The Gist

Leftover or fresh turkey is simmered and boned, then noodles and mushrooms are simmered in the stock. A fresh green goes in at the end.

Ingredients

a leftover turkey or chicken (or you can start with a whole, fresh chicken)

2 Tb. chicken stock base

2 cans straw mushrooms

your choice of fresh green (swiss chard, kale, chinese greens, etc.), chopped

1 lbs. dry whole wheat noodles (such as linguine)

Method

Remove the big chunks of meat from the leftover chicken or turkey and chop them. Place the remaining bones in a stock pot and add just enough water to cover. Add the chicken stock base and simmer for 30-45 minutes.

If you're using a whole, fresh chicken, cook it for 10-15 minutes extra, then remove it, let it cool, then remove and chop the meat.

Remove the bones from the broth with a strainer ladle, then bring the broth to a boil. Add the noodles and straw mushrooms and bring to a boil. Cook just until the noodles are barely tender.

Shut the heat off, add the greens, and give a stir. This heats the greens just enough to cook them while still leaving them crisp, and puts the soup at a ready-to-eat temperature. Add the chopped meat, stir and serve.

SMOKED TURKEY JOOK (RICE PORRIDGE)

A delicious new meal in itself. Please, don't call it "leftovers"!

An interesting twist on a traditional chinese rice porridge, this one packs a big dose of flavor with the leftovers and carcass from an Orange-Ginger Hickory Smoked Turkey.

The Gist

The carcass from a smoked turkey is simmered for stock, then brown rice is cooked until very soft. The boned meat from the carcass, water chestnuts, bamboo shoots, and chinese greens finish the soup.

Ingredients

carcass from an Orange-Ginger Hickory Smoked Turkey (or the carcass from any turkey)

3 cups short-grain brown rice

2 8-oz. cans sliced bamboo shoots

2 8-oz. cans sliced water chestnuts

3 lbs. chinese greens (or other greens, such as collard greens or mustard greens)

Method

Place the carcass any any other bony pieces (drumsticks, wings, etc.) in a large stock pot with just enough water to cover. Bring to a boil, then simmer for 1-2 hours. Remove all the pieces to a bowl to cool.

Add the rice to the simmer stock and simmer until the rice is very soft and thickening the broth. This will take around 3 hours. Towards the end, you'll need to scrape the bottom so the soft rice doesn't stick to it.

While you're waiting for the rice, open the water chestnut and bamboo shoot cans, wash and chop the greens, and bone out pieces.

When the rice porridge is ready, add the bamboo shoots, water chestnuts, boned out turkey meat, and greens. Heat through for a few minutes, then serve.

Notes

This porridge is much fuller flavored than traditional chinese rice porridges, which I find rather bland. I also like to add some chopped white meat from the turkey along with the meat boned out from the carcass. This full-flavored chunks add a nice texture in addition to the simmered and boned pieces of meat.

POZOLE

The whole corn and the corn tortillas make for a two-part hominy.

This traditional Mexican soup is very little work to make, requiring mostly time to simmer. An easy and perfect choice to make when you're around for a few hours before dinner time.

This Gist

Simmered pork is combined with hominy, red chile sauce, and salt. Chopped cabbage and yellow and green onions finish it off. Serve with corn tortillas.

Ingredients

3 lbs. pork shoulder or country style ribs

3 lbs. hominy (white or yellow), drained

1 cup red chile sauce

2 tbs. salt, or to taste

1/4 cup lemon juice

1 large head cabbage

1 bunch green onions, chopped

1 yellow onion, chopped

extra corn tortillas, white or yellow

> Any kind of red chile sauce would work, but make sure it is a puréed chile sauce and not some tomato concoction. Red sauce for enchiladas is what I buy, and it comes in cans.

Method

Place the pork in a large soup pot and add just enough water to cover. Bring to a boil, then simmer until just tender (about an hour). When done, remove the pork from the water and set on a plate to cool.

Add the drained hominy, chile sauce, and salt to the broth and bring back to a simmer. Cook until the hominy swells and "pops," about 30 minutes.

While the hominy is cooking chop the cabbage, green onions, and onions. By now, the pork should be cool enough to handle. Tear it into bite-sized hunks, removing and discarding excess chunks of fat as you do.

Add the pork hunks back to the broth, add the lemon juice, and bring to a simmer. Taste and adjust salt level. Traditionally, this soup is fairly salty.

Add the chopped cabbage, bring the soup back to a simmer, then shut off the burner. There will be enough heat in the broth to just cook the cabbage while still leaving it crisp.

Add the chopped green and yellow onions, then serve with the extra tortillas.

Notes

I like to tear the extra tortillas into pieces and mix them with the soup, but this is optional. It is also traditional to serve this with other chopped, raw vegetables for people to mix in with their hot soup. Possible choices include sliced radishes or jalapeño peppers, cilantro, or more green or yellow onion.

Using sliced pork shoulder reduces the cooking time and the work in tearing the meat.

To make this soup extra fancy, you could serve it with tortilla chips instead of whole, round tortillas, but this would increase the fat content.

Leftovers freeze very well.

Pozole is perfect when we have our El Salvadoran construction crew over.

HOT AND SOUR SOUP

Perfect for a cold winter night (or any other night, in my opinion!)

The Gist

Marinated pork is simmered in chicken broth and wood ear mushrooms, then finished with tofu, bamboo shoots, baby bok choy, eggs, green onions, and shrimp. Rice wine, rice vinegar, ground white pepper, and sesame oil provide the key seasonings. Noodles make the soup a complete meal.

Ingredients

20 or so dried lily buds

1.5 lbs. lean pork cut into long strips

2 Tb corn starch

2 Tb soy sauce

1 Tb vegetable oil

1 lb. raw, shelled and deveined shrimp

1 tsp. salt

2 Tb rice wine (or sherry)

1 lb. firm tofu, cut into long strips

6 cups water

6 Tb. chicken stock base

4 Tb rice wine (or sherry)

4-6 oz. fresh wood ear mushrooms, cut into strips (or half that amount dried mushrooms) soaked in water)

1 lb. whole wheat linguine

2 cans sliced bamboo shoots

2 lbs. baby bok choy, separated into leaves

2 Tb. corn starch

2 Tb. flour

6 eggs, beaten

4 Tb. rice vinegar (or cider vinegar)

2 Tb. sesame oil

2 tsp. ground white pepper

1 bunch green onions, chopped

Method

Soak the lily buds in a bowl of warm water. While they're soaking, mix the pork, 2 Tb corn starch, 2 Tb soy sauce, and 1 Tb oil together and let them marinate. Mix the shrimp with 1 tsp. salt and 2 Tb. rice wine and let them marinate.

Bring the water to a boil and mix in the chicken stock base. Add the 4 Tb. rice wine, pork, wood ear mushrooms, and lily buds. While this is simmering, bring another pot of water to boil to cook the linguine.

Simmer the soup for about 10 minutes, then add the tofu, bamboo shoots (along the way, feel free to start the linguine). When it comes to a boil, add the baby bok choy and bring back to a boil. Mix the 2 Tb. of corn starch with the 2 Tb. of flour, then add enough water to make a smooth paste, then whisk it in with a fork to thicken the soup. Turn the heat down.

Cook the linguine al dente, then drain.

Use the fork to mix the soup as you dizzle in the eggs, then turn the heat off. Add the drained linguine. Mix in the raw shrimp (there will be just enough heat in the broth to cook the shrimp perfectly). Add the 4 Tb. rice vinegar, 2 Tb. sesame oil, 2 tsp. white pepper, and the green onions.

Give it a final stir, then taste. Add more vinegar and white pepper if you like it more hot and sour. Serve and enjoy!

Notes

Noodles aren't traditional in hot and sour soup, but I like to add them to make it a complete meal like a japanese udon dish. Feel free to use brown rice noodles or another other type of whole grain pasta that suits your fancy.

PERSIAN YOGHURT SOUP

Not your typical soup! But wonderful on a warm day.

Packed with more of the great add-ins than a traditional yoghurt soup, this is an easy and elegant make-ahead soup.

The Gist

Yoghurt, half-and-half, salt and pepper are combined with golden raisins, minced green onions and walnuts, dill and grated cucumbers. No cooking required!

Ingredients

2 japanese cucumbers, grated

1/4 cup minced fresh dill

1/3 cup golden raisins

1/3 cup minced green onions

1/3 cup minced walnuts

3 cups yoghurt

1/2 cup half-and-half

3/4 tsp. salt

3/4 tsp. fresh ground black pepper

> Yoghurt keeps in the fridge for a long time and is great to always keep on hand—even if you're not planning on making this soup! I use it to substitute for part of the mayonnaise in any recipe.

Method

Grate the japanese cucumbers into a bowl big enough to hold everything (it's not necessary to peel them). Add the remaining ingredients and give a good stir. That's it!

Notes

If you like, you can save a little of the dill, green onions, walnuts and raisins for a garnish on top.

This soup can chill in the fridge several hours or even overnight before serving.

Traditionally, the golden raisins are soaked in water first and drained, but I find they plump up nicely with a few hours of chilling the soup in the fridge.

ÜBER-ONION SOUP

The rich and golden flavor deserves a platinum rim!

A classic french soup fortified with beef, greens and beans to make it a complete and healthy meal. This recipe is also great for giving a new life to leftover roast beef or steak.

The Gist

Onions are caramelized in butter, then simmered in beef broth with white beans. Fresh greens (collard greens in this version) are added at the end. The soup is then served with wheat bread toasted with cheese on top.

Ingredients

2-3 lbs. cubed beef (leftover roast or fresh)

2 quarts water

3 Tbs. beef stock base

1 stick butter

5 yellow onions, sliced

1 lbs. dry white beans (such as the Great Northern variety)

1 pkg. fresh thyme, minced

1/2 cup white wine or brandy

salt and pepper to taste

2 large bunches collard greens, chopped

8 slices whole wheat bread

1 cup mixed grated swiss and parmesan cheese

Leftover grilled or roasted beef is ideal for this recipe because it already has the searing step to bring out the flavor of the beef. If you're using fresh beef, be sure to sear it thoroughly over high heat before simmering.

Method

Cut the leftover or fresh beef into small cubes. If you're using leftover roast beef or steak from one of the marinated, grilled recipes in this book, it can immediately go into the water to start simmering. If you're using fresh beef, brown it in the stock pot over high heat first, then add the water.

Add the stock base to the water and bring it to a simmer. Leave it simmering while you prepare the onions. (The stock can also be prepared ahead and simmered for several hours, but 30-45 minutes will get you most of the flavor.)

Place the butter in the bottom of a large stock pot, then add the sliced onions. Heat the pan over medium heat until the butter is melted, then cover the pan and raise the heat to high. Stir the onions every few minutes as they give up their juices. After about 15 minutes, uncover the pan, turn the heat down to medium, and stir the onions every few minutes until golden brown. Be sure to scrape the bottom of the pan as you stir so it doesn't burn on the bottom. If the onions start to stick, add just a little water to unstick them.

Rinse the dry white beans thoroughly in a colander.

When the onions are golden and caramelized, add the beef stock and cubes, thyme, dry white beans, and the white wine or brandy. Bring the mixture to a simmer and taste for salt and pepper. If you're using marinated, leftover beef, you may not need any more salt or pepper.

Simmer the soup until the beans are tender (about 1-1/2 hours).

Lightly toast the slices of wheat bread. A toaster oven can do them all at once. Place the toasted slices on aluminum foil or a baking sheet and sprinkle the mixed, grated cheeses over them. Return them to the oven or toaster oven for a final toasting when you're ready to serve the soup.

Just before serving, add the greens and shut off the heat. Give the bread a final toasting, then serve. The greens will still be bright green and crunchy. Float a slice of toast on top of each bowl, or—for folks who like their toast crisp—serve it on the side for dipping.

Variations

I also like this soup with cannelloni beans (white kidney beans) and kale instead of collard greens. Any sturdy, cooking green would also do well. Mustard greens would be an interesting choice if you like mustard flavor with your beef.

CRAB-CORN SOUP

This is my version of a traditional, fancy chinese soup. Good enough to serve for the most elegant dinner! Always requested around our house for Christmas Eve.

Here's my bowl ready to go on Christmas Eve. Yum!

The Gist

Chicken stock is heated with creamed corn, then sautéed minced ginger, cilantro, green onion,and ham go in. The soup is thickened with corn starch and flour, then egg whites are whisked in. Cooked crab meat and white pepper finish it.

Ingredients

Optional for making your own chicken stock:

2 chickens

1 cup fresh ginger, sliced thin

1 bunch green onions, lightly pressed

water to cover

2 tsp. salt

or just 1 gallon good chicken stock

or 1 gallon water with chicken stock base to taste

4 15-oz. cans creamed corn

4 Tb peanut oil or chicken fat skimmed from the stock

1 bunch cilantro, minced

3 bunches green onions, chopped

4 Tb minced fresh ginger

1 cup minced ham

1/4 cup rice or white wine

6 egg whites, lightly beaten

4 Tb corn starch

4 Tb flour

1-1/2 lbs. cooked crab meat

1 tsp white pepper

additional salt to taste

Method

Thoroughly rinse the chickens in cool water, then place in a close-fitting stock pot. Add the ginger, green onions, salt, and water to cover. Bring to a simmer, then simmer for 1 to 4 hours. Remove the chicken, ginger slices, and green onion and discard (or eat if you like well-cooked chicken!). Add the creamed corn to the stock and keep it simmering on the stove.

If you like, reserve a little of the minced cilantro and green onion to garnish on each bowl as you serve them.

In a large sauté pan, heat the peanut oil or chicken fat over high heat. When hot, add the minced ginger and sizzle for a minute or two. Add the green onion and cilantro, give a few more stirs, then add the ham. When all is hot and sizzling, add the rice wine. Give a stir for a minute or two until all the alcohol has evaporated (no more alcohol smell in the steam). Add these ingredients to the simmering stock. Add all this to the stock and bring back to a simmer.

Mix the corn starch and flour together dry, then add just enough water to make a smooth pasted. Once all the lumps are out, add a little more water to make the mix thin and pourable. Whisk this paste into the simmering stock to thicken it. You should have a nice creamed soup consistency.

Drizzle and whisk in the beaten egg whites. Shut off the heat and add the crab meat. Add the white pepper, then adjust the salt and pepper to your taste.

This soup can be made ahead and kept warm till serving time. Don't boil it once finished as the consistency and crab will suffer as a result.

Notes

Homemade chicken stock delivers over-the-top flavor, but the other options for stock still make a great soup. Leftovers are also great. This soup does not freeze well. Freezing would make it runny and the crab tough.

SALAD MON AMOUR

The crop of tomatoes one good Saturday. Quick, pick some basil!

I love salads. Hence the title. A great salad can be a meal in itself or the overture to what follows.

Unfortunately, much of what passes for "salad" is best passed on altogether. In my experience, two villains carry much of the blame:

- Iceberg lettuce

- Bottled salad dressing

I suppose that iceberg lettuce must have gained its preeminent position because it is durable and crisp. All that it lacks is flavor and nutrition. I only eat it to be polite.

Thankfully, these days most grocery stores carry a wide variety of greens year-round—many in bags already washed and ready to go. Spring mix, baby spinach, romaine, butter lettuce, red leaf lettuce—I love them all. All (except iceberg!) are very high in fiber and nutrition and very low in calories. I advise people to eat as much of them as they like and not worry about it.

Unless, of course, you're combining those yummy greens with bottled dressing (the second villain). A few are good, but most bottled dressings are very high in calories and very low in flavor. There's nothing like a big glop of ranch dressing to turn a potentially great salad into calorie-laden, soupy mess.

A great salad dressing can be as easy as a little olive oil, balsamic vinegar, salt, and pepper. You don't have to mix or make it, just sprinkle a little on and toss. Done. If you're wary of proportions, the first recipe suggests some, but feel free to adjust to your taste.

Other recipes are somewhat more involved, but the result could change your opinion of salads forever.

Here's hoping you're on your way to making delicious salads a regular part of your meals.

ALMOST TOO-EASY TOSSED SALAD

A simple tossed salad arranged nicely for the photo. To eat this, I put it in a bowl and tossed it! What does go on off camera...

Better than ready made, and almost as fast. The trick is fresh, good ingredients.

The Gist

Toss your favorite greens with some tomatoes, another vegetable or two, extra virgin olive oil, balsamic vinegar, one herb (pick one), salt and pepper.

Ingredients

a bag of your favorite greens (washed and ready to go)

tomatoes

a red onion

a cucumber

extra virgin olive oil

balsamic vinegar

an herb (pick one)

salt

fresh ground black pepper

Method

Buy a bag of your favorite salad greens at the store. Spring mix, for example, comes in bags well-washed and ready to go. Sprinkle as much as you like into a bowl. Add tomatoes cut into bite-sized pieces, a little thin-sliced red onion, and some sliced cucumber. Pick one dried herb from your spice cabinet and add a few teaspoons-worth. Tarragon or oregano are good choices to start with.

Drizzle a little olive oil over the bowl, then toss. Start with just a little because it's easy too add too much. There should be just enough to barely coat the leaves. Adding the olive oil first helps keep the salad crisp.

Sprinkle a few teaspoons of balsamic vinegar over, then a little salt, then some fresh ground black pepper. Toss thoroughly, taste for salt and pepper, then serve.

Notes

An easier salad could hardly be imagined: construction takes all of ten minutes. And you still get something on par with the house salad at most restaurants.

Bagged greens are an easy choice because you just open the bag and pour some in. You could also buy greens (butter lettuce, romaine, endive, etc.). For those, wash and tear them into bite-sized pieces, then either toss with paper towels or spin in a salad spinner to remove the excess water.

For cucumbers, I prefer the flavor of the japanese cucumbers (the long, thin ones wrapped in plastic). I tend to use balsamic vinegar in a very simple salad like this because the flavor is milder. I save red wine vinegar, cider vinegar, etc., for richer salads which can stand up to their greater acidity.

If there are no decent tomatoes at all in your grocery store, a can of diced tomatoes in juice (drained) will work in a pinch.

You could also pick up a bunch of fresh herbs at the store in lieu of a dried herb. It would need to be washed and chopped, and you can generally get away with more fresh herbs than dried. For fresh herbs in this salad, I like thyme, oregano, tarragon, rosemary, or basil. Parsley by itself is a little too bland. Multiple herbs is also fine, but you have to pay attention to how all the flavors go along with your choice of greens and vegetables.

Black or green olives and avocados are also frequent additions to salads around our house. I will also sometimes sprinkle a little of the ever-handy grated cheese mix for pasta over the salad to zip it up.

Good ingredients are especially key for a good salad. Thankfully, quite good grape or cherry tomatoes in plastic boxes are available year round. I avoid the larger varieties because they tend to be bland. An easy way to tell: smell the tomato. If it smells like a tomato, it will taste like one!

I only use 100% pure extra virgin olive oil (the dark green kind). I find the flavor far superior to lighter varieties or blends and, to me, it has never seemed to strong. Little bottles can very expensive at the grocery store, but Costco, Trader Joe's , and Smart and Final all have large ones for very cheap. The large ones will stay good in your pantry until you finish them.

SECRET SPICE DRESSING

So simple and yet so good, this dressing is easy to make and will utterly baffle your guests as to its origins. Let it be your house secret!

The Gist

Regular ol' ketchup, olive oil, cider vinegar, salt, black pepper, cayenne, paprika, and granulated garlic combine to create a wonderfully spicy dressing that's moderate on the calories.

Ingredients

1/2 cup ketchup

1/4 cup olive oil

2 Tbs. cider vinegar

2 tsp. fresh ground black pepper

1 tsp. paprika

1/2 tsp. salt

1/2 tsp. granulated garlic

1/4 to 1/2 tsp. cayenne pepper

Method

Combine all ingredients and whisk together with a fork until creamy and smooth. Toss with your favorite salad fixings.

Almost as fast as a bottle, and so much better!

Variations

For a more complex spicy flavor, add 1/2 tsp. dry mustard powder or 1/2 tsp. ground ginger. (I've not tried both together, but why not?)

Fresh minced garlic would also be nice instead of the granulated garlic, but be sure the dressing has an hour or two before serving for the garlic flavor to disperse.

Notes

This dressing can be made well ahead of time, and you can easily double the recipe and store the extra in a glass jar in the fridge. It will keep for quite some time.

DILLY GRAND HI-LO DRESSING

High in flavor and lower in fat, this version of Thousand (a grand!) Islands Dressing gets an extra flavor punch from fresh dill. Great with a tomato, cucumber, and red onion salad

The Gist

Blend half-mayonnaise half-yoghurt together with ketchup, dry mustard powder, paprika, chinese chili garlic paste, Worcestershire, salt, pepper, and lots of chopped fresh dill.

Ingredients

1/2 cup mayonnaise

1/2 cup yoghurt

1/4 cup ketchup

1 tsp. dry mustard powder

1 tsp. paprika

1 tsp. chinese chili garlic paste

1 tsp. Worcestershire

1 tsp. fresh ground black pepper

1/2 tsp. salt

1/2 cup minced fresh dill

Easily a thousand islands of flavor.

> I almost always use half-mayonnaise and half-yoghurt whenever I use mayonnaise. You get the creaminess of mayonnaise with greatly reduced calories, plus a nice little tang from the yoghurt.

Method

Mix together all ingredients until smooth. Lightly dress your choice of salad ingredients with it.

Variations

This dressing can take lots of chopped add-ins to make the flavor even more complex. I sometimes will add one or more of the following:

- minced red onion
- minced hard boiled egg
- minced black or green olives (or both!)
- minced capers

On occasion, I have even been known to add all of these at once! Living la vida loca...

LOW-FAT HIGH-FLAVOR BLEU CHEESE DRESSING

This version uses my trick of yoghurt with a little mayonnaise to turn out a bleu cheese dressing vastly better than I've had elsewhere. A generous portion of real bleu cheese (too expensive for commercial varieties) is part of the secret.

The Gist

The bleu cheese is crumbled into the yoghurt and roughly mixed in, then the remaining ingredients are mixed in. That's it!

Ingredients

1 cup yoghurt

4 oz. bleu cheese

2 Tb. mayonnaise

1/2 tsp salt

1 tsp. fresh ground black pepper

1/2 tsp. granulated garlic

1/2 tsp. dry mustard powder

1/8 tsp. cayenne pepper

1 tsp. Worcestershire sauce

1 tsp. lemon juice or white balsamic or white wine vinegar

So much better than from a bottle.

Method

Place the yoghurt in a small mixing bowl. Crumble the bleu cheese into it and mix well with a sturdy fork, breaking up the larger lumps. Mix just enough to distribute the bleu cheese flavor, leaving some small pieces.

Add the remaining ingredients and mix well. Chill until ready to use. Will keep in the fridge for a week or more.

> Be sure to buy a hunk of bleu cheese instead of a container with it already crumbled. The crumbled cheese seems to lose a lot of flavor in the process.

Notes

The key to this recipe is a piece of good quality bleu cheese. It's expensive, but you only need a little. A good Stilton cheese would also work.

BLEU CHEESE VINAIGRETTE

This non-creamy variation on a bleu cheese dressing goes great with full-flavored greens like arugula and radicchio.

The Gist

Bleu cheese is crumbled into a cup, lightly mixed with a little extra virgin olive oil, then tossed into your choice of green salad. A little salt, pepper, and your choice of vinegar finishes it off.

Ingredients

1/4 cup bleu cheese

4 Tb. extra virgin olive oil

1/2 tsp. salt

1 tsp. fresh ground black pepper

1-2 Tb. your choice of vinegar, such as white balsamic vinegar

Method

Crumble the bleu cheese into a little cup and add the olive oil. Lightly mix with a fork, still leaving whole bits of cheese in it.

Pour this over your choice of green salad and toss. Sprinkle the salt, pepper, and vinegar over the salad and toss again. Serve immediately.

Crumbled bleu cheese mixed with a little extra virgin olive oil makes for the start of a great dressing.

Notes

If you like, you can mix all the dressing ingredients together and just toss the salad once. I find that tossing the oil first before adding the salt and vinegar seems to keep the greens crisper.

CAESAR ESCAPE SALAD

If Caesar had served this salad to the Roman Senate on that fateful day in March, no doubt he could have made his escape while they finished their salads!

The Gist

Toss romaine lettuce, alfalfa sprouts, red onions, tomatoes, avocados, and roasted garlic croutons with Caesar salad dressing.

Ingredients

1/2 head of romaine lettuce leaves, washed and torn

1 package alfalfa sprouts

1 ripe Haas avocado, cut into hunks

4 ripe tomatoes, roughly chopped

1/2 red onion, diced

4 slices of roasted garlic toast (see Recipe), cut into croutons

1/4 cup Caesar salad dressing (Recipe follows)

the rest of the anchovies from making the dressing, minced

"Et tu, crouton?"

Method

Wash the romaine leaves and tear them into bite-sized pieces. Rinse the alfalfa sprouts. Spin both in a salad spinner or blot damp-dry with paper towels.

If you're preparing this salad ahead of time, refrigerate the lettuce and sprouts in a bowl with damp paper towels on top. The rest of the ingredients (except for croutons) can go in a separate bowl in the fridge covered with plastic wrap. The salad will keep for several hours this way, and you can then toss all together when ready to serve.

Otherwise, toss the lettuce and sprouts with all remaining ingredients. Feel free to add a little more dressing if you like.

Variations

For a fancy, plated salad, keep the romaine leaves whole and arrange the rest of the ingredients on top of the whole leaves. Garnish with a little extra parmesan-romano grated cheese mix.

To turn this into an entrée salad, top with strips of grilled chicken or fish. Who needs a bistro?

Notes

I think anchovies are one of the key flavorings in Caesar salad, but if the flavor is not to your liking, feel free to use less or eliminate them entirely. The salad will still be delicious and far more flavorful than the typical restaurant Caesar salad.

CAESAR SALAD DRESSING

Much easier to make than you might think. Toss over some romaine lettuce leaves, add grated Parmesan-Romano cheese over it and some roasted garlic croutons (see Recipe) and you have an $8 salad right at home.

The Gist

Combine olive oil, coddled eggs, lemon juice, peppercorns, and oil from a can of anchovies in a blender.

Ingredients

1/2 cup extra virgin olive oil

2 coddled eggs

1/4 cup grated parmesan-romano cheese mix

2 Tbs. lemon juice (more to taste)

1 tsp. peppercorns

1/2 tsp. salt

olive oil from a can of anchovies

2 anchovy fillets

> Coddling the eggs takes care of any errant bacteria or concerns from using raw eggs. Be sure to heat the water just until a near-simmer so you don't end up with soft-boiled eggs!

Method

To coddle the eggs, place 2 eggs in a small saucepan with enough hot water to float the eggs. Place the pan on a burner over high heat and heat just until it's ready to simmer. Immediately remove the pan to the sink and flush it with cold water until cool.

Break the eggs into a blender container. Add the remaining ingredients and blend until smooth. Extra dressing keeps well in the fridge. Chop the rest of the anchovies to go into the salad.

Notes

I have many time made this dressing with raw eggs without making myself (or anyone else!) ill. However, concerns of food safety being what they are these days, I've added a coddling step for extra safety.

Adding the olive oil from the can of anchovies and two of the fillets brings a little of the wonderful anchovy flavor to the dressing. Blending with the grated cheese gives the dressing a creamy, cheese flavor without the goupy ingredients in commercial dressing.

HOLIDAY SURVIVAL SALAD

When it's the holiday time of year and calorific temptations abound, I'll often make what I call a "Holiday Survival Salad" to bring to a gathering. This is a salad so full of vegetables, nutrition, and fiber that it helps to average out even the most decadent dinner. Combine it with one of my dressings and you'll have a delicious and not-so-secret weapon for emerging from the holidays the same size you went in.

The Gist

Thow together whatever fresh, frozen, or canned vegetables you like and add a low-fat dressing. The list below is just an example.

Ingredients

1 bag ready-to go washed spinach

1 can julienne beats, drained

1 pint cherry or grape tomatoes

1 can garbonzo beans, drained

1 lb. carrots, cut on the diagonal into slices

1 bag frozen baby green beans

1 bag frozen sugar snap peas

> Brief blanching or steaming is the key to cooking many kinds of vegetables. You want just enough heat to eliminate the raw taste, while still leaving the vegetable crisp and bright.

I could just eat the whole thing! So I make sure to bring enough for everybody. :)

Method

The simplest way is to just open the cans, thaw the frozen vegetables, and construct your own creative arrangement. In the above photo, I put the spinach leaves on the bottom.

If you're up for taking a little extra time to improve the textures, a little blanching will do the trick. Bring a pot of water to a boil, then, one at a time, add a cookable vegetable, then use a strainer to scoop it into a colander. Immediately rinse it with cold water to hold the color and crispness. For this salad, I blanched the green beans, peas, and carrots. The beets and garbonzo beans are already cooked.

Serve with a low fat dressing on the side. Leftovers will stay good for a few days if not dressed.

Notes

Fresh green beans and snap peas also work well. I use the frozen when I'm short of time and don't want to remove strings or ends. If you have the time, the fresh vegetables have better flavor and consistency than the frozen ones.

VEGELICIOUS PASTA SALAD

A very different and very good pasta salad chock full of vegetables. Add the optional chopped, cooked chicken and it's a complete meal.

It's a pasta! It's a salad! No, it's Vegelicious Pasta Salad!

The Gist

Cooked whole wheat pasta is tossed with a complex and spicy dressing, then set aside to cool. Fresh chopped vegetables and herbs are tossed in after cooling to finish the salad.

Salad Ingredients

2 lbs. dry whole wheat pasta (penne or fusilli work well)

1 minced red onion

1 bunch chopped parsley

2 cups frozen peas

4 red bell peppers, chopped

4 yellow bell peppers, chopped

2 cans black olives, drained and sliced

1 28-oz can diced tomatoes in juice, drained

Dressing Ingredients

1/2 cup mayonaise

1/2 cup yoghurt

4 tbs. soy sauce

4 tbs. lemon juice

4 tbs. red wine vinegar

2 tsp. Dijon mustard

2 tsp. sugar

1 tsp. granulated garlic

1 tsp. paprika

1 tsp. ground ginger

1 tsp. fresh ground black pepper

1/4 tsp. cayenne pepper

Method

Contemplating a salad.

Set a big pot of salted water on to boil while you make the dressing.

Combine all dressing ingredients together in a bowl and whisk together until smooth.

Cook the pasta just until cooked but still a little tough (al denté). Drain in a colander, then pour into a large mixing bowl. Pour in the dressing over the hot pasta and toss thoroughly. Continue to toss the pasta every ten minutes or so as you chop the vegetables until the pasta is cool and all the dressing is absorbed into it.

Wash and chop all the vegetables. If you're ready to serve, toss the chopped vegetables into the pasta and serve.

This dish can also be prepared as far ahead of time as the day before. Store the pasta and vegetables in separate bowls in the fridge, then toss together for serving. This keeps the vegetables at maximum crispness for serving.

Notes

I prefer penne or fusilli pasta for this salad because it holds and absorbs the dressing well, but any variety would do in a pinch. Just be sure to slightly undercook the pasta so it doesn't get mushy as it absorbs the dressing.

Variations

Add up to 6 cups of chopped chicken or shrimp (or some of each) to turn this into a main dish salad.

If really good fresh tomatoes are available, you could chop and add them in lieu of the canned tomatoes. I find canned diced tomatoes to be a reliable, year-round ingredient. Be sure to drain them well before adding them.

For the over-the-top garnish, sprinkle the salad with grated pasta cheese mix.

ORANGE AND AVOCADO SALAD

This salad is an easier-to-make variation on a grapefruit and avocado salad. I love this salad with oranges (faster and easier to peel!) but do on occasion make it with grapefruit, too.

So delicious it's almost a dessert!

The Gist

Butter lettuce leaves are tossed in a dressing of walnut oil, white balsamic vinegar, salt and pepper. Orange sections, red onion, and mint are tossed in a dressing of olive oil, sherry vinegar, fruit vinegar, salt and pepper.

Ingredients

1 head butter lettuce

3 oranges, peeled and cut in sections

3 ripe Haas avocados, peeled and sliced

1 red onion, thinly sliced

4 Tb. fresh mint, minced

Dressing for lettuce:

4 Tb. walnut oil

1 Tb. white balsamic vinegar

1 tsp. fresh ground black pepper

1/4 tsp. salt

Dressing for oranges:

4 Tb. extra virgin olive oil

2 tsp. sherry vinegar or white balsamic vinegar

2 tsp. fruit vinegar (such as raspberry)

1 tsp. fresh ground black pepper

1/4 tsp. salt

> I like the rich, nutty flavor or Haas avocados more than any other variety. Thankfully, they are available year round with flights from southern places. The trick to peeling them easily is to let them ripen just until they are barely soft. Too hard or too soft and peeling is more difficult. Let them ripen more quickly on the counter, then put them in the fridge to slow the process down.

Delicious with grapefruit, too!

Method

Wash the butter lettuce and keep the leaves whole or tear them in small pieces, then spin them or toss them with paper towels to dry. Place the leaves in a bowl, cover with more paper towels, then place them in the fridge to chill.

Make the two separate dressings and whisk each together.

Lightly toss together the orange sections, sliced red onions, and mint. Gently toss in the avocado slices or leave them separate to arrange on the leaves. These can also chill in the fridge until you're ready to serve.

Toss the lettuce leaves with their dressing and arrange on plates. Toss the orange etc. with its dressing. Arrange the avocado slices on top of the leaves, then put a mound of the orange mix in the middle. Serve!

Notes

You can try tossing the orange sections and avocado together, but avocado slices are rather delicate and tend to break. If that doesn't bother you, then go for it! For a final garnish, you can sprinkle each plate with a little chopped fresh chives or some more minced fresh mint.

Variations

I do sometimes make this salad with grapefruit, but extracting the sections without the membrane takes some work. Here's a few hints.

First cut off the peel off a grapefruit with a knife (going all the way through the white membrane to the fruit), then gently tear it apart section by section to remove the fruit from the membrane. Don't worry if your fruit sections don't all stay whole (they probably won't). They'll still be delicious. The trick is to remove just about all the white membrane because it is so bitter.

I've tried using the containers of peeled, fresh grapefruit sections as a shortcut, but they contain so much of the bitter membrane that the flavor suffers considerably. Oranges are easy because the membrane isn't bitter, so no need to remove it.

TAPAS-STYLE POTATO SALAD

This recipe was inspired by a traditional tapas recipe. I added the green peas for the wonderful color and texture.

The Gist

Red potatoes, bell peppers, fresh peas, capers, and red onions are tossed with a dressing of olive oil, lemon juice, orange juice, dill, salt and pepper.

Ingredients

6 red skin potatoes, boiled and cubed

2 bell peppers (your choice of color), chopped

1 red onion, finely chopped

1 cup fresh or frozen green peas

1/4 cup small capers

1/4 cup extra virgin olive oil

2 Tb. lemon juice

4 Tb. orange juice

1/4 cup minced fresh dill

1/4 cup minced fresh parsley

2 tsp. salt

1 Tb. fresh ground black pepper

Almost a meal in itself, this is a refreshing change from usual potato salads.

Method

Combine the potatoes, bell peppers, red onion, peas and capers in a bowl. Combine the remaining ingredients in a bowl to make the dressing and whisk together. Pour the dressing over the salad and gently toss. Chill until serving.

Notes

Unlike many salads, this one can be made a few hours or even a day ahead and is still quite good.

WATERMELON SALAD

Not your typical salad, but oh-so-cool, delicious, and refreshing on a warm day. Best put together right before you eat it (if you can wait!).

The Gist

Watercress is tossed with walnut oil, lemon juice, mint, salt and pepper. Watermelon cubes are tossed with raspberry purée, olive oil, mint, salt and pepper and then go on top of the watercress.

Ingredients

2 bunches fresh watercress

1/2 cup fresh mint leaves, chopped

6 cups seedless watermelon, cubed

1 red onion, thinly sliced

1 pint fresh raspberries

1/4 cup extra virgin olive oil

1/2 tsp. salt

1/2 tsp. fresh ground black pepper

1/4 cup walnut oil

juice of 1 lemon

1/2 tsp. salt

1/2 tsp. fresh ground black pepper

A refreshing combination of sweet and piquant.

Method

Rinse and drain the raspberries thoroughly, then press them through a sieve to extra the purée. Combine the purée with half the mint, olive oil, salt and pepper. This is the dressing for the watermelon.

Combine the walnut oil, lemon juice, salt, pepper, and remaining mint to make the dressing for the watercress.

Wash the watercress and dry in a spinner or with paper towels, then chop it roughly and place it in a bowl.

Place the watermelon cubes in a bowl with the sliced red onions. At this point, the two bowls can hold in the fridge until you're ready to serve.

When you're ready to serve, toss the olive oil dressing with the watercress. Pour the raspberry dressing over the watermelon and red onion, then gently toss. To serve, place a generous portion of watercress on a plate and top with the watermelon.

Notes

The undressed ingredients can hold for several hours in the fridge until you're ready to serve, but should be dressed immediately before serving so nothing starts to get soggy.

This salad is almost a salad and between-courses fruit all in one. It's especially good to lighten up a dinner with a substantial entrée.

Attention salad-lovers: head for the pool!

NOODLING AROUND

I love pasta. Doesn't everybody? Only it's gotten such a rap with all the hooha about carbs. The truth is that whole grain carbs (including pasta) are great part of a healthy and weight-maintaining diet. I love them all and eat them all the time—mostly whole wheat pastas, but sometimes brown rice or buckwheat noodles, too. Thankfully, they are widely available these days.

All a great, whole grain pasta is something great to go with it, and the choices are wider than sauces. This chapter gives lots of different ways to turn a great noodle into a great dinner. Just don't spoil it with a super buttery cream sauce or oil drenched tomato sauce, please! This chapter gives some great, healthy sauces with just enough fat to fool the pickiest eater (I should know; I married one!).

Check out the recipe in Three Meals to Save Your Live for a very fast and easy pasta dinner. The ones in this chapter are for when you're in the mood for something more special.

> For best nutrition and flavor, be sure to buy whole grain pasta. The package, for example, should say "100% whole wheat." There are some pastas which say "whole grain" and are a blend of whole wheat and processed flours. These are okay in a pinch but not as good in my opinion.

PASTA À LA CARBONARA

Somewhat non-traditional, but delicious and fast.

The Gist

Onions and bacon are sautéed together, then tossed with cooked spaghetti and broccoli. A cheese, egg, salt and pepper purée is tossed in last.

Ingredients

1 lb. sliced bacon (1 package)

2 large yellow onions, finely chopped

1 lb. (dry) whole wheat spaghetti

6 eggs

1 cup grated cheese mix (romano-parmesan, see Recipe)

1 tsp. salt

1 tsp. fresh ground black pepper

another vegetable to go along

Method

Cut the bacon into pieces about an inch long. Place these in a large sauté pan and start them frying over medium heat. They'll need to cook until crisp.

Put a large pot of salted water on to boil (for the pasta). Peel and chop the onions, then place them in a bowl so they ready to go.

Combine the cheese, eggs, salt and pepper in a bowl and whisk together

When the bacon is crisp, turn off the heat and remove almost all the melted bacon fat. Tilting the pan and using a small gravy ladle works great for this. Turn the heat back on to medium and add the onions. They'll need to cook at least until transparent but, if the water's not boiling yet, you can keep them cooking until they're brown and caramelized.

When the water is boiling, add the spaghetti and cook until almost done, then drain the spaghetti in a colander.

Add the spaghetti to the bacon and onion pan and toss thoroughly to combine. Add the egg and cheese purée and toss to mix thoroughly. The heat of the ingredients will be just enough to turn the purée into a creamy egg and cheese sauce for the pasta.

Manga!

> I let the bacon fat cool a bit in a bowl, then keep it in a jar in the fridge for later frying. Nothing zips up eggs for breakfast or a fried rice like frying it in bacon fat instead of oil or butter! You can also use it instead of shortening or butter to grease a pan, such as for biscuits or corn bread.

Here's some Pasta à la Carbonara (linguine in this case), served with SuperFastEasy Grilled Chicken and Garlic-Roasted Brussels Sprouts. Who needs dessert?

Notes

This recipe makes a complete, one-dish meal. Omit the bacon and sauté the onions in a few tablespoons of olive oil if you're expecting vegetarians for dinner.

Frying the bacon until crisp is the most time consuming part of this recipe, but important both for flavor and for getting the fat content down to an acceptable level.

To make the frying go faster, you can start the bacon in a covered pan with a little water and cook it on high heat until the water is evaporated (it will escape around the cover). Then turn the heat down to medium and continue frying until crisp. This accelerates the process of melting the excess fat off of the bacon.

Although low in moisture, leftovers tend not to freeze well because the egg and cheese sauce separates.

Variations

If you like the sauce a little creamier, add a few tablespoons of milk or cream to the egg and cheese mixture.

Different varieties of pasta work just as well, though spaghetti is more traditional.

You can also fry a few chopped cloves of garlic along with the onions if you really miss it.

Other cheeses will work in a pinch, but do use a full-flavored variety (such as a sharp cheddar, dry jack, or gruyère) so the flavor stands up.

LA PASTA DELLA MIA CASA

This is the pasta I make most often when I'm just in the mood for all my favorites in a pasta dish. It's spicier and more aromatic than my Nona used to make, but I think she would approve.

The Gist

Cook hot italian sausages first, then remove them and use the fat to sauté red bell peppers, onions, garlic, basil, parsley, oregano, salt, black and red peper, Canned tomatoes to go in to finish the sauce, which I toss with the sausages over spinach and cooked pasta

Ingredients

2 lbs. dry whole wheat pasta

2 lbs. hot italian sausage

2 tbs. olive oil

8 red bell peppers, seeded and chopped

2 yellow onions, chopped

1/2 cup garlic, chopped

1 bunch fresh parsley, chopped

1 bunch fresh oregano, chopped

1 bunch fresh basil, chopped

2 28-oz cans ground tomatoes in heavy purée

1 28-oz can diced tomatoes in juice

> I always used canned tomatoes for sauces. Besides being much more convenient, I think the flavor is just as good as the best, vine-ripened tomatoes, and far better than most store-bought fresh tomatoes. If I have really good, vine-ripened tomatoes, I'll eat them in salads, sandwiches, or just plain!

2 tsp. salt

2 tsp. fresh ground black pepper

1/2 tsp. red pepper flakes

1 2-1/2 bag washed spinach

La pasta della mia case done with marinated, barbecued chicken pieces instead of sausages. It's also great without any meat at all!

Method

Wash and chop all the vegetables so they're ready to go (this takes most of the time).

Set a large pot of salted water on to boil.

Start heating a large pot over medium heat. Add the olive oil (this helps the sausages not to stick at first.) When hot, add the sausages. Cover the pot, When the sausages are browed on one side, flip them over and pierce them each several times with a fork. This helps the fat to melt and run out of the sausages.

Remove the sausages when thoroughly browned. They do not have to be completely cooked at this point.

Add the bell peppers and onions to the sausage pot and sauté them in the sausage fat over high heat until wilted. Add the garlic and stir for another minute. Add the herbs and stir for a minute more.

Turn the heat down to medium and add the tomatoes, salt, black and red peppers. Add the browned sausages and bring the sauce to a simmer.

Cook the pasta until just barely tender but still a little tough (al denté). Drain the pasta into a colander.

Empty the spinach into the hot pasta pot, then dump the hot pasta on top. Toss the mixture a bit to separate the spinach as it wilts.

Use a small sauce pan to scoop up the hot sauce and sausages and pour it on top of the pasta and spinach. When the tomato sauce pan is almost empty, you can just pour the rest in.

Toss the pasta, sauce and spinach thoroughly. Let it sit a few minutes to finish cooking the spinach and allow the sauce to absorb into the pasta. Enjoy with grated pasta cheese mix.

To make it extra fancy, you can sprinkle some reserved chopped (uncooked) herbs on at the end.

Notes

This pasta has all the things I like best in pasta: red bell peppers, garlic, basil, sausages, and spinach. It's a complete meal in itself without need for a salad or meat course. The browning reduces the fat in the sausages, which then furnishes frying oil and flavor back into the sauce.

Variations

Barbecued chicken pieces: marinate some boneless, skinless chicken thighs in salt, pepper, minced fresh garlic, and a little white wine. Barbecue just enough to sear, then add them to the sauce. The pasta in the photo is also sprinkled with toasted pine nuts. The nuts can be toasted either in a skillet or in the toaster oven at 350°F. Do watch them closely; they tend to burn quickly!

Easy Chicken cacciatore: to turn this into an easy chicken cacciatore (see Recipe for a fancier one), brown skinned pieces of chicken in the olive oil instead of the sausages and increase the amount of bell peppers. All green peppers is traditional, but I prefer a mix of red and green bell peppers.

Yellow bell peppers make the sauce more colorful.

Feel free to add sliced mushrooms with the bell peppers if you like those in your sauce.

I sometimes add fennel seeds and extra red pepper flakes for sweeter, hotter flavor.

A cup or two of red wine is also a nice addition. Add it before the tomatoes so all the alcohol has a chance to burn off.

SZECHUAN SHRIMPS PASTA

Inspired by a dish at one of my favorite chinese restaurants, I added the pasta to spread around the wonderful seared garlic and chili flavor of the shrimp.

The Gist

Fresh mince garlic and chinese chili garlic sauce are quickly seared in hot oil, then sautéed with shrimp, rice wine or sherry, a little salt and sugar, and some fresh greens. Hot cooked pasta is tossed in at the end.

Ingredients

2 lbs. uncooked, shelled shrimp

3 Tb. peanut oil

4 Tb. minced fresh garlic

2 Tb. chinese chili garlic sauce

2 Tb. dry rice wine or sherry

1 tsp. salt

> Unless you have a really good store for buying fresh shrimp, I normally just buy frozen shrimp and thaw them. Almost all shrimp is frozen on the boat and then thawed at the story anyway.

1/2 tsp. sugar

2 lbs. fresh green, such as baby bok choy

1 lb. dry whole wheat pasta, such as penne or fusili

1 bunch green onions, minced

Crisp, crunchy spicy and sweet—about all I could want from some shrimps!

Method

Start 3 quarts of salted water heating to a boil. Chop the garlic and green onions and have them ready in separate bowls. Wash and drain the baby bok choy and separate into individual leaves.

When the water comes to a boil, start the pasta and cook just until barely tender (al denté). When it is almost down, start the peanut oil heating in a large sauté pan. Pour the cooked pasta into a colander to drain while you stir fry everything else.

Turn the sauté pan with the peanut oil to high heat. When almost to smoking, add the garlic and give it a quick stir. Add the chili garlic sauce and toss again. Add the shrimp and toss, then add the rice wine or sherry and toss again. Add the salt and sugar.

Add the baby bok choy and cook just until it's warmed but still crisp. Shut the heat off and add the pasta. Mix thoroughly, then add the green onions. Serve immediately.

Notes

I normally use frozen shrimp for this recipe and thaw them first. They can be quickly thawed under cold running water, or thawed in a more leisurely fashion in a bowl on the countertop. The shrimp should be at room temperature before you cook them.

Completely shelled and deveined shrimp seem to hard to find, but you can often find them with just the tail on. It's then not too much trouble just to pull the tails off.

CHICKEN CACCIATORE

The fresh, bright flavors and colors distinguish this cacciatore from the rest!

Lots of fresh red, green, and yellow bell pepper, seared pieces of skinless chicken, plenty of herb and garlic—and I just couldn't resist browning some italian sausages, too. They're optional!

The Gist

Brown sausages and skinless chicken pieces in a little olive oil, remove and then sauté onions, garlic, red, green, and yellow bell peppers, basil, oregano, and parsley. Add canned tomatoes and the meat, simmer till done, toss with your favorite pasta—and be assured no one will leave hungry!

Ingredients

leg and breast pieces from 2 chickens, skin removed

2 lbs. hot italian sausages

3 Tb. extra virgin olive oil

4 yellow onions, chopped

1/3 cup fresh garlic, chopped

2 lbs fresh mushrooms, sliced

4 each red, green, and yellow bell peppers, seeded and chopped

1 cup fresh parsley, minced

1/2 cup fresh basil leaves, chopped

1/4 cup fresh oregano

1 28 oz. can chopped tomatoes in juice

1 28 oz. can ground tomatoes in heavy purée

2 lbs. dry whole wheat pasta (your choice of variety)

Method

I usually start with two whole chickens, cut them up and use the breast pieces and legs for the cacciatore while leaving the wings and backs to barbecue. You can also just buy ready-to go chicken pieces. Just be sure to remove the skin (too much fat!).

Brown the sausages in the olive oil. Halfway through, poke them with a fork to let the excess fat melt off. This fat helps to sauté everything else and flavors the sauce. Remove the sausages when done and similarly brown the chicken pieces on both sides. Remove the chicken.

Start with browning the onions in the fat and cook until well -browned and caramelized. Add the garlic, toss for a minute, then add the mushrooms and cook just to where they start to release their juices. Add the bell peppers and herbs. Sauté over medium high heat until the peppers start to wilt.

Add the tomatoes, sausages, and chicken pieces, turn the heat down to medium and bring the sauce to a simmer. Check for salt and pepper. The chicken will only need to simmer another 15 minutes or so to cook through, but you can cook longer if you like your chicken falling off the bone.

While the sauce is simmering, bring 3 quarts of salted water to boil. Cook the pasta until just barely no longer tough (al denté).

Toss the pasta with the sauce and serve with my parmesan-romano grated cheese mix.

Notes

I like my cacciatore cooked just to where the chicken is done but still juicy and the peppers are still a little crisp and with bright colors. Long simmering seems to make everything soft and about the same color, but feel free if that's how your Nona used to make it!

Variations

If I'm thinking that far ahead (which I not always am!), I'll toss the chicken pieces in 2 Tb. salt, 1 Tb. fresh ground black pepper, and 1 Tb. granulated garlic and let them marinate on the counter for a few hours or overnight in the fridge. This gives the spices time to penetrate the pieces and, once they've simmered in the sauce, provide all the salt and pepper the sauce needs. A little extra time, but the difference in the chicken is worth it!

MAC'N'CHEESE

**Mac'n'cheese made with a little craft, instead of the usual variety!
Elegant enough to serve to company.**

This dish is such a huge improvement over the usual macaroni and cheese it seems unfair to call it by the same name. You may even be able to slip a few vegetables into your house's biggest veggie skeptics!

The Gist

A really simple (as you can make for sure make it!) sauce is tossed with cooked pasta and broccoli and cauliflower pieces. A little breadcrumbs on top and the whole thing is baked for a bit.

Ingredients

3 Tb butter

3 Tb flour

2 cups milk, warmed

1 tsp salt

1/2 tsp. fresh ground white pepper

1/2 tsp. mustard powder

1 tsp. dried tarragon (or other herb)

a big pinch of nutmeg

1 cup of your choice of cheese, grated

1 lb. whole wheat macaroni

1 head broccoli

1 head cauliflower

1/2 cup whole wheat breadcrumbs

Method

Start a big pot of salted water heating to a boil. Cut the broccoli and cauliflower into florets. Butter a baking dish big enough to hold everything. Preheat the oven to 350°F.

Heat the butter and flour together in a sauce pan over medium heat until thoroughly bubbling. Whisk to make sure the flour is evenly distributed. While that's heating, heat the milk in the microwave until warm.

Use the whisk to beat the warm milk into the butter and flour mixture. Heat just to a simmer, whisking every minute or two to make sure no lumps form. Turn off the heat, then beat in the salt, pepper, mustard powder, tarragon, and nutmeg. Stir in the cheese (it will melt in). Cover the pan to stay warm.

When the water is boiling, add the pasta and cook to al denté (still a little tough). Dump the broccoli and cauliflower into the boiling water, stir for a minute or two, then drain everything into a colander.

Transfer the pasta and vegetables to a mixing bowl and add the sauce. Toss thoroughly, then pour the mixture into your baking dish. Top with the breadcrumbs, then bake uncovered for 45 minutes.

Notes

For cheese, I like to do 3/4 cup of grated swiss and 1/4 cup of my all-purpose mixed grated cheese (parmesan and romano). You could use any full-flavored cheese, such as a sharp cheddar or an aged jack. A handful of crumpled bleu cheese is also good instead of the grated pasta cheese mix.

If you don't have whole wheat breadcrumbs on hand, just toast three slices of whole wheat bread, then crumble them with a rolling pin (or in your hands).

Variations

Endless variation are possible by changing the cheese (as noted above), the vegetables, or the herb. Basil or parsley would be good in lieu of the tarragon. Frozen peas would also be good as a vegetable, or even a medley of frozen vegetables.

IMPERIAL NOODLES

Good enough for an emperor, in my opinion. I like to serve them with crisp, blanched vegetables people can mix in.

The Gist

Cooked noodles are tossed with soy sauce, sesame oil, black or balsamic vinegar, salt, sugar, chili, and green onions. Serve with your favorite blanched vegetables.

Ingredients

2 lbs. dry brown rice or whole wheat noodles

1 bunch green onions, minced

2 lbs. bean sprouts

2 lbs. green beans

2 lbs. carrots, cut into sticks

Sauce Ingredients:

1/2 cup sesame oil

1/2 cup black or regular soy sauce

1/4 cup chinese black vinegar or balsamic vinegar

4 Tb. sugar

1 Tb. salt

2 tsp. chinese chili garlic paste (more to taste)

All ready to dig in. Chopsticks are optional!

Method

Whisk together all the sauce ingredients.

Bring a big pot of water to boil. One at a time, dump in the vegetables, stir for just a minute or two, then use a strainer spoon to remove them to a colander. Rinse immediately with cold water. This keeps the vegetables crisp and gives them intensely bright colors. Bring the water back to a boil before doing the next vegetable.

When you're finished blanching the vegetables, bring the same pot of water back to a boil for cooking the noodles.

Cook the noodles in boiling water until just tender and still a little tough. Drain in a colander and rinse briefly with hot tap water. Shake to drain thoroughly, then dump into a bowl and pour the sauce over them. Toss to thoroughly coat the noodles. Continue to toss every ten minutes or so as the noodles cool and absorb the sauce. When the noodles have cooled, toss in the minced green onions.

Arrange the noodles and blanched vegetables as you like and serve.

Notes

This dish is great served at room temperature, and can be made up hours or even days ahead of time. Store in the fridge if made up days ahead, and bring to room temperature before serving.

Japanese buckwheat soba noodles also go well with the sauce.

Variations

I like to use vegetables of bright, contrasting colors, and lots of different vegetables would do. For green vegetables, pea pods or asparagus work well. Red or yellow bell peppers would also be delicious.

TURKEY AL DENTE

This recipe turns a turkey into an italian dinner to feed a crowd for a very buon giorno meal. Vegetarians also get a luscious and complete meal by passing on the sausages and turkey pieces. This recipe will seriously feed twenty hungry people, so feel free to cut it in half and use a smaller turkey (or several chickens) if you're expecting fewer.

The Gist

The sauce is a combination of garbanzo beans (chickpeas) stewed in tomato and garlic, seared turkey pieces and hot italian sausages, fresh herbs, onions, carrots, and red bell peppers. At the end, it's tossed with whole wheat linguine and fresh spinach and served with romano-parmesan cheese mix.

Ingredients

4 cups dry garbanzo beans (chickpeas)

1 cup garlic cloves

1 6-oz. can tomato paste

1 tsp. salt

1 tsp. fresh ground black pepper

4 lbs. hot italian sausage

1 10-12 lb. turkey, thawed

1 Tb. salt

1 Tb. fresh ground black pepper

1 Tb. garlic powder

1 cup fresh parsley, chopped

1 cup fresh oregano, chopped

1 cup fresh basil, chopped

8 red bell peppers, chopped

3 yellow onions, chopped

3 lb. carrots, sliced

4 Tb. extra virgin olive oil

2 28-oz. cans crushed tomatoes in heavy purée

1 28-oz. can diced tomatoes in juice

1 Tb. red pepper flakes

3 lbs. whole wheat linguine (uncooked)

1 2.5 lb. bag washed spinach

A delicious combination of linguine, turkey, sausage, carrots, red bell peppers, garbanzo beans, herbs and spinach. Who needs a salad?

Method

Rinse the garbanzo beans well in a colander, then set them in a large sauce pan filled with warm water for about an hour. The beans will swell up. After an hour, discard the soaking water, then add more warm water to cover the beans plus about 1/2-inch over them. Add the garlic cloves and 1 tsp. each salt and pepper. Bring the mixture to a simmer and cook until the beans are tender (about 2 hours). After the first hour, all the garlic cloves will be floating on the top. Use a fork to mash them against the sides of the pot, then stir them back in. This helps the cooked garlic almost dissolve in the sauce.

While the beans are cooking, cut the legs and wings off of the raw, thawed turkey. Cut the legs into drumsticks and thighs, then remove the skin from them. Remove the skin from the breast, then cut the breasts off of the turkey. You'll want to end up with the breast meat cut into serving-sized pieces, so whether you remove the entire breast before slicing it or simply cut the breast off in pieces is up to you. Put the leg and breast pieces in a bowl. Mix together the 1 Tb. each of salt, pepper, and garlic powder, sprinkle it over the turkey pieces, then toss them well to evenly coat them. Set them aside to marinate while you chop vegetables. Save the carcass and wings for soup.

Chop herbs and set them in a bowl. Chop the bell peppers, carrots, and onions and set them in a bowl. Open the cans of tomatoes. Start a large pot of salted water heating for cooking the linguine.

Heat the olive oil in a large pot over medium high heat. When hot, add the sausages and brown them on both sides. As they cook, pierce them with a sharp carving fork so some of the fat melts off and drains into the pan.

Remove the sausages when browned to a bowl. A few at a time, brown the turkey pieces in the hot olive oil and sausage fat. They don't need to be cooked through, just briefly seared on both sides. As you sear them, removed the finished piece to the bowl with the sausages.

Pour the chopped bell peppers, onions, and carrots into the pot and sauté them until the onions are just starting to wilt. Add the herbs and red pepper flakes and toss of another minute or two.

Add the sausages and turkey pieces to the pot, then the garbanzo beans with their sauce, then the canned tomatoes. Gently stir the whole mixture, then leave it on a temperature that will heat it through to a simmer without scorching. Depending on your stove and pots, this is probably either medium or medium high. Check the sauce for seasoning. The salt and pepper from the garbanzo sauce and the turkey pieces is probably enough.

I'm going to be hungry for some pasta after this!

While the completed sauce is heating, cook the linguine until just barely tender and still a little tough and underdone. It will soften more and finish cooking as it absorbs the sauce. Drain the slightly underdone linguine into a colander. Empty the bag of spinach into the (now empty) pasta cooking pot. Dump the cooked pasta on top. With a large ladle or cup, spoon a good portion of the sauce mixture on top of the pasta and spinach. Toss it as you do so to distribute the spinach throughout the pasta. The heat from the pasta, the pot, and the sauce will be enough to just wilt the spinach, leaving it bright green and still a little crunchy. There's enough sauce in the pot when you can move the pasta and still see 3 or 4 inches of sauce on the bottom. Toss the pasta again five or ten minutes leave so the sauce soaks evenly into the pasta.

Plate up some pasta, a sausage, and a piece of turkey on each plate (or whatever your guests like!). Make sure everyone gets a good helping of the beans, spinach, and carrots. Top with the romano-parmesan cheese mixture (see Recipe). Enjoy!

Notes

This recipe will easily serve twenty hungry people and can be completed before anyone arrives. The pot of pasta and sauce will stay warm on the cooktop with the burner off for at least an hour. If you've a smaller group to feed, feel free to cut the ingredients in half and use a smaller turkey, or to substitute two or three chickens instead of a turkey.

SAGE LINGUINE WITH LENTILS AND CARROTS

This was a daring choice to pair a sage-flavored pasta and lentils with black bean salmon but, judging by what was *not* left on the plates, it was a hit!

This flavorful, hearty pasta can stand on its own but, for a special lunch, I paired it with Black Bean Steamed Salmon. Perfect for people who didn't realize how much they like vegetables!

The Gist

Lentils are stewed with sautéed onions and garlic, bacon, chicken stock, and sage. Carrots go in at the end. This goes on top of linguine tossed with olive oil and more sage.

Ingredients

2 Tb. extra virgin olive oil

1/2 cup chopped bacon

2 yellow onions, chopped

8 cloves garlic, minced

1 lb. teeny weeny lentils (typically french or italian varieties)

2 Tb. chicken stock base

4 Tb. fresh sage, minced

4 cups diced carrots

1 tsp. salt

2 tsp. fresh ground black pepper

1 lb. whole wheat linguine

2 Tb. extra virgin olive oil

1 tsp. salt

1 tsp. fresh ground black pepper

2 Tb. fresh sage, minced

Method

Fry the bacon with 2 Tb. olive oil in a medium-sized pot until crisp. Add the onions and garlic and sauté until the onions are transparent. Add the lentils, chicken stock base, 4 Tb. sage, 1 tsp. salt and 2 tsp. pepper. Add enough water to cover the lentils by about 1 inch.

Simmer until the lentils are tender, around 20-30 minutes. They will absorb most of the water during this time. Add a little more water if they're drying out and not yet done.

When the lentils are completely done, add the carrots, mix them in, and shut off the heat. The heat in the lentils will cook the carrots enough to make them done but still crisp.

Start a large pot of salted water boiling. Cook the linguine until just barely tender (al dente). Drain, return to the pot, and toss with the 2 Tb. olive oil, 1 tsp. salt, 1 tsp. pepper, and 2 Tb. sage.

Serve with linguine on the bottom and a generous portion of carrots and lentils on top.

Notes

If you're not serving this with the salmon, a little of my grated parmesan-romano cheese mix on top is great. I tend not to like fish with cheese unless tomatoes are also involved.

Variations

To turn this into an all-in-one dinner without the steamed salmon, add 1-2 cups diced lean ham with the carrots.

FOOLPROOF HOMEMADE WHOLE WHEAT PASTA

I've worked out the kinks to find a nearly foolproof method for whole wheat noodles. They match commercially made fresh whole wheat noodles in quality—if you can find them!

The Gist

One part each whole wheat pastry flour and semolina gets combined with a little gluten flour and salt, then enough egg and water to make the dough come together (exact proportions follow). Then knead and roll out the dough.

Ingredients

2 cups whole wheat pastry flour

2 cups semolina flour

2 tsp. salt

4 tsp. gluten flour

4 eggs

4 tsp. water

Method

In a sturdy mixer with a paddle attachment (a Kitchenaid works great), combine the three flours and salt. Mix for 1-2 minutes until thoroughly mixed.

Beat together the eggs and water. While the mixer is running, slowly drizzle in the egg and water mixture. The dough will start to come together as you do so. Be ready to stop the mixer as the dough makes a ball. The dough is very stout and could jam the mixer.

This should be enough liquid so that the flours just form a dough ball. Too little water and a ball won't form. Too much water and the dough will stick together as you try to roll it out.

Pasta sheets in process...

You may need a little more liquid if your flour is very dry or it's a warm dry day (yes, it really does make a difference.) If you need a little more, add a few additional teaspoons of water to your egg bowl, swirl it around to pick up some of the egg, then continue drizzling it in until the dough ball forms.

Put the dough hook on the mixer and knead the dough for 5-10 minutes until it's somewhat soft and elastic. It should be about the consistency of your earlobe. If you pull the dough apart a little it should hold together well and show strands from the gluten. If in doubt, see if you can make a little noodle with your fingers that will hold together.

Let the dough rest an hour or more (no hurry here). Cut the dough ball into 1/2-inch thick slices with a knife, then roll each slice a little with a rolling pin so it's thin enough to feed into your pasta machine (1/4-3/8-inch thick).

Start with your pasta machine on the thickest setting for the rollers and roll all the dough through it. Reset your machine on a thinner setting and send all the pieces through. They will be turning into sheets of pasta dough as you go through this process. Repeat until you have the desired thinness.

With a good dough or a warm, dry day, you won't need extra flour as you're going through this process. If the dough starts to stick, dust it with a little extra whole wheat pastry flour.

When your pasta sheets are the desired thinness, put a noodle cutter on your machine and feed each sheet through to cut the noodles. Toss each batch with extra flour as it goes through the machine.

The noodles can then sit until you're ready to cook them. Give them an occasional toss so they don't stick together.

When you're ready to cook the noodles, bring a large quantity of salted water to a boil. More is better. Add the noodles all at once and keep stirring on high heat as you bring the water back to a boil.

As soon as the water boils, the noodles are done. Drain them immediately in a colander, then toss them with sauce, butter or olive oil.

...then ready to go!

Notes

Unlike dried noodles, fresh ones don't have to boil for a bit to be cooked. They're done as soon as the water comes back to a boil.

Fresh noodles do have a more delicate texture, though. They need to be immediately tossed with sauce, butter, or olive oil so they don't stick together. Probably you could also rinse them thoroughly with cold water in the colander and keep them for later, but I haven't tried this.

Some cookbooks say one can take the uncooked noodles tossed with flour and freeze them for later. This hasn't worked for me. I end up with noodles stuck together. And what's the point of making fresh pasta if you're just going to freeze it?

Wider noodles (like fettucine or linguine) are easier to start with than spaghetti. Angel hair pasta (the thinnest spaghetti) always gives me trouble. If I want angel hair pasta, I just use a package of commercial pasta.

If the dough gives you trouble the first time through, don't despair. Making fresh pasta is a little tricky. I spent endless hours experimenting with mixtures and methods before arriving at this one. Just remember to add the liquids slowly and stop as soon as the dough makes a ball. You can always add more water, but you can't take it out (and adding more flour just doesn't work).

Once I worked out this formula, I get a perfect dough every time. And the delicate texture and flavor of the noodles is just something you'll have to experience yourself.

DE-LICIOUS DE-LUXE LASAGNA

Mangiamo!
(That's Italian for "Let's Eat!")

This very special lasagna is suitable for the fanciest occasions and easily feeds a crowd. I would recommend making the cheese mixture, tomato sauce, and Béchamel sauce the day before you construct and cook the lasagna so you don't feel rushed the day of.

The Gist

Homemade pasta sheets are layered with Béchamel sauce, a ricotta cheese filling, sautéed red and yellow bell peppers and spinach, a tomato sauce, and hot italian sausage with grated mozzarella.

Ingredients

Note: these quantities will fill a standard-sized lasagna pan. The photos below show a double recipe made in a large, party-sized pan.

For the ricotta filling:

1 32-oz. container ricotta cheese

2 cups grated Parmesan-Romano cheese mix

1 bunch italian parsley, minced

3 eggs

grated rind of 1 lemon

1 tsp. salt

2 tsp. fresh ground black pepper

large pinch of nutmeg

For the tomato sauce:

1 28-oz. can crushed tomatoes in heavy purée

1 28-oz. can diced tomatoes in juice

2 yellow onions, diced

10 cloves garlic, minced

3-4 Tb. extra virgin olive oil

1 bunch fresh italian parsley, minced

1 bunch fresh oregano, minced

2 tsp. salt

1 Tb. fresh ground black pepper

1 tsp. red pepper flakes

1 tsp. sugar

1/4 tsp. cinnamon

1 cup red wine

For the Béchamel sauce:

3 Tb. butter

3 Tb. flour

3 cups milk

1/2 tsp. salt

1/4 tsp. fresh ground black pepper

pinch of nutmeg

For the sautéed vegetable layer:

2 lbs. baby spinach leaves

3 red bell peppers, diced

3 yellow bell peppers, diced

1 yellow onion, diced

6 cloves garlic, minced

1 tsp. salt

2 tsp. fresh ground black pepper

1 tsp. sugar

This needs one more noodle to go on top of the bottom Béchamel sauce layer

Here's the vegetable layer as we're covering it with sauce. Another layer of cut-to-fit noodles goes on top.

4 Tb. extra virgin olive oil

Everything else:

1 lb. mozzarella cheese, grated

1-1/2 lbs. hot italian sausage, cut in 1/2-inch slices

3 recipes fresh whole wheat pasta dough

Method

Combine all ingredients for the ricotta filling and mix together thoroughly. If making a day ahead, cover the bowl and set it in the fridge.

For the tomato sauce, sauté the onions and garlic in olive oil until the onions are transparent. Add the parsley, oregano, salt, black pepper, red pepper flakes, cinnamon and sugar and cook for another minute or two. Add the red wine and cook until all the alcohol has boiled off. (You can tell by the smell.) Add the two cans of tomatoes and bring the sauce to a simmer. Test for seasoning. The sauce can simmer for a few another hour or two if you have time, or let cool and refrigerate overnight.

For the Béchamel sauce, microwave the milk until very warm, then set next to the stove. Melt the butter in a sauce pan. Add the flour and whisk over medium heat until bubbly. Add the warmed milk in a steady stream, whisking as you do to create smooth sauce. Add the salt, pepper, and nutmeg and bring the mixture to simmer. Simmer for another 10-15 minutes. Likewise, this can go in the fridge overnight. Before setting it in the fridge, though, let it cool, then set a sheet of plastic wrap right on top of the sauce so a thick skin doesn't form.

Make the pasta dough. Wrap it in plastic and let rest at least 30 minutes before rolling it out.

For the sautéed vegetable layer, heat the olive oil in a large pot. Add the onions, garlic, and red and yellow bell peppers and sauté over high heat until the onions are transparent and the whole mixture is hot (about 5 minutes). Add the spinach and quickly toss over high heat just until the

Sausages arranged on the noodle layer, grated cheese next, then the remaining sauce on top of the cheese.

spinach starts to wilt. Shut the burner off and continue to toss as the spinach finishes wilting. Add the salt, pepper, and sugar and toss together thoroughly.

Slice the (uncooked) italian sausages into 1/2-inch slices. Grate the mozzarella.

Roll out the pasta dough to the thinnest setting on your machine. Set the whole pasta sheets aside.

Butter your lasagne pan. Preheat the oven to 350°. Now you're ready to assemble.

Spread half the Béchamel sauce in the bottom of the pan, then lay a layer of noodles over the sauce, leaving the long ends trailing over the edges. Those we'll fold over onto the top when all assembled.

Spread the ricotta filling on top of the noodles, then add another layer of noodles on top. These you should cut to fit inside of your pan.

Spread the sautéed vegetable layer on top of the noodles. Add about half of the tomato sauce on top of the vegetables. Any extra juice from sautéing the spinach and vegetables goes in, too.

Arrange the sausage slices on top of the noodle layer, then sprinkle the grated mozzarella cheese over this. Spread the remaining tomato sauce on top.

Fold the long noodles from the bottom on top of the sauce/cheese sausage layer. Use the rest of the cut noodles to fill in the top. Spread the remaining Béchamel sauce on top of the noodles. It's almost ready to go in the oven!

Cover the pan tightly with aluminum foil and place it in the middle of a hot 350ºF oven. Cook it covered for 1 hour, then uncover and cook for another 30 minutes. (Note: this is cooking time for a standard-sized lasagne pan. The large, double-recipe pan shown in the photos cooked covered for 1-1/2 hours, then uncovered for 30 minutes.)

Let the lasagne rest 10-20 minutes before serving. You can also recover with aluminum foil and it will stay hot for an hour before serving. You could even cover it and place it back in a warm oven to say warm for several hours before serving.

Notes

There will be a fair amount of juice that comes out when you sauté the spinach and vegetable, and it may seem like too much liquid to go in the pan. But, because we haven't pre-boiled the noodles, they will absorb almost all of the juice as the lasagne

The rest of the noodles are folded onto the top, gaps filled in with remaining noodles, then remaining Béchamel sauce spread on top.

cooks. The last 30 minutes of uncovered cooking browns the top and evaporates excess water.

This lasagne is a complete meal in itself. I might possibly do an appetizer and salad beforehand for a fancy dinner party, but then the lasagne is served by itself as the entrée.

Variations

If you omit the sausages, this becomes a gourmet vegetarian lasagne which will please even your most devoted carnivorous friends.

PIZZA PARTIES

These recipes are called "pizza parties" because I think whenever you're making pizza, it's a party! And great fun to do with guests over helping out. Everyone can customize their pizza just how they like it.

Also, I think the pizza you make at home is so much better than most of what you can order out. Most pizzas have just dizzying fat and calorie contents. Two slices can wipe out a week of watching what you eat. Plus very few places have whole wheat pizza dough, which I prefer and which is so much better for you (fiber, nutrition, etc.)

I use a stone in the oven to cook pizza on and highly recommend it. A stone shortens the cooking time and gives you that authentic, crusty, pizzaria bottom. A pizza peel (basically a big, flat wooden paddle for handling pizzas) also helps. A wooden cutting board works almost as well.

Start making your pizzas on the small side so it's easier to slide them from the cutting board or peel onto the stone. That's the hardest part. A little back-and-forth shaking and a spatula do the trick for me. Once cooked, the pizza is firm enough to push off the stone very easily.

I, of course, usually make my pizzas as big as my peel and stone can handle, and usually load on perhaps more toppings than what makes for easy handling. These big pizzas sometimes come to a little grief getting onto the stone, but no big deal. A little poking to fix it and maybe a little sauce spills on the stone. It's still delicious!

Here's a few recipes to get you started on creating. Once you get the hang of the dough (much easier than you think!), your imagination is only the limit.

EASY HOMEMADE PIZZA DOUGH

This roughly makes enough for three 14-inch pizzas (as big as my pizza peel), or more smaller ones. Sometimes you can also find ready-to-go whole wheat pizza dough in stores, but this one is so easy I no longer bother to look.

The Gist

Yeast gets proofed with warm water, milk, and a little sugar. Then add salt, olive oil, and enough flour to make a dough. Knead with a heavy duty mixer, then put in a warm place and let rise while you make the sauce and toppings.

Ingredients

1 cup warm water

1 cup warm milk

1 tsp. sugar

2 tbs. active dry yeast

1 tsp. salt

2 tbs. olive oil

enough whole wheat flour to make a dough

> Any kind of whole wheat flour seems to work fine for this. If you're making it for the first time and are worried about it coming out, use 1-2 cups of whole wheat white flour along with the regular whole wheat.

Method

Combine the water, milk, and sugar in the mixing bowl of a heavy duty, dough-kneader mixer (like a Kitchenaid). Stir to dissolve the sugar. The liquid should feel very warm to the touch (not uncomfortably hot). If you need it a little warmer and the bowl is metal, you can place it directly on a very low heat burner to warm it up.

Sprinkle the yeast on top, then stir to dissolve it. Cover the bowl with plastic wrap and set it in a warm spot. The back of the stovetop works well if you've started heating your oven already. Let sit for 10-15 minutes while you start on pizza toppings. The yeast should start growing and form a foam on top of the liquid.

When the liquids are foamy, set the bowl in your mixer, add the salt, olive oil, and 1 cup of flour, then start mixing with the paddle attachment. When thoroughly mixed, add a second cup of flour and let this mix for 2-3 minutes. It should be a thickish batter that starts getting stringy as you continue mixing it. This is the gluten developing which makes the dough elastic and light. I find that starting it this way gives you a head start on kneading.

Continue adding flour a half-cup at a time, letting each addition mix in thoroughly. When the dough comes together and forms a ball, switch to the dough hook. Continue adding flour a little at a time until the dough forms a ball which no longer sticks to the side of the pan. Let the dough hook do the work for you as it kneads the dough for perhaps an additional 5 minutes. The dough should be smooth and elastic. You made need to drizzle in a little more flour if it starts to stick.

Cover the bowl with plastic wrap and set in a warm spot to rise. It will take about 20 minutes to double in bulk. If you're not ready to construct pizzas at that time, just punch it down and let it rise again.

The pizza stone goes on the top rack in your oven, and the oven needs to preheat to 450°F for at least 30 minutes.

Proceed to make your pizzas.

Notes

The trick to this recipe is gradually adding enough flour for the dough to form a ball, and just enough additional flour so the ball doesn't stick to the sides of the bowl. With the pre-mixing with the 2 cups of flour at the beginning, I get away with no hand kneading at all.

Some books say to coat the dough in a little olive oil to keep it moist while rising. I used to do this, but then had oily dough to roll out. Covering the bowl with plastic wrap works just as well.

The liquid and then the dough need to stay somewhere around 80-90°F for the yeast to be really feisty. The back of the stove top near the oven vent does this for me. Alternately, you could turn a second oven on warm for a few minutes, then turn it off and put the bowl in there.

On warm days, of course, it's not a problem!

HAWAIIAN PIZZA

**We traditionally serve Hawaiian Pizza for our Oscar-watching party.
It makes for an award-winning evening!**

With very easy toppings, this is a good pizza to start with. Just brimming with aloha.

The Gist

The sauce is chopped tomatoes, chopped fresh garlic, salt and pepper. Any kind of mild cheese works. The toppings are chunks of ham and pineapple.

Ingredients

1 recipe pizza dough

1 28-oz. can diced tomatoes in juice

8 cloves finely chopped garlic

1/2 tsp. salt

1 tsp. freshly ground black pepper

generous dash of red pepper flakes

3 cups of grated, mild cheese (mozzarella, provolone, jack, or a mix)

3 cups diced ham

3 cups pineapple chunks (about 2 cans)

> No, I've never successfully tossed the dough in the air to make it round. I've tried it a few times, but it never seemed to work for me. I just roll it out instead. Maybe gravity is just too strong in my area!

Method

Place your pizza stone in the oven and start the oven preheating to 450°F.

Make the dough and let it rise.

Drain the juice from the diced tomatoes, then combine them in a bowl with the garlic, salt, pepper, and red pepper flakes. Mix well.

Grate the cheese. Chop the ham. Open and drain the pineapple chunks.

> I think getting the pizza on and off the stone is half the fun! But, if you're nervous about it or just starting out, just make and bake your pizza on a non-stick cookie sheet. It will still be delicious!

Divide the dough into three or four equal-sized hunks (we'll assume 3). Place the remaining two back in the dough bowl. Roll out one hunk into a circle on a floured pizza peel. Roll the dough to around 1/8 to 1/4-inch thick. The first few times through, making the dough a little thicker makes it easier to handle.

Fold up and pinch the edges to make an edge. Give the peel an occasional shake back and forth to make sure the dough isn't sticking.

Brush the crust with 1 tbs. of olive oil (this helps keep it crisp). Spread 1/3 of the sauce over it, then 1/3 of the cheese, then 1/3 each of the ham and pineapple.

Slide the pizza onto the pizza stone. A little back and forth shimmy-shaking does it for me.

Bake the pizza for 8-12 minutes, or until the edges are browned and the toppings are hot and bubbly.

While it's cooking, start making the next one. By the time the first one is done, the second will be ready to go into the oven. I use the wooden peel for making the pizzas and sliding them in, then a second wood cutting board for putting them on when I take them out. A nylon cutting board would lose the crispness of the crust.

Notes

Smaller pizzas are easier to handle than larger ones, and thicker crusts are easier than thin ones. More toppings also make the pizza heavier and harder to move. As much as I try to do something different, though, I always seem to end up with a large, thin crusted pizza with lots of toppings! I guess I must just like them that way. As long as I put enough flour on the pizza peel and give the pizza a shake bake and forth as I'm making it (to ensure it's not sticking), they do come out beautifully.

I make all the pizzas at once and keep extra, whole pizzas on round serving platters in the fridge (covered with plastic wrap). Then, to reheat them, I heat the stone up again and slide the cooked pizza onto the stone. This re-crisps the crust and heats up the whole pizza in 4 or 5 minutes. They're just as good this way as when freshly made.

PEPPERONATA PIZZA

A very good, colorful, and fairly easy pizza. The basic version is vegetarian, but see the optional meat toppings under variations. The pizza in the photo is topped with hot italian sausage.

The Gist

The sauce is red and yellow bell peppers sautéed with garlic, salt, pepper, thyme or basil, and canned tomatoes. Mozzarella and provolone cheeses are the topping.

An unidentified italian object has landed in the kitchen. Proceed with forks and caution.

Ingredients

1 recipe pizza dough

3 yellow bell peppers

3 red bell peppers

6 cloves garlic, finely chopped

3-4 tbs. chopped fresh thyme or basil

2 tbs. extra virgin olive oil

1 28-oz. can crushed tomatoes in purée

1 tsp. salt

1 tsp. pepper

generous dash of red pepper flakes

> Fresh pimentos can be used in place of red bell peppers, and you can use just red if the yellow ones aren't available. If you can't find fresh ones, look for roasted red or yellow peppers in jars and reduce the cooking time for the sauce.

1-1/2 cups grated mozzarella

1-1/2 cups grated provolone

optional topping #1: sliced yellow tomatoes

optional topping #2: fresh chopped basil

Method

Sauté the bell peppers and olive oil over high heat for a few minutes. Add the garlic, give it a good stir, then turn the heat down to medium. Add the tomatoes, thyme or basil, salt, pepper, and red pepper. Heat until bubbling, then turn the heat off.

Grate the cheeses. Slice the yellow tomatoes if you're using them.

Divide ingredients into 3 or 4 portions, depending on how many pizzas you're making.

Roll out the dough for the first pizza. Brush it with a tablespoon of olive oil. Add the bell pepper sauce, then cheeses. Yellow tomatoes go on top.

Bake of 8-12 minutes or until the edges are browned and the toppings are hot. See the Hawaiian pizza recipe for more detail on construction and on getting your pizza onto and off of a pizza stone.

Top with the optional basil after the pizza comes out of the oven.

Variations

Other cheeses: some folks go for the "fresh" mozzarella. This comes in plastic bags with some liquid in them. Many stores also carry smoked fresh mozzarella. They're great for other uses but, for pizza, I find them too soft to grate and very difficult to slice thinly enough.

Instead, smoked gouda is good choice for a smoked cheese. Substitute it for the provolone.

Seared sausage pizza: cut raw, hot italian sausage into coins. Dot these on top of the pizza last of all. By the time the pizza is done, the sausage will be seared and just cooked and contributing its juices to the pizza.

Seared chicken pizza: cut some boneless skinless breast or thigh pieces (or some of both) into bite-sized pieces. Marinate in salt, pepper, chopped fresh garlic and rosemary, and a few dashes of red pepper flakes. Place raw chicken pieces on top of the pizza. The chicken pieces will also sear and contribute their juices.

Seared shrimp pizza: marinate whole, peeled and deveined shrimp in salt, pepper, chopped fresh garlic, and little rice wine or sherry, and a few dashes of red pepper flakes. Likewise, place the raw shrimp on top of the pizza so they sear as the pizza cooks.

BARBECUE CHICKEN PIZZA

The Gist

A whole wheat pizza crust gets brushed with a little olive oil, then topped with sliced red onions, chopped red bell peppers, grated smoked Gouda cheese, and chunks of marinated chicken breast. Minced cilantro goes on top after it comes out of the oven.

This recipe makes 2 large or 3 smaller pizzas.

Ingredients

1 recipe whole wheat pizza dough

2 boneless chicken breasts, cut into hunks

1 tsp. salt

1 tsp. granulated garlic

1 tsp. fresh ground black pepper

1 tsp. New Mexico chile powder

3 Tb. barbecue sauce (pick your favorite!)

1 tsp. Chipotle Chile purée

1 red onion, thinly sliced

3 red bell peppers, chopped

3 cups shredded smoked Gouda cheese

extra virgin olive oil

1/2 cup fresh cilantro, chopped

> There is something about the flavor and consistency of frozen, boned chicken pieces from the store I find unappealing—like they've been through some extensive processing to get there. Get yours from a good meat department or extract them from a chicken yourself. It's easier than you might think!

So good you'll hardly believe it's good for you, too!

Method

Start the pizza dough (the water, milk, sugar, and yeast part) and set aside to let the yeast get foamy. Put your pizza stone in the oven and start the oven heating to 450°F.

Combine the salt, garlic, pepper, and chile powder and mix thoroughly. Sprinkle over the chicken hunks and mix. Combine the barbecue sauce and Chipotle purée, then pour over the chicken and mix again until the spices are evenly distributed.

Finish the pizza dough and set aside to rise. (The back of the stove with the heat from the oven is a good place.)

Prepare the red onion, red bell peppers, and cilantro. Grate the cheese.

Divide the dough into halves or thirds. Roll out a piece to a size that conveniently fits on your stone. Be sure to adequately flour the bottom so the dough will slide.

Slip the dough onto a floured pizza peel (or a floured wooden cutting board) and pinch some of the edge together to make a raised border around the pizza. Give your pizza an occasional shake throughout this process to make sure it's still sliding.

Add 1-2 Tb. of extra virgin olive oil on top of the crust and distribute with a pastry brush to coat thoroughly. Add half (or a third if you're making three) of the red onions, then a similar proportion of the bell peppers, then likewise for the cheese. Top with chicken chunks.

Slide the pizza onto your stone (a spatula sometimes helps the process) and bake until the crust is crisp, about 20 minutes. Remove the pizza from the oven. Usually, you can slide it directly onto your wood cutting board with a spatula. Sprinkle with half the cilantro.

Let the pizza settle for a few minutes while you make the second pizza and get it in the oven. Cut and enjoy!

SHRIMP SCAMPI PIZZA

The Gist

A whole wheat pizza crust gets topped with sautéed leeks, garlic, and parsley, then grated mozzarella and provolone cheese, then shrimp marinated in garlic, salt, pepper, and sweet white wine. Delish! This recipe makes 2 large or 3 smaller pizzas.

Ingredients

1 lb. large, raw shrimp, peeled and deveined

1 tsp. salt

1 tsp. fresh ground black pepper

10 cloves fresh garlic, minced

2 Tb. sweet white wine, such as Gewürtraminer

4 Tb. extra virgin olive oil

4 leeks, chopped

10 cloves garlic, minced

1 bunch parsley, minced (reserve 1/2 cup for garnish)

1/2 cup dry white wine

grated zest of 2 lemons

1-1/2 cups grated provolone cheese

1-1/2 cups grated mozzarella cheese

1/3 cup grated parmesan-romano cheese mix

2 pints cherry tomatoes, preferably mixed red and yellow

Authentic Shrimp Scampi flavor in a pizza. What's not to love?

Method

Start the pizza dough (the water, milk, sugar, and yeast part) and set aside to let the yeast get foamy. Put your pizza stone in the oven and start the oven heating to 450°F.

Sprinkle the salt, pepper, first batch of 10 minced garlic cloves, and sweet white wine over the shrimp. Mix thoroughly and set aside.

Finish the pizza dough and set aside to rise. (The back of the stove with the heat from the oven is a good place.)

Heat the olive oil in a sauté pan over high heat. Add the leeks, second batch of garlic, and parsley (making sure to reserve 1/2 cup). Sauté until the leeks are well softened. Add the 1/2 cup dry white wine and continue to cook and toss until the mixture is fairly dry. Shut off the heat.

Combine the reserved 1/2 cup minced parsley with the grated lemon zest and mix thoroughly. Grate the cheeses and mix them together.

Divide the dough in half. Roll out half the dough to a size that conveniently fits on your stone. Be sure to adequately flour the bottom so the dough will slide.

Slip the dough onto a floured pizza peel (or a floured wooden cutting board) and pinch some of the edge together to make a raised border around the pizza. Give your pizza an occasional shake throughout this process to make sure it's still sliding.

Add 1-2 Tb. of extra virgin olive oil on top of the crust and distribute with a pastry brush to coat thoroughly. Add half the leeks mixture, then half the cheese, then half the shrimp. Top with half of the cherry tomatoes.

Slide the pizza onto your stone (a spatula sometimes helps the process) and bake until the crust is crisp, about 20 minutes. Remove the pizza from the oven. Usually, you can slide it directly onto your wood cutting board with a spatula. Sprinkle with half the parsley and lemon zest.

Let the pizza settle for a few minutes while you make the second pizza and get it in the oven. Cut and enjoy!

Notes

Be sure to use raw shrimp on the pizza rather than cooked shrimp. This way, the shrimp will be perfectly done when the pizza is. Pre-cooked shrimp, unfortunately, will come out shrunken, dry, and very sad.

PIZZA SUPER DELIZIOSA

Almost too yummy and different to call it "pizza"!

The Gist

The crust is grated zucchini, flour, eggs, and cheese. It gets baked first, then diced Pasilla chiles, chopped tomatoes with basil and garlic, marinated shrimp, grated provolone and smoked Gouda cheese and chunks of Italian sausage meat are layered on top. Yummy!

Ingredients

For the crust:

2 very large or 8 small zucchini, grated

2 tsp. salt

6 eggs

2 tsp. fresh ground black pepper

1 cup grated mix of romano and parmesan cheeses

3 cups whole wheat flour

extra virgin olive oil

For the shrimp:

2 lbs. shelled raw shrimp

8 cloves fresh garlic, minced

2 Tb Mirin (sweet rice wine) or sweet sherry

2 Tb chinese chili-garlic paste

2 tsp. fresh ground black pepper

1 tsp. salt

For the sauce:

3-14.5 oz cans of roasted chopped tomatoes

1/2 cup fresh basil roughly chopped

1 Tb. fresh ground black pepper

3 cloves fresh garlic, minced

Everything else:

6 fresh Pasilla chiles, seeded and sliced

1/2 lb. provolone cheese, grated

1/2 lb. smoked Gouda cheese, grated

2 lb. bulk Italian sausage meat (sweet or spicy)

Method

Combine the grated zucchini with the 2 tsp. of salt and mix well. Let stand for 10-30 minutes or so. This is a good time to get the rest of the chopping and grating done. Preheat your oven to 350°F.

Mix all the shrimp ingredients together and let them marinate.

Drain the zucchini in a fine mesh basket or with several layers of cheese cloth. Add the rest of the crust ingredients except for the olive oil, which is used to oil one large or two smaller baking pans (I used a turkey roasting pan). Place in the oven and bake until the top is dry, about 30 minutes.

While that's baking, mix your sauce ingredients together and finish any chopping or grating.

When the crust is done (leave the oven on!), remove it from the oven and layer the remaining ingredients in this order:

1. Pasilla chiles

2. sauce

3. shrimp

4. grated cheeses

5. sausage meat, in chunks

Bake until browned on the top and warm and bubbly through, about 20-30 more minutes.

Slice and serve. Enjoy!

Notes

Putting the sausage pieces on the very top gets them browned and crispy, while having the shrimp farther done cooks them through without overcooking them.

This crust is also a good base for assembling your own fantasy pizza with your choice of ingredients. Fresh red and yellow cherry tomatoes and pesto, anyone?

Here's how it all looks through assembly:

1. The crisped zucchini crust

4. The marinated shrimp layer

2. The Pasilla chile layer

5. The grated provolone, smoked Gouda, and Italian sausage layer

3. The tomato, garlic, basil layer

6. Done!

BIRDS OF A FEATHER

A roast chicken so delicious and easy you'll want to make it a regular. A roast turkey so flavorful and juicy that other turkeys you've had will seem mummified by comparison (Turtankahem, I call them!). Birdies done right! Move on to the next chapter if you're in the mood for some Moo! Oink! or Baaa!

Here I'm about to carve an Orange Ginger Hickory Smoked Turkey fresh off the grill. Thankfully, my spouse set the table whilst I was cooking!

CHICKEN

"Tastes like chicken." I'm sure you've heard that. And what's wrong with that. I love chicken. One just has to get the fat down to an acceptable level. Of course, that's easier than you might think. Most of the fat is in the skin. The cooking methods here show you how to get the fat down so the chicken tastes downright great and you can eat the skin. (Okay, maybe don't eat just the skin!). I even have a guilt-free fried chicken recipe.

So, grab those chickens on sale and chick-away! They're cheaper than gasoline, after all.

EASY SEASONED OVEN ROAST CHICKEN

Roast chicken seasoned and then ready after 45 minutes at 450ºF. Note all the fat that has drained off to the bottom—plus all the skin is crisp.

Fast, easy, and so much better than the take-out birds.

Roast chicken in about an hour, and much moister and tastier than a packaged roast chicken from the store. The cooking method and spice rub make the difference.

The Gist

Chickens get rubbed with salt, pepper, and garlic powder, then roasted at high heat on vertical racks for about 45 minutes.

Ingredients

2 chickens

2 tbs. salt

1 tbs. granulated garlic

1 tbs. fresh ground pepper

aluminum foil

> The vertical roasting racks are key. They let the chicken cook evenly and the skin brown on all sides. The bird cooks much faster and more evenly this way. I love to watch all the fat melt and drip off of it as it cooks!

Method

Start your oven preheating to 450°F.

Wash the chickens. Remove and discard the extra fat in the body cavity and neck opening. Pat them dry-ish with paper towels. If you like, save the neck, gizzard, and heart in a bag in the freezer for gravy later, and the liver separately for pâté.

Combine the salt, granulated garlic, and fresh ground pepper and rub it evenly inside and outside of the chicken. Set the chickens on the vertical racks. If they're sagging low on the racks, put a ball of crumpled aluminum foil in the cavity, then set the birds on the rack to prop them up higher. If you like, use a poultry skewer to close the skin over the neck opening. This helps keep the breast meat moister.

> There seems to be two types of garlic powder in stores: a finely powdered variety, and a so-called "granulated" garlic. I prefer the granulated variety because it seems to have more garlic flavor. Feel free to use the powdered variety if that's all you can find.

Set each racked chicken in a low baking dish. Add about 1/4-inch of water. This keeps the drippings from burning as it cooks.

Place it dish and chicken in the even. Be careful not to burn yourself because the oven will be very hot.

The chickens will be done and the skin crisped on all sides in about 45 minutes. Remove them from the oven and let rest for 10-15 minutes before you remove them from the racks and carve them.

Notes

This method produces a beautifully roasted and crisped chicken without drying out the breast meat or undercooking the thighs. There may be hints of pink as you carve it. This is not only okay, it's desirable! The meat will be tender and much moister than you've had before, and perfectly safe to eat. The combination of washing first and rubbing salt all over the outside are extra precautions. I've made hundreds of chickens this way and, though people sometimes balk at the pink, no one's ever gotten sick!

I always make 2 or 3 chickens at a time, though we only ever eat one on the first night. The oven's hot, it's very little extra work, and the leftovers are great. I cut pieces off and reheat them under the broiler, then make sandwiches from slices of the breast meat.

Variations

If you're starting a day or two ahead, use chopped fresh garlic instead of the granulated garlic powder and add an accent herb to the rub. Chopped fresh rosemary or tarragon are good choices. Marinate the chickens at least overnight and up to 3 or 4 days. This makes a very special and richly flavored roast chicken with very little advance work.

Variations

Although I love the way a simple salt, pepper, and garlic marinade accents the flavor of the chicken, a more complex spice combination works well and varies the flavor. For example, the spice combination from the no-rotisserie rotisserie chicken (see Recipe) works great when roasting on vertical racks in the oven instead of on the barbecue.

SUPERFASTEASY GRILLED CHICKEN

Here's this recipe with boneless, skinless chicken thighs and fresh rosemary as the herb. Served here with Pasta à la Carbonara and Garlic Roasted Brussels Sprouts

This chicken can be on the table less than 30 minutes before you start—just enough time for a cocktail!

This Gist

Chicken pieces are tossed in salt, fresh ground black pepper, granulated garlic, and an herb, then grilled for about 2 minutes a side on the grill.

Ingredients

2 lbs. boneless, skinless chicken pieces (see Note for pieces with bone-in and skin-on)

1 Tb. salt

2 tsp. granulated garlic

2 tsp. fresh ground black pepper

1 Tb. an herb (your choice, fresh or dried)

Method

Start your grill heating on high. Mix together the salt, granulated garlic, pepper, and herb, then sprinkle over the chicken. Toss thoroughly to distribute the seasonings.

Grill the chicken pieces for about 2 minutes per side with the grill cover closed (a little longer if your grill has no cover). Serve and enjoy!

Notes

Boneless skinless pieces cook the fastest on the grill with the least fussing: they won't get torched with the fat melting off like pieces with the skin will. But this recipe works just as well with bone-in, skin-on pieces. You'll just need to watch them for flare-ups and cook for a few minutes longer.

Variations

Greek Grilled Chicken: If you use oregano for the herb and add a teaspoon of lemon pepper, this makes my version of Greek Grilled chicken. For this variation, I like to use whole chicken legs.

FIESTA TACO

This recipe came together in about 15 minutes one day from what was on hand in the fridge. Even if a stop at the store is required, it still makes a fast and delicious lunch or dinner.

The Gist

Saute together marinated, chopped chicken breast and onions. Spoon on corn tortillas warmed in the microwave and top with salsa fresca and guacamole.

Ingredients

2 boneless chicken breasts

1/2 tsp. salt

1/2 tsp. fresh ground black pepper

1/2 tsp. granulated garlic

1/2 tsp. chili powder

1/2 tsp. Chipotle chili powder

1 yellow onion, chopped

1 Tb. extra virgin olive oil

12 corn tortillas

salsa fresca (store bought or see Recipe)

guacamole (store bought or see Recipe)

Method

Chop the chicken breasts into bite-sized pieces, then toss together with the salt, pepper, garlic, chili and Chipotle chile powders. Set aside to marinate for a few minutes.

Place the tortillas on a plate, cover with a sheet of plastic wrap, then microwave for about a minute and a half to warm.

Heat a skillet with the olive oil over high heat. Add the onions and saute over high heat until the onions are browned (the pan will be getting very hot as you do this). Add the marinated chicken pieces and toss. Pour a few tablespoons of water in the pan (step back from the steam as you do this), and continue to toss for another minute. The water will pick up any spices or chicken that was sticking and quickly cook the chicken (for culinary types, this is called "deglazing" the pan). Shut the heat off. The heat remaining in the pan will finish cooking the chicken while still leaving it juicy, and keep it warm.

Serve this right from the pan. Place a little chicken on a tortilla, then top with salsa and guacamole and enjoy. Delish!

I could almost eat the photo—though four or five real ones would be better!

Variations

If you like, sprinkle a little grated extra sharp cheddar on top of the chicken and tortilla, then top with salsa and guacamole.

EMPEROR'S LUNCH POACHED CHICKEN

Here's six breasts sliced, drizzled with Spicy Szechuan Oil, and served on a bed of Stir-Fry Garlic Spinach. If it doesn't impress your in-laws, there's no hope!

This chinese-inspired recipe makes a wonderfully flavored, moist chicken. For a truly elegant lunch or dinner, serve it on a bed of Stir-Fry Garlic Spinach and drizzle Spicy Szchuan Oil (see Recipes for both) over the top.

The Gist

Bring salted water, sliced fresh ginger, green onions, and a splash of sherry to a boil, drop in the chicken, shut off the heat, and let it sit for a bit. That's all!

Ingredients

4 chicken breasts (boneless or bone-in)

1/2 cup thin sliced fresh ginger

6 green onions, cut in pieces and lightly mashed

2 tsp. salt

1 Tb. sherry

1 quart water

Method

Wash the ginger and thinly slide enough to make 1/2 cup. It's not necessary to peel the ginger. Cut the green onions into pieces which fit conveniently into your pan and mash then lightly with the flat side of your knife.

Put the water, ginger, green onions, salt and sherry in a sauce pan big enough to hold the chicken breasts, too. Bring to a boil. Drop in the chicken breasts and poke them a bit to get them under water. Cover the pan and shut the heat off. In about 30 minutes (while you do something else!), the chicken will be perfectly cooked.

For a little extra spice, serve the chicken with Spicy Szechuan Oil drizzled over the top.

Notes

This dish can be made up well ahead of time and the chicken left to sit in the water until you're ready. It's also great served at room temp. If you're making this a day or two ahead of time, store the whole thing (water, ginger, and all) in a container in the fridge for extra flavor in the chicken.

The stock is very good for other chinese soups or dishes.

NO-ROTISSERIE ROTISSERIE CHICKEN

No, Miss Kitty. This isn't for you!

Here's a rotisserie-style chicken without the bother of a rotisserie. Crisper and more moist by far than store-bought varieties.

The Gist

The chicken gets marinated whole in a spice mixture, then barbecued whole. The result is a rotisserie-style chicken without the bother of a rotisserie.

Ingredients

2 whole chickens

2 Tb. salt

1 Tb. fresh ground black pepper

1 Tb. granulated garlic

1 Tb. paprika

1 Tb. ground dry chile Chipotle

1 Tb. onion powder

1 Tb. dried thyme

> The trick I've found to doing whole chickens on the barbecue is turning them after no more than 5 minutes, then again after 5 more minutes. If you leave them longer, the skin sticks to the grills. After that, you just mainly need to watch for fires and turn them as they cook.

Method

Wash the chickens. Remove and discard the extra fat in the body cavity and neck opening. Pat them dry-ish with paper towels. If you like, save the neck, gizzard, and heart in a bag in the freezer for gravy later, and the liver separately for pâté.

Combine all the dry spice ingredients, then rub them thoroughly inside and outside the chickens. Put the chickens in the fridge to marinate for a day or two, or just go ahead and cook them.

Heat the barbecue. For my 5-burner gas barbecue, put the two in the middle on low, and the rest (2 on one end, 1 on the other) on high. Let preheat for 15 minutes or so.

Place the whole chickens on grills over the burners that are on low. Close the cover, leave for 5 minutes, then flip the whole birds over. Close the cover, leave them another 5 minutes, then flip them again.

Continue to flip the chickens over every 10 minutes or so. They will be completely done in about 30 minutes. If the fat dripping off starts to catch fire under the chickens, move them out of the fire if there's space. If not, just shut off the burner(s) under the chicken.

When done, let the chickens rest for 10-15 minutes before carving.

Variations

The spice mixture can be varied almost infinitely, so feel free to experiment. For example, either sage or rosemary works well in lieu of the thyme.

Notes

I actually have a rotisserie and separate rotisserie burner on my barbecue, but found it very tricky to use. Set the rotisserie burner too high and the chickens catch on fire. Turn it too low and the chickens are cooked before the skin is crisped. Playing with settings on the main burners didn't help, either. This method works for me reliably and with much less fuss.

This method would probably work with a charcoal barbecue with cover. Make the mound of charcoals in the center so you can keep the chickens on the edge: next to the hot coals, but not over them.

This recipe is endlessly variable by changing the marinade. See the next recipe for one very different marinade.

I always do two chickens because it's just as easy and then one is left over for another night.

No-Rotisserie Teriyaki Chicken

The Gist

Same method as for the regular no-rotisserie chicken, but a teriyaki-style marinade substitutes for the dry spice mixture.

Ingredients

2 chickens

2 cups plum jam

1/2 cup fresh ginger slices

1/2 cup garlic cloves

1/4 cup soy sauce

2 tsp. salt

1 tbs. fresh ground black pepper

The key to this recipe is a good quality plum jam. Try to find one that's all fruit and doesn't have too much sugar. Most varieties are too sweet for my taste, but you may like the chicken very sweet, so feel free! I use my homemade plum jam for this. It has just enough sugar to cut the tartness of the cooked plums.

Method

Wash the chickens. Remove and discard the extra fat in the body cavity and neck opening. Pat them dry-ish with paper towels. If you like, save the neck, gizzard, and heart in a bag in the freezer for gravy later, and the liver separately for pâté.

Combine all remaining ingredients in a blender and blend until smooth. This makes a thick marinade paste. Pour over the two chickens, then turn and rub to distribute the marinade evenly. Let the chickens marinate for 1-2 days in the fridge, then cook as directed for the other no-rotisserie chicken.

Beware fruit marinades on poultry and fish. More marination time is usually better, but, after a day or two, the ascorbic acid in fruits (and especially in lemon juice) starts to break down the meat fibers and make the meat pasty. This is especially true with fish, so limit the soaking time to 1 day for chicken and 1-2 hours for fish. Beef and pork can handle more time.

Notes

This marinade is fast to make, but, if you're really short of time, just buy a prepared teriyaki sauce and use that. They tend to be very salty and sweet, so use just enough to give the chickens a good coating. The flavor won't be as intense, but the chicken will still be good.

Double-Herbie Chickie Stew with Dumplings

Perfect comfort food for a cold Saturday afternoon. Herbs are in the broth and in the dumplings (hence the double herbie!). Leftovers will get you through a good part of the week when simmering time is scarce.

The Gist

Chicken pieces are simmered with herbs, then boned and finished with leeks, cabbage, peas and carrots. Whole wheat dumplings to on top to finish it.

Just like a chicken pot pie—without the bother of a crust!

Ingredients

2 chickens, cut into pieces

chicken broth or water plus base to cover

1 bunch fresh parsley, chopped

1 bunch fresh thyme, minced

1 head cabbage, chopped

4 leeks, sliced

1 2-lb. bag frozen peas and carrots

salt and pepper to taste

1 recipe herbed dumplings (see Recipe)

> There are lots of ways to cut up a chicken. Here's an easy method that disposes of a bird in about 2 minutes.
> 1. Cut off the wings.
> 2. Cut off the legs. If desired, cut the legs into a drumstick and a thigh.
> 3. Cut the carcass lengthwise to separate the back from the breast.
> 4. If desired, split the breast lengthwise along the breast bone (not necessary for stew.)

Method

Cut the chicken into pieces (or start with 2 cut-up chickens. Place in a large pot with a tight-fitting lid and enough chicken stock (or water plus chicken stock base) to cover the chicken pieces. Add the parsley, thyme, and some fresh ground black pepper. If your broth or chicken base is already salty, you may not need any more salt. Bring the mixture to a boil over high heat, then simmer for 30 minutes.

While the chicken is simmering, wash and cut the cabbage and leeks. Take the peas and carrots out of the freezer to start thawing.

When the chicken is done, remove the pieces from the broth and set them in a large bowl or platter to cool so you can bone the chicken. Prepare the dumplings while the chicken is cooling.

Bone the chicken. If you like, set aside the skin, backs, and wings for Chicklins (recipe follows). These pieces are great crisped up, but in my opinion have too little meat to be worth boning out.

Return the boned chicken chunks to the broth and bring to a boil over high heat. Add the vegetables and check the broth for salt and pepper.

As soon as the mixture boils, turn the heat down to a simmer and drop big dollops of the dumping batter on top of the simmering broth. Cover and simmer until the dumplings are done, about 15-20 minutes.

Serve to hungry people on a cold night. Yum!

Variations

Feel free to vary the herbs, or to add more. For a particularly elegant stew, add chopped fresh tarragon and 2 cups of dry, white wine when simmering the chicken. So good it's almost french!

> For some reason, leeks always seem to be filled with dirt hiding in the leaves. The best way I've found to clean them is to cut them lengthwise, then rinse thoroughly under cold, running water. Cutting them lengthwise lets you partially peel back the leaves to get at the hidden dirt.

Notes

Thickening the broth is not necessary because it will be thickened by some of the flour from the dumpling batter.

The vegetables will be quite done and soft by the time the dumplings are done. If you'd like the vegetables a little crisp, add the vegetables to the boiling broth and chicken, then shut off the heat. Spoon a few cups of the broth into a separate pan to cook the dumplings.

CHICKLINS

This recipe was inspired by what to do with the backs, wings, and skin pieces left over from making a stock. Although not quite as a good as fried chicken, it's very tasty!

The Gist

Leftover chicken pieces from stock are sprinkled with salt, pepper, and granulated garlic and roasted on racks in a 450°F oven until crisp.

Ingredients

Leftover chicken pieces from making a stew or soup (such as backs, wings, and skin)

salt

fresh ground black pepper

granulated garlic

Method

Start your oven preheating to 450°F. Place the chicken and skin pieces on racks on a baking sheet, or on the rack of a broiler pan. Add some water in the bottom of the pan so the fat won't burn as it drips off. Sprinkle the pieces well with salt, fresh ground black pepper, and granulated garlic.

Roast the pieces in the oven for 30 minutes, then remove them from the oven and turn them over. Roast for another 30 minutes. Keep an eye on them for the last 30 minutes so they don't burn.

Drain on paper towels and serve. My honey loves to have these with Hoisun sauce like Peking Duck!

**Here's a whole mess o' Chicklins—two chickens worth! Decadent, but oh so good.
No, I wouldn't have these every day!**

Notes

Okay, I'll grant these puppies are on the fatty side. But they sure are good, and a lot of the fat does melt off during the roasting process. I serve this as a very indulgent appetizer to an otherwise low fat meal.

COUNTRY BRAISED CHICKEN

This very elegant braised chicken is almost a white wine version of classic coq au vin. Easy enough to make for yourselves, but sure to be a hit with dinner guests.

The Gist

The legs and breast halves from two chickens are marinated in salt, pepper, and garlic, then seared in oil and butter, then simmered with wine, parsley, thyme, water, and chicken stock base. I like to make Herbie Dumplings on top as it simmers and serve on a base of steamed cauliflower.

Ingredients

leg and breast pieces from 2 chickens (skin removed)

1 Tb. salt

2 tsp. fresh ground black pepper

2 tsp. granulated garlic

2 Tb. butter

2 Tb. olive oil

2 leeks, chopped

2 lbs. sliced mushrooms

1/2 cup fresh parsley, chopped

1 Tb. fresh thyme, minced

2 cups white wine

water to cover

2 Tb. chicken stock base

salt and pepper to taste

2 heads cauliflower, cut into florets

Herbie Dumplings (optional, see Recipe)

A delectable combination of chicken, broth, and vegetables—with an herbed dumpling to boot!

Method

You can either buy the chicken pieces (4 legs and four breast haves would do it), or cut up two chickens for the pieces. If you cut them up yourself, the extra backs, wings, and skin are great for a mess o' Chiklins (see Recipe).

Remove the skin from the chicken pieces. Mix together the salt, pepper, and granulated garlic, then sprinkle it over the pieces and toss thoroughly. (If you do this step a few hours ahead of time, the spices will have time to penetrate through the pieces).

If you're making the Herbie Dumplings, make the batter now. I like to add a teaspoon of dried (or tablespoon of fresh) tarragon as the herb with this recipe.

Heat the butter and olive oil in a large skillet. Brown the chicken pieces on both sides in the hot oil (probably in 2 or 3 batches). Remove the browned pieces to a bowl.

Add the leeks and mushrooms to the skillet and sauté over high heat until the mushroom start to give up their juice. Add the parsley and thyme and toss for another minute. Add the chicken pieces back in and toss in the vegetables. Add the white wine and boil, cover off, until the alcohol smell is gone. Add just enough water to barely cover the chicken pieces, plus the chicken stock base.

Stir thoroughly and test for salt and paper (you probably won't need any more). Turn the heat down to a simmer and add dollops of the Herbie Dumpling batter on top if you're making them. Cover the pan and simmer for twenty minutes.

While the chicken is simmering, steam the cauliflower just until crisp.

Serve the braised chicken on a bed of steamed cauliflower with a dumpling on this side. This makes a complete meal in itself.

Variations

As noted, you can make this either with or without the Herbie Dumplings. If you're not making the dumplings, serve with a loaf of good whole wheat bread for dunking in the broth.

Although I like this dish on top of steamed cauliflower, Garlic Mashed Potatoes (see Recipe) would also be great on the bottom.

Notes

If you have the time, letting the chicken pieces marinate overnight in the fridge would be ideal. Otherwise, just go ahead and make it all in one shot.

GUILTLESS FRIED CHICKEN

Eliminating the breaded coating drastically reduces the fat content. Good, hot peanut oil crisps it and melts off some of the fat. The marinade adds exceptional flavor.

The Gist

Cut the chicken into pieces and marinate it with the spice mix. Fry a few pieces at a time in smoking hot peanut oil, keeping the finished pieces warm in a warm oven.

Ingredients

2 whole chickens, washed and cut up

2 tbs. salt

1 Tb. fresh ground black pepper

1 tsp. ground white pepper

I always use peanut oil for deep frying because it can get the hottest of any oil before it starts to smoke. More expensive than corn or soy oil, but worth it when you're going to this much trouble. Stores like Smart and Final have it by the gallon for much cheaper than the little bottles in your typical grocery store.

1/2 tsp. cayenne pepper

1 Tb. garlic granulated garlic

1 Tb. dried granulated onion

2 tsp. dried thyme

peanut oil

Get those fingers ready for some lickin'!

Method

Thoroughly rinse the whole chickens in cool water, pulling out any feather remnants. Drain and pat them dry with paper towels, then cut them up. I like to cut the pieces like this: wings, then legs (thigh and drumstick together), then cut lengthwise to separate the back from the breast side, then breasts in half lengthwise along the breast bone, than cross-wise into breast quarters. This keeps the pieces around the same size so they cook in about the same time. I save the back and giblets for stock or soup.

Alternatively, you could buy chicken already cut up in the store. Do still give it a good rinsing.

Mix the dry spice ingredients together, then sprinkle them over the chicken pieces and toss together thoroughly. If you're cooking the chicken that day, leave it on the counter to marinate. Otherwise, put it in the fridge to marinate for up to two or three days. Give it a mixing once a day or so to distribute the spices evenly.

Before cooking the chicken, take it out of the fridge and bring it to room temperature.

Use a tall-sided pot for frying to contain at least some of the spatters. Put in enough peanut oil for a depth of 2 or 3 inches. Heat it over high heat until it starts you can see the fumes coming off the oil. (A burnt smell is too much.) Have ready tongs for adding and removing the chicken pieces. Put your hood fan on high. Heat your oven to warm (150 or 200ºF). Have a plate or tray ready with several layers of paper towels on it.

Once the oil is fuming, carefully put three or four pieces into the hot oil, stepping back so you don't get spattered. There will be clouds of hot steam, so be careful. Cook the chicken until brown and crispy. The time depends on how hot your burner is. If your burner is really hot (such as with a commercial stove), you may need to turn the heat down so the chicken doesn't burn.

When the first batch is done, remove the chicken, place on the paper-toweled tray, and put the tray in the oven to keep the chicken warm and crisp. Use a mesh implement to fish any odd pieces out of the oil. then reheat it to smoking and proceed with the next batch.

Notes

Traditionally, a southern fried chicken dinner would be served with mashed potatoes, gravy, biscuits, and honey for the biscuits. With lots of breading on the chicken and butter in the potatoes, it's a big waistline builder. This recipe reduces the fat by eliminating the breading. If you were feeling really puritanical, you could remove the skin, but I like the crispy skin. Plus, with no breading to hold the fat, more of the fat from the skin and melts into the peanut oil.

Lots of recipes call for using a thermometer to keep track of the temperature of the oil, but I don't find it necessary. It takes a lot of heat to get peanut oil to burn, and you can just watch for the fumes rising off of it instead. I've never yet actually burned peanut oil, but it's easier to do with other oils. So just save your peanut oil for frying!

With great, crispy-skinned but still fried chicken, to make the meal work from a fat content standpoint I round it out with a big, tossed salad and a warmed loaf of whole wheat bread. In my book, nothing is better than munching a hunky of crispy fried chicken on a slice of crusty wheat bread. (Okay, duck would be good, too.)

I like to use dry rather than fresh spices for this recipe because they help to keep the moisture content down. Putting a wet piece of chicken in hot oil is not a good idea. With all the steam and spattering, it's really easy to get burned.

Feel free to experiment and create your own favorite spice mixture. You could play around with onion powder, chipotle chile powder, or different herbs.

If you have high blood pressure, reduce the salt and do all the marination in the fridge. The salt (plus rinsing) is what makes it safe to marinate the chicken at room temp for up to 24 hours.

Lastly, use a big tray to keep the chicken warm so you don't have to pile pieces on top of each other. This helps with draining excess oil, keeps the pieces crisper while waiting, and makes for a dramatic presentation when you're ready to eat!

BLACK BEAN CHICKEN ENCHILADA BAKE

I usually make this when I've made a batch of Southwestern Black Beans (see Recipe) and want to feed a crowd. Even when I make it just for us, though, leftovers freeze quite well.

The Gist

Tortillas, black beans, sautéed fresh chiles and onions, marinated chicken pieces, and chile sauce are all layered together and topped with grated cheese, green onions, and black olives to make a lasagne-like version of an enchilada.

Sure to feed a hungry amigo!

Ingredients

Note: amounts for ingredients are approximate. There's a lot of room for variation!

2 dozen whole wheat or corn tortillas

3 cups Red'N'Ready Chili Sauce (see Recipe) or canned red chili sauce

4 cups Southwestern Black Beans (see Recipe)

4 fresh Pasilla chiles, seeded and chopped

4 fresh Anaheim chiles, seeded and chopped

1 white onion, chopped

6 cloves garlic, minced

2 Tb. extra virgin olive oil

2 16-oz. cans of corn, drained

2 lbs. boneless raw chicken pieces (white or dark), chopped

2 tsp. salt

2 tsp. granulated garlic

1 Tb. fresh ground black pepper

2 cups jack cheese, grated

2 cups extra sharp cheddar cheese, grated

2 bunches green onions, chopped

2 16-oz. cans black olives, drained and sliced

Method

Mix the chicken pieces with the salt, granulated garlic, and pepper in a bowl. Sauté olive oil, chopped Pasilla and Anaheim chiles, white onion, and garlic together until just barely wilted, then mix in the two drained cans of corn.

Using your favorite high-sided lasagne pan, very lightly oil it with a little olive oil. Spread one-third of the chili sauce on the bottom, then set down a layer of tortillas. Spread the Southwestern Black Beans on top, then make another layer of tortillas.

Spread the sautéed chiles, onions, and corn on top of the tortillas, then add the grated jack cheese on top. Lay down another layer of tortillas, then top with the chicken pieces. Add another third of the chili sauce, then a final layer of tortillas

Spread the remaining chili sauce on top of the tortillas, then sprinkle with the grated cheddar cheese. Top with the green onions and black olives.

Bake in a 350°F degree oven until well-heated through and bubbling, which takes about an hour.

Notes

Although the chicken pieces go in raw, they'll cook thoroughly in the oven and contribute their delicious juices to the mix, while remaining moist and tender. Delish!

FIVE-STAR COQ AU VIN

See the Variations for an easy version of this recipe that will be ready for your family and guests to love in under an hour. This version can hold it's place on the table at the finest restaurants (and it's lower in fat, to boot!).

The Gist

Skinned chicken pieces are marinated in salt, pepper, and garlic powder, then browned in bacon fat. Onions and mushrooms are also browned in the fat. Everything gets flambéed in cognac, then simmered with red wine, beef broth, garlic, tomato paste, thyme, and parsley. The broth is thickened, then sliced carrots go in at the end.

Ingredients

breast and leg pieces from 2 chickens, skinned

1 Tb salt

2 tsp. fresh ground black pepper

2 tsp. granulated garlic

1 pound of bacon, chopped

2 yellow onions, sliced

2 pounds mushrooms, sliced

1/4 brandy or cognac

1 bottle robust red wine

2 cups water

4 Tb. beef broth base

8 cloves garlic, minced

2 Tb. fresh thyme, minced

1/2 cup fresh parsley, chopped

1 6-oz. can tomato paste (check can size)

4 cups sliced carrots

4 Tb. flour

A very substantial portion of Coq au Vin served over my favorite whole wheat penne. Non-traditional, but delish!

Method

For the chicken pieces, I like to keep the legs whole (thigh and drumstick together), but cut the breasts into four pieces (halved and then quartered). A half of a breast from a large chicken (the only kind I buy!), seems a lot for most people, but a quarter is quite manageable. But do piece the chicken up any way you like.

Mix the salt, pepper, and garlic powder together, then sprinkle over the chicken pieces and toss thoroughly. Set aside.

Fry the bacon over medium heat until the pieces are crisp. While the bacon is frying, chop the onions, mushrooms, garlic and herbs.

When the bacon is crisp, remove the pieces from the hot bacon fat. Remove the excess melted fat (about 2/3 of it). Brown the chicken pieces on both sides in the remaining hot bacon fat a few at time. Depending on how hot your stove is, medium high or even high will keep the fat hot. Move them around frequently so they don't stick. About 2-3 minutes per side for the chicken pieces should do it. Remove the browned pieces to another bowl as you do this.

When the chicken pieces are all browned, add the onions to the bacon fat and fry until golden brown. Right when you first add the onions, a little water is often helpful to help unstick anything stuck to the bottom of the pan (a.k.a. deglazing the pan).

When the onions are golden brown, return the browned chicken pieces and crisped bacon pieces to the pan. Your burner should still be on medium high or so. Have a lighter ready and turn your fan on if it isn't on already. Sprinkle the cognac over the chicken pieces, then *lean back!* and gingerly insert your lit lighter over the pan. The alcohol fumes from the brandy will instantly alight with a very hot blue flame. Shake the pan back and forth a bit as the alcohol burns off. This is the flambé step and it adds a wonderfully unique seared flavor to the dish.

Add the wine, water, beef broth, garlic, thyme, and parsley. Bring the pot to a boil, scraping the bottom a bit in case anything has stuck. Cook uncovered over high heat until you don't smell any more alcohol in the steam coming off the pan. This will take about 20 minutes or so. Once the alcohol has burned off, add the tomato paste (adding it earlier seems to make the alcohol take longer to burn off.)

As the mixture boils, begin to skim off the fat. You will probably be able to skim off as much as a cup of fat, which is from the bacon and the chicken. It's done its flavoring job at this point, but a little will be added back in for richness. When you're done skimming the fat, turn the heat down to medium and add the carrots.

Check the flavor for salt and pepper. The salt and pepper from the chicken should be enough, but add more if you think it's required.

Remove about 1/4 cup of the warm, liquid fat to a small cup and stir in the flour. It will make a smooth, thick paste. Whisk this in to the still simmering broth. It should thicken it nicely without lumps. Make sure the mixture is still simmering to cook the flour, then turn the heat off and put the cover on the pot.

The coq au vin is now ready and will stay hot for serving for at least an hour. Serve over garlic mashed potatoes or (my favorite!) whole wheat penne pasta.

Notes

Most of the time in this recipe is for browning everything one at a time. See the variations for a quicker version.

I've also been known to marinate the chicken in the salt, pepper, and garlic powder overnight in the fridge. This gives the spices time to completely penetrate the chicken.

You can also make this dish most of the way a day ahead. After the alcohol has burned off the broth, turn off the heat and add the tomato paste and carrots. Let the mixture cool, then refrigerate it. The next day, it's very easy to skim off the hardened fat layer on top. To finish it, just skim the congealed fat, reheat to a simmer, then thicken as described above (you will need to microwave the 1/4 cup of fat to melt it). This makes for a no-stress finish on party day for a very fancy entrée.

Variations

Easy Coq au Vin: put all the ingredients except the bacon, tomato paste, and flour in a big pot. Bring to a boil. When all the alcohol has evaporated, add the tomato paste. Cook until the chicken is done (20-30 minutes). Thicken with the flour and enjoy!

TURKEY

Turkeys intimidate many chefs. First of all, there's the weight of one (another reason to go to the gym!). Second is how long to cook it. Too much and it dries out. Not enough and people worry.

Read on to discover my foolproof methods for turning out a spectacularly scrumptious turkey every time. But, for starters, how about an utterly simple way to serve delicious turkey! That's Bubba's Mississippi Meatballs.

BUBBA'S MISSISSIPPI MEATBALLS

Bubba's Mississippi Meatballs (in the raised dish) had a starring spot at our annual Christmas Party. I was too slow to try one—there were gone before I got to them!

These meatballs are so great they stand on their own as a dish. Partner them perhaps with some brown rice or whole wheat pasta and your choice of vegetable for an elegant casserole or one-pot dinner. To save time, just use your favorite store-bought turkey meatballs to start with!

The Gist

Meatballs are browned, then tossed in a sauce of sautéed onions, red wine, Coca-Cola(!), balsamic vinegar, Dijon mustard, dark brown sugar, cinnamon, and a little of your favorite barbecue sauce.

Ingredients

For homemade meatballs (or use store-bought turkey meatballs):

2 lb. lean ground turkey

1/2 cup plain bread crumbs

1 egg

1 onion minced

3 gloves garlic minced

1/4 cup chopped parsley

2 teaspoon kosher salt

1/2 teaspoon pepper

1 Tb. Worcestershire sauce

1/4 Cup Barbecue sauce

1/2 Cup Parmesan Reggiano cheese cut into small cubes * (optional)

Splash of Hot Sauce

4 Tb. extra virgin olive oil

For the sauce:

1 yellow or red onion, minced

4 Tb. extra virgin olive oil

1/4 cup red wine

1/4 cup Coca-Cola

3 Tb. balsamic vinegar

2 Tb Dijon mustard

2 Tb. dark brown sugar

1/4 tsp. cinnamon

1/4 cup of your favorite barbecue sauce

Method

Combine the meatball ingredients and make into balls, or just thaw store-bought. Heat the olive oil in a large skillet and brown on all sides. Cover and simmer for 10-15 minutes until thoroughly cooked (not necessary if using store-bought fully cooked meatballs). Set aside.

In a saucepan, sauté the minced onion in olive until translucent. Add the red wine, Coca-Cola, and balsamic vinegar. Bring to a boil and reduce to 1/2 the original volume. Add the Dijon mustard, dark brown sugar, cinnamon, and barbecue sauce. Heat to a simmer, then pour over the meatballs in the skillet. Simmer on low until ready to serve.

Notes

For our party, we put these on the raised dish and stuck toothpicks in them so folks could just grab them. Considering how fast they went, maybe we should have required people to use chopsticks instead!

On to the Big Birds!

I love turkey and eat it all the time. Why wait for Thanksgiving? For less than the cost of a large pizza you can have a bird that will feed your family for an entire week. And check out my many recipes (like Turkey Barley Mushroom Soup) for what to do with the leftovers. You can even turn my Chicken Enchilada Bake into a Turkey Enchilada Bake. Why not?

Of course, many people are put off by cooking a turkey and save the dreaded chore for once a year when it's required. No need to be so put off. You can have a great turkey by following just one secret: don't overcook it! See the next recipe for details.

SUPERB STUFFED ROAST TURKEY

A finished, stuffed 20-pound bird ready to carve: crisp on all sides, moist inside and delish!

Brining the turkey, then cooking at high heat and turning it yields a mind-bogglingly flavorful, moist and tender turkey. Not overcooking it is key.

The Gist

The turkey gets marinated for one or more days in a strong salt, pepper, and herb brine, then stuffed and roasted at 450°F. At this temperature, it has to be flipped part way through to be cooked evenly, but will cook faster. If you're not up to flipping it, turn the temperature down to 350°F and cook it longer.

Ingredients

A Turkey (as big as you can lift comfortably)

1 cup salt

1/3-cup fresh ground pepper

1 cup chopped fresh rosemary or sage

approximately 1 gallon of cool water

a 16-quart stock pot or 5 gallon bucket

stuffing (recipe follows)

4-6 poultry skewers

Method

Thaw the frozen turkey. Overnight in cold water will do it (a big garage sink works wonderfully for this). In the fridge, it will take several days to thaw.

Once, the turkey is thawed, rinse thoroughly in cool water. Reserve the giblets and neck for gravy. Then combine the salt, pepper, and herb in the stock pot. Add about a gallon of cool water and stir until the salt is dissolved. There should be just enough water that the turkey would be submerged when pressed down, though it will actually float. That's fine because it gets turned over through the marination process.

Give the turkey a few turns to get it thoroughly drenched on all sides, then marinate for 24 hours at room temperature, flipping every 6 hours or so. If you have time (and I highly recommend this), it can soak for days more in the fridge. I find that a minimum of 3 days is required to get the flavors to penetrate all the way.

On Thanksgiving day, take the pot out of the fridge and set on the counter first thing in the morning so the turkey can begin to warm up.

Start your oven preheating to to 450ºF, then make the stuffing while the oven is heating. Remove the turkey from the marinade and discard the marinade (no re-using!). Stuff the turkey and use the poultry skewers to pull the skin together over the openings. I like to stuff the main cavity and to put some in the front. There's usually plenty of skin around the neck to make a pocket and, in my opinion, the stuffing roasted in the neck cavity directly under crisped skin is the best part. You could use thread to close the openings, but I find the skewers much easier to use and remove after cooking. Before putting the turkey in the oven, add about 1/4-inch

Many people spend a lot of extra money for a fresh turkey instead of a far less expensive frozen one. I've never really been able discern any flavor difference between the two. On the other hand, how you cook it (and how much!) makes a huge difference. My advice is to save your money, buy a frozen turkey, and do it right!

Ms. Bird in her 3-day beauty bath. A flip once or twice a day does the trick.

Here she is after the first 90 minutes: crisped and browned on the back side, and ready for a flip.

of cold water to the bottom of the roasting pan so the drippings don't burn.

Set the turkey in a roasting rack, put the rack in the roasting pan, then roast it breast down for 1 to 1-1/2 hours, depending on how big it is.

Remove the roasting pan from the oven. Have a turkey-sized platter ready. Using several layers of paper towels in each hand so you don't get burned, lift the turkey and rack out of the pan and flip them together onto the platter. Then lift the rack off the turkey and set it back in the roasting pan. Still using the paper towels, flip the turkey over and set it breast side up on the rack.

> If you have trouble flipping the turkey, remove the rack and turkey to a big platter next to the sink, then just roll the whole thing over. Set your roasting rack in the sink, then slide the turkey back onto the rack. The rack then goes back in the roasting pan.

Roast for another 1 to 1-1/2 hours. Replenish the water in the bottom of the pan if necessary. The turkey is done when a piercing in the deepest part of the thigh produces juice with just the faintest hint of pink. Or, if you have a meat thermometer, roast to an internal temperature of 150°F.

Remove from the oven and let rest at least 30 minutes. A full hour is better, and the bird will still be warm two hours later.

Scrape the drippings and add them to the gravy. Remove the stuffing and put it in your serving dish. Carve the turkey as nicely or not as your inclined to (it tastes great in any shape!), then you're ready to eat.

Notes

The skin over the stuffing in the neck cavity will turn very dark during the cooking process, but won't actually burn. If you like, cover just this area with foil to keep it lighter in color.

I usually do a turkey weighing somewhere in the mid-20's. It's big enough to feed up to around 15 or 20 people and small enough that I can still flip it over. If I'm expecting more people than that, I'll usually do the non-traditional Thanksgiving menu with smoked turkeys instead of roasted stuffed turkeys because they cook faster and it's not too bad to do one after the other. Two roasted stuffed turkey is really hard unless you have two large ovens.

The chilled drippings from the pan tell the story: about 3 cups of fat melted off the turkey, while almost all of the juices were sealed in by the high heat. Gotta love it!

I usually get a frozen turkey. Fresh are a lot more expensive and I don't see the difference in the result. Most turkeys are dry because people overcook them. There should still be hints of pink in the finished result. An overcooked fresh turkey is just as dry as an overcooked frozen one.

If you're nervous about telling when the turkey is done, use a meat thermometer. However, only roast to an internal temperature of 150°F—not the 180°F temperature commonly recommended these days. Cooking to 180°F will give you Roast Turtankahem (mummified turkey) for sure, and now amount of gravy will erase the impression that you're eating something which was not alive any time recently. 150°F really is cooked enough to eat safely. In addition, out of "an overabundance of caution" as the lawyers would say, we're being extra-safe by: (1) thoroughly rinsing first; and (2) soaking in a brine salty enough to kill bacteria.

I've cooked hundreds of turkeys over the years, and no one's gotten sick yet. But, everyone does say "Your turkey is so moist! What did you do?"

It's simple: don't overcook it. There will be hints of pink. Blame it on the marinade.

I also don't bother with covering with cheesecloth or anything else, or with basting. Both interfere with the skin browning. In addition, with enough marinading time, the flavor's already in the meat. And basting is not necessary if, again, you just don't overcook it.

The cooking method given here of using high heat and flipping the bird gives you a result similar to a fried turkey without the bother of special turkey fryer and all that hot oil. The finished bird is beautifully browned and crisp on all sides while still juicy and moist inside. It's not that hard if you just use enough paper towels to insulate your hands against the heat.

If it's more than you'd like to try, just reduce the oven to 350°F and roast the turkey breast down. That's right: breast down. I know this is contrary to all the photos and recipes you've seen. I've tried it many times both ways and find that, breast up, the white meat is dry by the time the thighs are done. Roasting breast down gives you wonderfully moist breast meat when the bird is done. Sure, it won't look as pretty if you flip if over. Just don't!

ORANGE-GINGER HICKORY SMOKED TURKEY

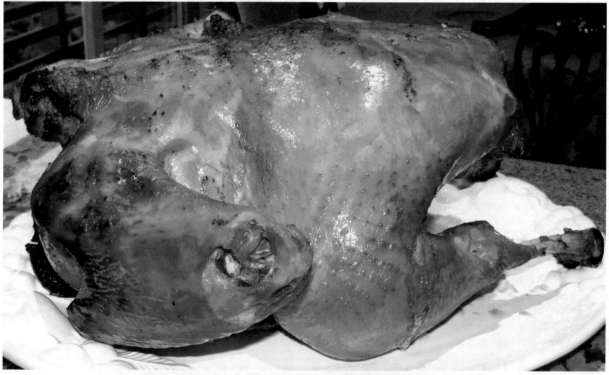

**Here's a finished 20-lb. bird ready to transport to my sister-in-law's.
Yes, I'm looking for a spot I can sneak a bite!**

Here's a delicious, different way to prepare a turkey for any festive gathering from Thanksgiving to a mid-summer pool party. For our family, this is a regular request for the Thanksgiving table.

The Gist

The turkey is brined in water, salt, pepper, sugar, ginger, orange rind, and cinnamon, then hickory-smoked on the barbecue.

Ingredients

1 gallon cool water

1 15-20 lb. turkey

1 cup salt

1 cup sugar

1/3 cup fresh ground black pepper

1/4 ground cinnamon

1 cup thinly sliced fresh ginger root

1/2 cup orange rind, minced

hickory smoking chips

> To flip a turkey on the barbecue, use a quadruple layer of paper towels in each hand and flip it by hand. These work as disposable pot holders. Using tongs, etc. (my former method) tends to tear the skin. This method keeps it perfect!

Method

If using a frozen turkey (I usually do!), thaw it first. Overnight in a sink of cold water or 3 days in the fridge will do the trick. Rinse it thoroughly in cool water, remove excess fat around the openings (front and back), and set the giblets aside for gravy.

Combine the water, salt, sugar, pepper, cinnamon, ginger, and orange rind in a large stock pot or 5-gallon plastic bucket. Stir thoroughly until the sugar and salt are dissolved. Put the turkey in the brine and turn a few times to expose all sides to the brine. Cover the pot or bucket with plastic wrap and set the turkey in the fridge for a minimum of 1 day, though 3 days are better so the flavor penetrates all the way. Flip the turkey over every 12-24 hours so it marinates evenly.

My do-it-yourself, disposable smoker box filled with hickory chips and ready to go.

The day you're cooking it, take the turkey out of the brine and set it on the counter in a large tray so it can come to room temperature before cooking. This will take several hours. Discard the brine.

When you're ready to cook the turkey, set up your smoking arrangement. I use a gas barbecue. On the turkey side, I set a the bottom of a broiler pan with a little water in it under the grill to catch the drippings. The turkey then goes on the grill over the broiler pan. The burners under that side of the grill I leave turned off.

The burners on the other side of the grill (not under the drip pan), I turn to high. My grill takes about 20 minutes to heat up, reaching a temperature of about 400° (on half the burners!).

For the smoking chips, I fill a small, disposable aluminum loaf pan with smoking chips, enclose the while thing in aluminum foil (excess folded tight), then poke holes in the top. This works greats for smoking, then it can be discarded.

When I'm ready to cook the turkey, it goes on the grill over the drip pan, and the smoking chip pan goes on the hot side.

The turkey will need to be turned around or flipped every 30 minutes or so in order to brown evenly on all sides. It will be done in about 2 hours. The end-to-end turning is necessary because the end closest to the burners tends to brown more.

When done, remove it to a platter and let rest for at least 30 minutes before carving it. When I'm taking it elsewhere for Thanksgiving, I put the cooked bird in a covered roaster for transporting. It will stay warm this way for several hours.

Carve and enjoy!

My brother-in-law Doug does a beautiful job carving and presenting the bird—and I'm happy to delegate!

Notes

Because the flavors of this turkey are so unusual, I developed a special giblet gravy and dressing to go along with it. See my recipes for Bacon-Onion Giblet Gravy and for Spicy Cajun Cornbread Dressing.

If at all possible, save the carcass and bones for Smoked Turkey Jook (rice porridge). Worth spiriting away the carcass after the meat is carved from it!

SZECHUAN TURKEY

This turkey is a variation on Peking Duck, with slightly different flavoring and without the final crisping step. Utterly delicious and a show-stopper entrée. It takes some time, but not a lot of skill. Plan to start at least two days ahead of when you plan to serve it, with the first day for marinating and the second for it to sit overnight after steaming.

The Gist

A turkey gets marinated, then steamed, then smoked, then totally wows your relatives.

Ingredients

1 12 or 13 lb. turkey

1/3 cup salt

1/3 cup peppercorns, roasted and ground

minced rind from 1 orange

1/2 cup loose black tea

1/2 cup brown rice

1/2 cup brown sugar

2 Tb. peppercorns

2 Tb. anise seeds

4 sticks cinnamon or canela, broken into small pieces

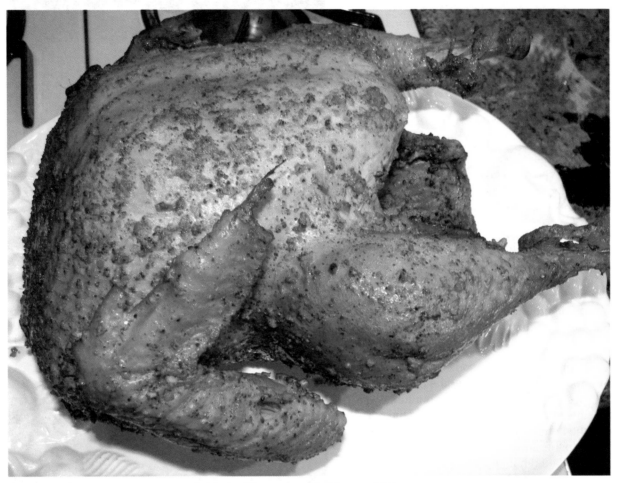

A bird with an out-of-this-world flavor.

Method

Wash the turkey thoroughly in cool water and pat dry with paper towels. Set in a bowl or container big enough to hold it while marinating.

Set the peppercorns in a skillet over medium heat and roast just until they start to pop and smoke a bit. Immediately remove from the burner and let cool for a bit, then grind. While it's cooling, use a vegetable peeler to peel the rind from an orange, then mince the rind.

Combine the salt, ground pepper, and orange rind. Rub thoroughly inside and outside the turkey, distributing the marinade evenly. Marinate the turkey for 24 hours at room temperature or up to 3 days in the refrigerator. Flip the turkey and redistribute the marinade every 12 hours or so to marinate evenly.

To steam the turkey, I use a 20-quart stock pot, vertical turkey rack, and top the pot with a dome of aluminum foil crimped tightly around the edges. The important part is to have the turkey above and not in the steaming water and to have a tight enough seal that it gets really hot inside. Any sort of pot and rack combination would work. For the vertical rack I use, I stuff a wadded up ball of aluminum foil inside the turkey to help it sit higher on the rack and above the steaming water.

Once you have the turkey set up in your steamer, add about 1/2 inch of water in the bottom of your pot and apply your seal (aluminum foil or a lid). Be sure that the turkey is above the steaming water and that there's space over it for the steam to circulate.

Set your stove to high heat. Once the turkey is hot and steaming (a little steam will be seeping out from somewhere), steam it over high heat for 45 minutes, then shut the burner off and let the turkey sit overnight. The heat from steaming will thoroughly cook the turkey, but it needs time to penetrate and then cool.

After cooling overnight, the turkey can go in the fridge if you're not going to have it that day. When you take the turkey out of the pot, be sure to save the delicious aspic-like juices from the bottom for soup.

Here's the birdie steaming away. The aluminum foil puffing out let you know you have a good seal on the edges.

On smokin' and eatin' day, ready your pot and rack again. They should be clean and dry. Line the bottom of your pot with a single piece of heavy duty aluminum foil or two pieces of regular strength. Wrap a strip of foil around the bottom of the rack so the smoking mixture won't stick to it.

Combine the tea, brown rice, brown sugar, peppercorns, anise, and cinnamon pieces. Spread them evenly over the bottom of the pot (on top of the foil). Set your turkey on the rack and place these back in the pot. If the bottom of the drumsticks are sticking into the smoking mixture, you can wrap a little aluminum foil around these, too.

Set your burner to high. Once the smoking mixture begins to smoke, clamp on your foil or lid (smoking may start fairly quickly, depending on how hot your stove is). Your lid should be tight enough that little wisps of smoke escape, but no more. It's probably a good idea to turn your fan on.

The turkey needs to smoke for 12-15 minutes. My stove (a commercial-type range) needs to go somewhere between medium high and high to keep the smoke coming. A steady stream of smoke wisps tells you it's hot enough. It's important to get a fast, hot heat to get the smoking going. Too slow a process and the turkey starts to heat up and drip juices into the bottom of the pot, quenching the smoking.

Ms. Birdie is done her steam bath and ready for smokin'.

When finished, shut the burner off, move the pot off the hot burner (turn your fan on high!) and carefully remove the lid. The turkey should be beautiful caramel brown color like the photo, and the smoking mixture should be brown-black like the photo.

If the turkey isn't smoked enough and the smoking mixture is still dry, you can restart the smoking over high heat. If the smoking mixture has gotten soggy, you'll need to make a new smoking mix—or call it enough and enjoy it as is! It will still be delicious.

Remove the turkey, set it on a platter, give yourself a pat on the back, and wait for your guests to be totally impressed.

Notes

The only trouble I've ever had with making this is when the pan doesn't get hot enough quick enough or the turkey juices start to drip. Starting with high heat and watching for the continuous wisps of smoke seems to take care of this. Letting the turkey sit in the pot overnight after steaming took care of the juices problem by allowing the turkey to thoroughly cool and set.

And even when things didn't come out exactly right, it still tasted great! I suspect I was the only one who knew the difference.

Here's the residue from smoking—it will be black! Note the foil on the bottom of the rack so the smoking mixture won't stick to it.

DUCK

Usually, I stick to chicken or turkeys because, when you're having chicken, you don't have to explain to your guests that it tastes like chicken! However, I am very fond of chinese-style duck this recipe. I have a bunch of other duck recipes I really like, so will have to get them and some Cornish game hens in the next book!

PEKING DUCK

This version of Peking Duck produces a fabulously flavored and crisp bird remarkably free of fat. Love without guilt! What's not to like about it?

The Gist

A duck is marinated with salt, pepper, anise, fennel, cinnamon, and cloves, then steamed, then deep fried.

Ingredients

1 duck

3 Tb. salt

2-1/2 Tb. peppercorns, roasted and ground

1/2 tsp. anise seeds

1/2 tsp. fennel seeds

1/2 tsp. cinnamon

1/4 tsp. cloves

4 Tb. dry rice wine or sherry

8 slices fresh ginger

4 green onions, cut in half and smashed lightly with a knife

3 tb. soy sauce

flour

peanut oil to reach 3" depth in a pot (approximately 6-8 cups)

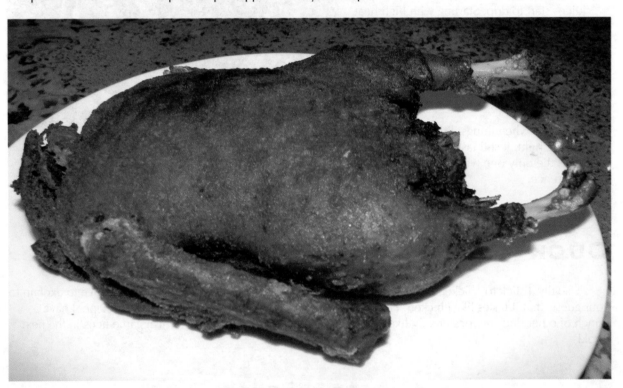

When you want a meal fit for an emperor (or empress!)

Method

This duck needs to start at least a day ahead of time (which is why one needs to call ahead!), but you can stretch it out over several days if you like.

If you're starting with a frozen duck (which is what most stores have), thaw it first. A day or two in the fridge or an afternoon in the sink in cool water will do it.

Rinse the duck thoroughly in cool water and pat dry. If your duck still has its complete wings, cut off and discard the end sections.

Roast the peppercorns in a skillet over medium heat just until they start to crackle and smoke slightly. Remove from the heat and let cool, then grind them with the anise and fennel seeds. Combine with the salt, cinnamon, and cloves.

Rub this mixture thoroughly inside and outside the duck. Let marinate at room temperature for 24 hours, flipping 2 or 3 times along the way. It can then be steamed, or marinate another day or two in the fridge.

Place the duck in a tray with high sides or a bowl (to hold the juices). Rub it thoroughly with the rice wine or sherry. Place half the ginger slices and green onions inside and half arranged over the top.

Place the duck in bowl in a steamer and begin steaming. It will steam for 3 hours in total. After 30 minutes, use a baster to drain off the accumulated juices and melted fat. Drain again after 30 more minutes (at the 1 hour mark), then again at the 2 hour mark. In this process, most of the duck fat will melt and drain off, leaving a remarkably defatted duck.

Remove the duck from the bowl and place on a rack to dry thoroughly. The process can be expedited in a 150°F oven if you like.

The duck can go into the fridge at this point until you're ready to serve, or go right to frying.

Start your peanut oil heating in a pan big enough to hold the duck and with sides high enough to catch the splatters. Heat the oil to a dense haze (almost smoking).

Rub the soy sauce evenly on the outside of the duck, then dust the duck lightly with flour. Shake off the excess.

Using implements (like two slotted metal spoons), carefully lower the duck into the hot oil. It will splatter and give off steam, so be careful! Press it down every minute or so to make sure the top crisps, too, and cook until golden brown in color (about 5 minutes).

Remove the duck, being careful to tip it a bit so the hot oil drains out from the inside. Set the duck on a rack to drain and heat the oil back to a dense haze (almost smoking).

Carefully use your implements to lower the duck a second time into the hot oil. If you can manage it, flipping it over for the second frying would be a good idea. This second frying makes it extra crisp, and will only take 2-3 minutes. Remove when the duck is a deep brown color.

Set the duck back on the rack to drain and cool for a few minutes, then carve and serve.

Notes

This duck is traditionally served with slivered green onions, hoisin sauce, and buns of some sort. A good, whole wheat dinner roll or chinese bun would be great, or try my recipe for Potato Rosemary Rolls for a special accompaniment.

All of the preparation can be done ahead of time except the final deep frying, which should be done right before serving.

MOO, OINK & BAAA

BEEF

Yes, I love beef, too! I just don't like the fatty varieties—of anything, for that matter!

Granted, lots of folks shy away from red meat because of the fat and cholesterol content. And I'm not recommended you go totally beefy if your cholesterol is a problem. But, you can have great cholesterol levels and still eat beef if you follow my Bite It and Burn It motto and watch my Three Secrets of Power Foods. I eat a lot of beef and my cholesterol levels are so great my doctor doesn't know what to make of them. That's his problem!

BEST BARBECUE STEAK

Here's some ribeye steaks cooked medium well for my honey (on the left), and New York sirloin steaks (on the right) cooked medium rare for me. Extras are easy to do on the hot grill and reheat really well with a minute or two in the microwave.

Perhaps the title is a bit presumptuous, but so many people have called this the best steak they've ever had that I'll stick with it. The secret is a marinade that "disappears,"—leaving only exceptionally fully flavored and tender BEEF.

The Gist

Marinate steaks for 1-2 hours in a slurry of vodka, salt, and pepper. Grill briefly over high heat and serve.

Ingredients

4-5 steaks, about 4 lbs. total (see Notes for thoughts on cuts of steak)

vodka

1 Tb. salt

1 Tb. fresh ground black pepper

Method

Combine the salt and pepper in a tray or baking dish big enough to hold the steaks. Splash on just enough vodka to make a thick slurry of the salt and pepper. Less is better than too much or your steaks will taste like vodka!

Add the steaks, toss thoroughly, then let marinate at room temperature for 1-2 hours.

Pre-heat grill to maximum temperature. Grill briefly (with 1 or 2 flips) until desired degree of doneness. Medium-rare will be slightly firmer than raw, about the consistency of your earlobe.

Remember that the steaks will continue to cook about one degree of doneness more after you take them off. So, if you would like medium rare and want to make a cut to take a peak, they should still look rare when you take them off.

Let the steaks sit for 1-2 minutes (to finish cooking), then serve.

Notes

This recipe produces a beautifully flavored and juicy steak. The vodka helps to tenderize the meat and helps the salt and pepper penetrate. It then burns off in cooking. The salt and pepper is just enough to accent the flavor of the meat without overpowering it. The resulting flavor simply says "BEEF!"

People are always asking me what the best cut of steak is. My answer is: "it depends!"

If you prefer the best flavor, I would suggest New York sirloin, either boneless on on the bone. If you prefer the most tender steak, that would be rib eye (which usually comes with a rib bone attached).

Some folks might object that they prefer filet mignon. Yes, it is very tender, but to me it is not nearly as flavorful as either the rib eye or the New York sirloin. See the next recipe for how to fix this!

Top sirloin is tasty, but tough. It and tri-tip sirloin I would save for hamburger (they do make excellent hamburgers!).

High temperature and short cooking times are essential for steak. Purists will insists on charcoal, but, for convenience, a gas grill wins hands-down for me. Pre-heat it enough to reach its maximum temperature before you put the steaks on. Mine will get over 600°F (that's as high as the gauge goes!) in about 20 minutes.

For medium rare, I would then cook them 1-2 minutes per side, with the cover closed.

If someone prefers their steak well done, then by all means put it on 2-4 minutes early. It should then be done around the same time as the remaining steaks.

One caveat: when eating out, save ordering your steak well done for the better restaurants. There's a saying in the restaurant world that when a raw steak is almost old enough to discard, they "save it for the well done!"

Some folks will still want steak sauce with their steak. Oh, dear.

WESTERN TENDERLOIN

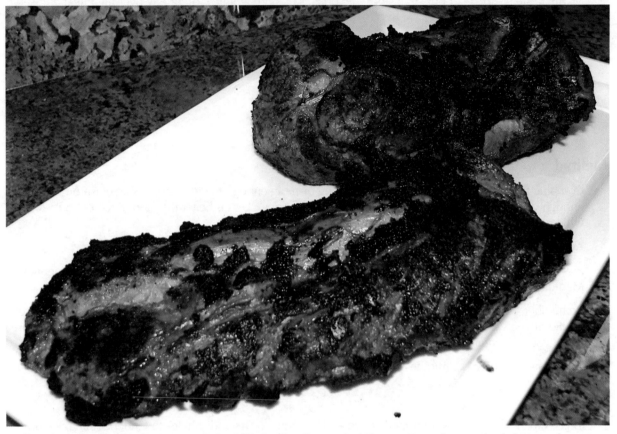

Ready to feed a hungry crowd. And it's better than what I've gotten at any steak house, in my opinion!

Beef tenderloin is marvelously tender, but not as flavorful as other cuts of beef. This recipe spices it up just enough to make it great. I get rave reviews for this—even from die-hard ribeye lovers!

The Gist

Marinate a tenderloin in salt, pepper, granulated garlic and Chipotle chile powder, then grill.

Ingredients

2 Tb. salt

2 Tb. fresh ground black pepper

1 Tb. granulated garlic

1 Tb. Chipotle chile powder

1 whole beef tenderloin

Method

Mix together all the spices. Cut the tenderloin in half lengthwise, both to make it easier to handle and so you can cook the smaller piece a little longer for folks who like their beef more done.

Rub the spice mixture evenly on all sides of the beef. If you have time, set it in the fridge to marinate for a day or two so the spices have time to penetrate. Let it come to room temperature before grilling.

Heat your grill to very hot. Sear the beef for 5 minutes on each side, then cook to desired degree of doneness, flipping every 5 minutes or so. 15-20 minutes in total should do it for medium rare.

Let the beef sit for 5 minutes before carving.

Notes

Although the smaller end of the beef will cook more because it's smaller, you can put it on 5 minutes before the larger end if you have folks who prefer their beef medium well. With how tender this cut is, I have found that even more-done folks like it medium rare!

BAY & GARLIC BARBECUED BEEF TENDERLOIN

Much easier to do than you might think, and very impressive for guests. It does need to start a few days ahead of time for marinating. This is perhaps more traditional than the Western tenderloin (previous recipe).

The Gist

Same basic marinade as for the steaks, but with fresh bay leaves or chopped garlic for additional flavor. More cooking time is required, but I still do it over high heat on the barbecue and flip every 5 or 10 minutes.

Ingredients

1 whole beef tenderloin

2 Tb. salt

2 Tb. fresh ground black pepper

a dozen fresh bay leaves *or* 1/2 cup chopped fresh garlic

vodka

Check for fresh bay leaves in the herb section of your grocery store. Dry ones won't do because they're not nearly as aromatic as fresh ones. If you can't find fresh ones, just garlic will work just fine instead. I get fresh bay leaves off of my bay tree. Then again, I live in California!

Method

Cut the tenderloin in half so you get two shorter pieces instead of one very long piece. This makes it easier to handle.

Mix the salt and pepper. Add just enough vodka to make a thick paste of it. Add the bay leaves or garlic.

Place the large tenderloin pieces in something you can cover and put in the fridge. I have very large plastic containers on hand for things like this. Rub the marinade well into all sides of the meat, then put it in the fridge.

Marinate the beef at least overnight, and preferably for 2 or 3 days. With such a thick piece of meat, it takes this long for the marinate to penetrate evenly through the meat. Once or twice a day, take the meat out of the fridge and give it a good turning and rubbing in the marinade to make sure it's evenly flavored.

The day you're cooking it, take it out of the fridge a few hours ahead of time to bring the meat to room temperature. Start the barbecue heating to high.

Place the meat on the hot barbecue and put the cover on. Flip it every 5 or 10 minutes, depending on how hot your barbecue is. It will take 20 to 30 minutes to cook. Remember to take it off when it's one step less done than you like because it will keep cooking after you remove it (e.g, cook to rare for medium rare final doneness).

Place the two roast pieces on a serving platter and let rest for 10-15 minutes before carving (so the juices don't all run out!). Carve pieces across the grain (the grain runs lengthwise through the meat).

Notes

Besides being very dramatic to serve, a whole beef tenderloin is a very convenient entrée for a large group for a lot of reasons. It's an easy way to do a large quantity for a crowd. And, because the meat goes from narrow at one end to thicker at the other, you'll end up with well done at the small end, rare at the large, and medium in the middle—so everybody can have exactly what they like without having to vary cooking times. That's what makes cooking steaks for a crowd so challenging.

I add the extra marinade ingredients of bay leaves or garlic because, to my taste, tenderloin is on the bland side. Feel free to experiment with other accent flavors. For example, rosemary would also work, but people might think you were making lamb!

ROAST PRIME RIB OF BEEF

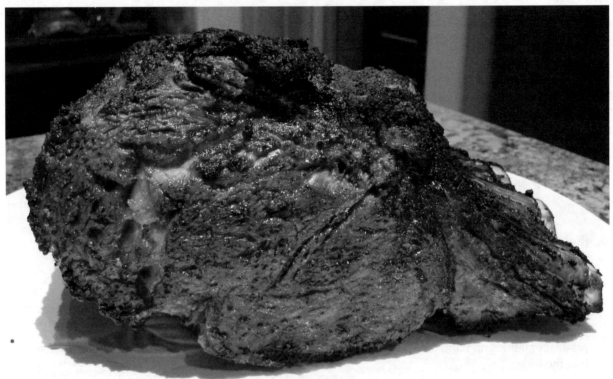

The high temperature-and-flip method produces a beautiful brown crust on all sides of the roast. Yummy!

Although many people are intimidated by cooking a prime rib (it is an expensive roast, after all), you can have a great roast every time by allowing enough time for the marinade and use a good meat thermometer. Give it a try next Christmas!

The Gist

Marinate the roast for 2-3 days in salt, pepper, fresh bay leaves, and vodka. Roast at 450°F till done, flipping the roast every hour.

Ingredients

1 6-8 lb. rib roast

2 Tb. salt

2 Tb. fresh ground black pepper

1 dozen fresh bay leaves

vodka

Method

Combine the salt and pepper. Add just enough vodka to create a thick paste. Rub this paste thoroughly into all sides of the roast. Press the bay leaves against all sides and set the roast in a covered bowl in the fridge for 2-3 days. This gives the spices enough time to penetrate all the way through the roast.

2-3 hours before cooking, take the roast out of the fridge so it can warm to room temperature.

Preheat your oven to 450°F. Set the roast on a rack over a pan to catch the drippings. Add about 1/4-inch of water in the bottom of the pan so the drippings don't burn.

Using a good meat thermometer, roast to an internal temperature of 120°F for rare, or 130°F for medium rare. This will take around 1-1/2 hours, longer for a larger roast. Flip the roast over about once an hour so it cooks evenly.

When the roast has reached the desired internal temperature, remove it from the oven, cover it loosely with aluminum foil, and let it rest for at least 30 minutes. It will continue to cook as it rests, and will still be hot an hour after you remove it from the oven.

Carve and serve.

Notes

Flipping the roast is necessary with using the high roasting temperature the entire time. You could reduce the temperature to 325°F after the first 30 minutes and skip flipping it, but it won't be as nicely browned on all sides. I like to start the roast with the fattest side down, then end it with the fattest side up so as much of the fat melts off as possible.

This recipe is one of the few for which I always use a thermometer because I find it so hard to tell when the roast is done. Skip it if you feel able!

Variations

Because a rib roast has a milder flavor than sirloin, it can take a wide variety of marinades. Instead of the bay leaves, try using a tablespoon of dry mustard powder or 1/2 cup of minced fresh garlic. After the first time through, you can adjust quantities if you'd like the flavor of the accent spice more or less pronounced.

SUPER BURGERS

Add cheddar cheese, crisped bacon, avocado slices, and bleu cheese dressing on the bun for an $18 burger.

I think these burgers are better than any I've had elsewhere. The secrets are good meat and just enough seasoning to accent but not overwhelm it.

The Gist

Ground sirloin with a little minced red onion, parsley, salt, pepper, soy, and Worcestershire.

Ingredients

1 4-lb. piece of top sirloin

1/4 cup finely minced red onion

2 tbs. finely minced parsley

1 tsp. salt

1 tsp. fresh ground black pepper

2 tsp. soy sauce

1 tsp. Worcestershire

> It's the beef! (And the flavorings.) Most ready ground beef in the store is way too fatty for my tastes. If you can't find ground sirloin and don't want to grind it, do look around for a leaner variety of ground beef, which many stores now have. The leanest is probably fine.

Method

Cut the meat into chunks and grind it in a meat grinder or in several batches in a food processor. Or just open the package of ground sirloin if that's what you bought.

Add the remaining ingredients and mix well. Form into 6 patties and grill to desired degree of doneness. Serve with your favorite burger condiments. For me, that always includes whole wheat burger buns. The burger in the photo also has cheddar cheese and bacon. Yum!

Notes

People disagree on the best cut of beef for hamburgers. Some folks call for chuck, but I think it has way too much fat. Top sirloin has a good balance of flavor and fat. It's way too tough to have as a steak, but perfect ground for burgers. With more expensive cuts of meat (such as New York sirloin), you're paying for tenderness which is lost in ground beef.

SOUTHWESTERN BARBECUE TRI-TIP

A moderately spicy dry rub puts a tri-tip roast on par with steak. This is a great dish for parties which can be cooked before your guests arrive. Do start the marinading 2-3 days ahead of time so the flavors have time to penetrate the roast.

The Gist

A dry mixture of salt, pepper, garlic powder, and Chipotle chili powder is rubbed over the roast, which is then marinated. The roast is cooked on the barbecue over high heat, then placed in a covered metal pan or pot to set and finish cooking.

Ingredients

2 whole tri-tip roasts

4 Tb. cup salt

4 Tb. cup fresh ground black pepper

4 Tb. cup granulated garlic

2-4 Tbs. Chipotle chili powder

> Tri-tips are not my favorite cut of roast beef because of the high fat content, but this recipe produces a very good roast and is great for groups. Well worth it when you don't want to spring for a prime rib roast or a beef tenderloin.

Method

Mix all the spices together, then rub them even all over the outsides of the roasts. Place the roasts in a container in the fridge and marinate 1 to 3 days. Once a day, flip the roasts and rub the spices around for even marination.

Heat a covered barbecue to high heat. Place the roasts on the grill and cover. Flip them every 5 minutes, for a total cooking time of around 25 minutes (depending on how hot your grill is). For medium rare, they should be about earlobe-firm when done. Also do keep an eye on the smoke level and move the roasts out of any flare-ups. These are likely as the fat on the outside melts.

Remove the roasts from the grill and immediately place them in a covered, heavy duty roasting pan or pot. Let them rest at least 30 minutes so the heat on the outside can finish cooking the inside. They will still warm this way for at least an hour.

Carve the roasts into slices across the grain (the short way rather than the long way of the roast), and serve.

Notes

The covered setting time at the end is essential to finish cooking the roasts and set the juices. Especially with roasts on the barbecue, they will be underdone when you take them off and need the set time to finish. Rare off the grill will turn to medium rare after 30 minutes of setting.

Vary the amount of Chipotle chili powder according to how spicy you like it.

Tri-tips are good for accommodating folks who like different degrees of doneness. The narrower end will be more on the well-done side, while the thicker end will be more rare.

Variations

This dry rub mixture will work on any roast beef, and the roast can be cooked uncovered in the oven on a rack. Even with oven cooking, the Chipotle (smoked jalapeño) will give the roast a nice, smoky flavor.

BOEUF BOURGUIGNON

Here it is in a little bowl of Garlic Mashed Potatoes with a crown of steamed green beans sprinkled with almonds. Your guests will be expecting a big bill!

Here's my version of the french classic. Be sure to check out the variations for an extra fancy version!

The Gist

Bacon gets crisped, then onions, mushrooms, and beef. A brief flambé, then simmered in red wine with parsley, thyme, and a little tomato paste until done. Carrot coins go in at the end. Too good to call it "stew!"

Ingredients

1/2 lb bacon, chopped

2 yellow onions, peeled and chopped

5 cloves garlic, minced

1-1/5 mushrooms, sliced

3 lbs. stew beef, cut in cubes

1/4 cup cognac

1 750-ml bottle dry red wine

2 tsp salt

1 Tb fresh ground black pepper

1/2 cup fresh parsley, chopped

3 Tb fresh thyme, minced

4 Tb tomato paste

4 Tb beef stock base

3 cups carrots, sliced into coins

Method

Fry the bacon over medium heat until crisp. Shut off the heat, tilt the pan and spoon out part of the melted fat, leaving a few tablespoons in the pot. Turn the heat back on and fry the onions until well browned. Add the garlic, toss for a minute, then add the mushrooms and sauté until browned. Add and brown the beef.

Turn your fan on high, STAND BACK, then add the 1/4 cup cognac and light it! Give the pan a good shake to distribute the flames. It will burn out by itself, or you can put the lid on to douse the flames.

Add the bottle of wine, parsley, thyme, salt, and pepper and cook over high heat until all the alcohol smell is gone (10-15 minutes, depending on how hot your stove is). Turn the heat down, add the tomato paste and beef stock base, then simmer until the beef is tender. Add the carrot coins and turn off the heat.

Serve with your favorite mashed potatoes (such as Garlic Mashed Potatoes) and your choice of green vegetable.

Notes

This recipe takes the classic french version and does all the browning in one pan instead of separately. Definitely a time saver, and still tastes great!

Variations

For a more intense grilled flavor, I'll sometimes cut the beef in large hunks, rub with salt and pepper, then sear them on a grill before cutting them into small pieces. They then don't need to be browned further when you add them.

For a super intense beef flavor, sear beef ribs and on the grill and then simmer them to make your own stock. Strain and discard the bones and excess fat. To take it to the gourmet level, simmer them with carrots, onions, and parsley and reduce the stock well to concentrate it.

BEEFY BORSCHT

A very simple and special one-dish dinner for the coldest night!

I love beets, and love the flavor of beets with beef in borscht. This is a hearty enough recipe, though, that you can omit the beef and make a wonderful vegetarian version.

The Gist

Beef is browned in butter along with soaked and sliced shiitake mushrooms, beef stock base, celery, and canned tomatoes. Beets and chopped purple cabbage go in to finish it.

Ingredients

2 lbs. lean beef (such as top round), cubed

2 Tb. butter

3 Tb. beef stock base

1 dozen dried shiitake mushrooms

4 cloves garlic, sliced

4 celery stocks, chopped

1 28-oz. canned diced tomatoes in juice

1 Tb. salt

> Canned beets are one of the vegetables I find just as good as fresh. I usually just buy fresh beets when I plan to cook them with the leaves. See my recipe for this.

1 Tb. fresh ground black pepper

6 carrots, sliced

2 lbs. beets (fresh or canned), sliced

2 Tb. lemon juice

1 Tb. sugar

4 Tb. fresh dill, minced

1 head purple cabbage, chopped

sour cream and extra dill to garnish

Method

Put the shiitake mushrooms in warm water to soak. When soft, cut them in slices. Save most of the soaking water, but discard any grit at the bottom which has come off of the mushrooms.

Heat the butter in a large stock pot. Sauté the beef until browned. Add the mushroom soaking water, mushrooms, beef stock base, garlic, celery, salt, pepper, and canned tomatoes. Add just enough water to barely cover the beef and bring to a simmer. Cook until the beef is tender, about 30 minutes.

If using fresh beets, add them now, along with the lemon juice, sugar, and dill and simmer for ten minutes, then add the carrots.

If using canned beets, cook the carrots, lemon juice, sugar, and dill for five or ten minutes, then add the beets. Be sure to add the juice from the beets can.

Add the chopped purple cabbage, simmer for another five minutes, then shut the heat off. Serve with a sour cream and dill garnish on top.

Notes

Although sliced potatoes are often included in borscht, I prefer to omit them. Feel free to include them if you're so inclined. The would go in along with fresh beets, or cooked for a few minutes before adding fresh carrots and canned beets so the potatoes are nice and tender at the end.

PORK

Pork is a favorite American food (just ask Congress!). From bacon to a slab of Bubba's Baby Back Ribs, it's a sure crowd-pleaser. The trick—as with beef and chicken—is to keep the fat content down, and to balance it out with low fat, high fiber foods. Ribs with a big green salad—what could be better?

Part of maintaining the balance is being selective about your cuts of pork to keep the fat down. I love pork loin for this reason and make it a lot. A pork shoulder is also a fairly lean cut. Some stores sell boneless pork shoulders, which make a great roast or source of chunks for something else. Pork butts, on the other hand, are too fatty for my tastes. I'll leave those for other folks!

Other tricks to keeping the fat down are careful trimming and how you cook it. By trimming the outer fat off a ham, for example, you'll get rid of a lot of the fat. This is easier to do now that whole hams seldom come with the complete skin and fat layer any more. For that inescapably fatty and favorite pork (bacon!), I'll cook it until crisp and drain the fat off. Not lean in the end by any means, but surely great and a reasonably accompaniment to whole wheat pancakes.

No reason not to make lean cuts of well-trimmed pork a regular part of great and healthy meals at your house!

Okay, the very first recipe (Bubba's ribs) doesn't look so lean. Don't forget the huge green salad to go along with it!

BUBBA'S BABY BACK RIBS

This amount of ribs will serve one hungry Bubba. Have some corn muffins to go along!

Perfect to satisfy all the hungry Bubba's in your life. Be forewarned, though: they'll want some extra sauce for dipping!

The Gist

Make some Barbecue MegaSauce (see Recipe), marinate some ribs in it, then grill 'em as much as you like.

Ingredients

1 recipe of Barbecue MegaSauce (see Recipe)

2 racks of baby back pork ribs

Method

Make the sauce, then douse the ribs thoroughly with the sauce. Some marinating time would be ideal (a few hours at room temperature or overnight in the fridge), but, if you're in a hurry, go ahead and grill them.

> Pork ribs are inescapably fatty, so make sure your have them with lots of vegetables (like a huge tossed salad) to balance out the nutrition and fat content of this meal.

The ribs will take about 10 minutes per side on a very hot grill for medium, a little longer for well done. Be sure to keep an eye on them and move them around if melting fat flares up. Cut the ribs into serving pieces to serve, or give each Bubba a slab of his own!

Notes

I like my ribs medium with just a hint of pink to them, but lots of other folks like them well done. Please don't overcook or even these saucy ribs will dry out.

These ribs can be grilled ahead of time and kept warm in a covered pan in the oven for quite some time.

Most Bubba's will want extra sauce for dipping. If some extra simmered Barbecue MegaSauce won't do the trick, your favorite bottled barbecue sauce is perfectly acceptable. It's a free country!

KAILUA PORK

Served on a bed of steamed black rice and chinese stir-fried spinach with charred garlic, this one is a real crowd pleaser.

Although a requisite luau food, authentic kailua pork from a whole roasted pig is not terribly practical to make at home. This version packs all the flavor, less of the fat, and serves a crowd. Mahalo!

The Gist

A whole boneless pork roast is marinated in a whole mix of stuff, then cooked on the grill.

Ingredients

1 9-10 lb. whole boneless pork loin

1 Tb. salt

1 Tb. Worcestershire sauce

1 tsp. ground cayenne pepper

1 Tb. fresh ground black pepper

1/2 cup soy sauce

1/4 cup minced fresh garlic

1/4 cup minced fresh ginger

1 tsp. liquid smoke seasoning

> If a whole pork loin is just too big for your family, either invite over a bunch of friends (my favorite option!) or cook half in this recipe and use the other half for something else. Twice Cooked Pork is a good choice because you can simmer the pork and let it sit in the juice in the fridge until you're ready to make it.

Method

Combine all ingredients together except the pork and mix thoroughly. Place the pork in a container large enough for it to marinate in. You may want to cut the pork loin into two pieces to make it easier to handle.

Pour the marinade over the pork and turn a few times to evenly distribute the marinade. Marinate the pork in the fridge for at least 24 hours, or up to a few days.

Heat a barbecue grill with cover to very hot. Grill the pork over high heat with the cover closed, flipping it every 5 minutes or so. You may want to move it around the grill to escape the flames if some of the melting fat starts to flare up. The pork will be perfectly done to a faint shade of pink in 20-30 minutes, depending on how hot your grill is.

Slice and serve. The pieces from the small end of the loin will be more done for people who like their pork that way.

Notes

If you'd rather, you can roast the pork loins in a 450°F oven on a rack instead of grilling them. Cooking time will be about the same.

Traditionally, kailua pork is cooked until falling apart, but this results in a very dry roast unless you use a fairly fatty cut of pork. A good pork loin benefits greatly from more discretion.

I like to serve this with rice and stir-fried spinach with charred garlic (see Recipe) for an all-in-one dinner.

MAPLE GINGER PORK LOIN

So impressive and delicious no one will guess how simple it is to make!

This is another really simple way to prepare a whole pork loin. The maple, ginger, smoky flavor is utterly outstanding.

The Gist

Marinate a whole pork loin in maple syrup, minced fresh ginger, salt, fresh ground black pepper, and cayenne. Grill.

Ingredients

1 whole pork loin

1/2 cup maple syrup

1/4 cup fresh ginger, finely minced

2 Tb. salt

1 Tb. fresh ground black pepper

1 tsp. cayenne pepper

Method

Combine the maple syrup, ginger, salt, black and cayenne peppers to make the marinade. Set the pork loin in a pan for marination and pour the marinade over it. Turn several times to coat thoroughly.

Marinate for an afternoon on the counter, or up to several days in the fridge. It really takes 24 hours or more for the flavors to penetrate completely. Bring to room temperature before cooking.

Heat a grill to very hot (mine goes to 600°F). Set the loin on it and turn every five minutes or so, moving it around the grill to avoid the flames as the fat melts off. Turn the grill down a bit if it gets too hot.

The loin will be done in about 30 minutes. Let rest at least 20 minutes before serving, then slice and serve.

Notes

Because a whole loin takes a while to marinade, if I'm in a hurry I'll use pork chops or cut the loin into thick slices. This way, an hour or two will do for marinading and cooking time will be ten minutes or so.

Variations

For a more complex smoky flavor, set a smoking box filled with smoking chips directly on the bottom of the grill. Your choice of apple wood, hickory, cherry, or mesquite chips. Be sure to close the cover so the smoky flavor gets into the meat. As a quick and easy alternative, a little liquid smoke seasoning (about 1 tsp.) is also good (but not as good as real smoking!).

PORK CHOP CHILI

Thick and hearty enough to stand up by itself. Where are the tortillas?

This recipe came out of wanting a good, red chile (a chile colorado) and having some pork chops on hand. Other cuts of pork would do, but I liked the name! See the next two recipes for my versions of a green chile.

The Gist

Pork chops get marinated, then grilled. Pinto beans are simmered with red chile sauce, canned tomatoes, and garlic. It all goes together with caramelized yellow onions and sautéed fresh poblano chiles.

Ingredients

2 lbs. pork chops

2 tsp. salt

1 Tb. fresh ground black pepper

1 Tb. granulated garlic

1 Tb. chile powder

2 lbs. dry pinto beans

1 28-oz. can red chile sauce (chile colorado sauce)

1 28-oz. can ground tomatoes in heavy purée

1/2 cup garlic cloves, lightly mashed

2 Tb. chicken stock base

1 Tb. puréed Chipotle chiles (or 1 whole chile)

2 yellow onions, diced

6 fresh poblano chiles, seeded and chopped

2 Tb. bacon fat or olive oil

salt to taste

> Soaking beans overnight in water, then discarding the water before cooking them seems to do two things. First, they swell up so you know how big a pot to get and they'll cook faster. Second, this method seems to eliminate any gas problems from eating beans. No scenes from "Blazing Saddles," please!

Method

Rinse the pinto beans thoroughly in a colander to remove any dirt, then put them in something big enough to cover with 3-4 inches of water. Let them soak for a few hours or overnight.

Combine the salt, pepper, granulated garlic, and chile powder. Sprinkle over the pork chops and toss to coat them evenly. Let these marinate while the beans cook (or let them marinate overnight in the fridge).

Drain the beans, then put them in a big pot with the red chile sauce, tomatoes, garlic, chicken stock base, and Chipotle chile. If necessary, add just enough water to cover the beans. Bring them to a simmer and cook until the beans are tender (an hour or more).

Heat a grill to very hot and barbecue the pork chops for 2-3 minutes per side (just enough to sear them). Place them in a bowl to cool.

Chop the onions and seeded poblano chiles. Be careful with removing the chile seeds because they are very hot. Wash your hands thoroughly with dish soap to remove some of the chile oil from your hands.

Cut the meat from the pork chops into chunks. Add the bones to the beans if they're still simmering.

Heat the bacon fat or olive oil in a pot big enough to hold everything. Cook the onions over medium high heat until golden brown and caramelized. Add the chopped poblano chiles and sauté until they are just starting to wilt and change color.

Add the beans and cubed pork and heat to a simmer. Check for salt. The chile is ready to eat immediately, or can simmer for another hour. If you pot is oven-proof, it can also go into a 250°F oven until you're ready to eat.

Notes

To expedite the process, you can skip grilling the pork chops and just add the chopped meat at the end (be sure to cook thoroughly). It's faster, but you will lose the extra flavor from the grilled meat.

Pork loin or sliced pork shoulder would also work well.

Variations

I've not tried this recipe with beef because I like the flavor of pork and beans, but, if a beef chile is more to your liking, go ahead and substitute beef. Something like a top sirloin would be perfect. It's a little tough to have as a steak in my opinion, but it would be perfect in chile.

BRATWURST AND SAUERKRAUT

All it needs is a beer. Your choice of beer.

This meal takes some time to bake, but preparation time is minimal. Perfect to have baking while you watch a movie!

The Gist

Ingredients

2 lbs. fresh bratwurst

1 large jar of sauerkraut

1 Tb. caraway seeds

2 tsp. fresh ground black pepper

1 tsp. sugar

Method

Start your oven preheating to 400ºF.

Drain the sauerkraut thoroughly, then toss in a bowl with the caraway seeds, black pepper, and sugar. Layer this in the bottom of a covered baking dish, then layer the bratwurst on top.

Place the cover on the pot and bake for around 45 minutes. Remove the top and broil the tops of the bratwurst until browned. Serve with garlic mashed potatoes.

Notes

Since the oven is on anyway, the easiest way to make the mashed potatoes is to place the potatoes and garlic in a heavy, covered pot and bake them in the oven along with the bratwurst. The potatoes will be ready to be mashed when the bratwurst is done!

TWICE COOKED PORK

Chinese restaurant taste brought right to your table—and it's not from a carton!

I've had many versions of Twice Cooked Pork in Chinese restaurants, some great and some not so. After many experiments, I came up with this version that captures the flavors and textures I love in this dish. It is best started a day or two ahead, but can be made all at once.

The Gist

Pork loin is simmered with fresh ginger and green onions, then sliced. It is then stir fried with garlic, carrots, greens, bamboo shoots, and topped with reduced broth mixed with two chinese sauces.

Ingredients

1 section of pork loin, approximately 3 lbs. in weight (this is about half of a whole pork loin)

1/2 cup fresh ginger, thinly sliced

4 green onions

4 Tb. rice wine

water to cover

3 Tb. Chinese barbecue sauce (Char Sui sauce)

3 Tb. Chinese Chile Bean sauce (Toban Djan)

3 Tb. flour

4 Tb. bacon fat or peanut oil

10 cloves garlic, minced

6 carrots, sliced into coins on the diagonal

4 Tb. rice wine

3 lbs. chopped greens, such as cabbage, mustard, or Chinese greens

2 cans bamboo shoots drained

1 bunch green onions, minced

brown rice or whole wheat noodles

Method

Cut the pork loin into two pieces and place them in a tight filling saucepan. Add the ginger slices. Cut the green onions in half, then mash them lightly with the side of your knife. Add them to the pot, along with the rice wine. Add just enough water to barely cover the pork and bring to a simmer. Simmer for 30 minutes.

If you are starting ahead, leave the pork with broth and flavorings in the fridge for a day or two so the flavors can really penetrate the meat.

Start your brown rice cooking, or the water boiling to make noodles. Have these cooked and ready to go when you start stir frying.

Remove the pork from the broth, cut into thin slices and set aside. Discard the ginger and onion pieces. Reduce down the broth on the stove until you have about a cup left. Add the Chinese barbecue and chile bean sauces. Stir thoroughly. Mix the flour with a little water, then whisk it into the simmering broth. You should have a slightly thickened, intensely flavored broth. Keep it warm on low heat.

If you haven't already, cut the carrots on the diagonal into thin coins. Chop the greens.

Heat the bacon fat or peanut oil in a large sauté pan over high heat. Add the garlic and toss for a minute or two. Add the carrot coins and toss for another two minutes. Add the pork slices and toss until the pork is warmed. Add the second 4 Tb. of rice wine and toss.

Add the greens and bamboo shoots and toss until the greens are cooked. Add the sauce and toss. Turn off the heat and mix in the green onions.

Serve over brown rice or the noodles.

Notes

Most recipes I've seen for Twice Cooked Pork call for Hoisin sauce and soy sauce for flavorings, plus minced ginger in the stir fry. I find this makes it too sweet for me. The barbecue and chile bean sauce seems to me to perfectly capture the elusive taste of the best versions of this I've had.

The minced ginger in the stir fry I skip because there's enough intense ginger flavor in the reduced broth to flavor the whole dish.

Variations

This is also quite good with dried shiitake mushrooms added to the pork simmering sauce. Save the mushrooms, slice them, and sauté them with the carrots.

EASY CHILE VERDE

I love chile verde and order it often in Mexican restaurants. Here's a very easy and delicious version you can make at home.

The Gist

White onions are sautéed in a little oil, then with pork chunks and garlic. Add canned green chile sauce, chopped fresh cilantro, cumin, Mexican oregano, and salt to finish.

Ingredients

1 Tb. peanut oil

2 lbs. cubed pork (shoulder or loin)

2 white onions, chopped

6 cloves garlic, minced

1 28-oz. can green enchilada sauce

2 tsp. ground cumin

2 tsp. Mexican oregano (or regular oregano)

1/2 cup fresh cilantro, chopped

2 tsp. salt

corn tortillas

Method

Heat the oil in a medium-sized pot over high heat. When hot, add the onions and sauté until browned. Add the garlic and toss together. Add the pork and toss until the pork is browned.

Turn the heat down to medium and add the remaining ingredients. Simmer until the pork is tender about 20-30 minutes. Serve with warmed corn tortillas (a minute in the microwave will do it. Also good with Frijoles (see Recipe).

Notes

Use pork loin for a leaner dish. If using pork shoulder, trim off the excess fat.

Traditionally, folks would dunk whole, rolled up corn tortillas into their chile. This works fine, but I prefer to break the tortillas into little pieces, mix them with the chile in my bowl, and eat with a spoon. So good.

Variations

See the Alcalde's Chile Verde (next Recipe) for the best chile verde you've ever had.

ALCALDE'S CHILE VERDE

Chile Verde fit for the alcalde. Guaranteed to generate rave reviews.

This dish takes some extra time to prepare the pork and chiles, but has such fantastic flavor it can easily take center stage for a very fancy dinner—perfect if the alcalde is coming!

The Gist

White onions are browned in a little oil, then simmered with marinated roasted pork, puréed roasted chiles and tomatillos, chopped fresh cilantro, roasted ground cumin, coriander and Mexican oregano.

Ingredients

1 lb. dried Mexican mayacabo beans (or other white beans)

6 cloves garlic, smashed

2 Tb. chicken stock base

2 lbs. pork (shoulder or loin) cut into 1-2 inch thick slices

1 Tb. salt

2 tsp. fresh ground black pepper

2 tsp. granulated garlic

4 fresh Pasilla chiles

4 fresh Anaheim chiles

1 lb. fresh tomatillos

2 tsp. cumin seeds

1 tsp. coriander seeds

2 tsp. Mexican oregano (or regular oregano)

1 Tb. peanut oil

2 white onions, chopped

1/2 cup fresh cilantro, chopped

corn tortillas

Method

Rinse the beans thoroughly in a colander and pick out any small stones or dirt pieces. Cover with at least 3-inches of water and soak for at least 4 hours, preferably overnight.

Combine the 1 Tb. salt, pepper and granulated garlic and mix thoroughly. Sprinkle over the pork slices and toss to coat evenly. Marinate at least an hour at room temperature, or overnight in the fridge.

Drain and rinse the beans, then place in a stock pot with just enough water to cover. Add the garlic cloves and chicken stock base and bring to a simmer. If soaked overnight, the beans will be tender in about an hour.

Heat your grill to very hot. Roast the chiles on the grill (or under a broiler) until the skins are blistered and a little blackened on all sides. You'll need to turn them as they cook. Set in a metal bowl and cover tightly with aluminum foil to steam.

While your grill is still hot, sear the pork slices for 2-3 minutes per side, then set in a bowl to cool.

Start a pot of water big enough to hold the tomatillos to boil. Remove the husks from the tomatillos, rinse them, then cook them in the boiling water until soft (about 5 minutes). Remove and set in a bowl to cool.

Heat the cumin and coriander seeds in a small pan over medium heat. When they smell very roasty toasty, turn off the heat and add the oregano, Stir together, then set aside to cool.

Peel and seed the chiles. Dice half of the chiles and set aside in a bowl. Purée the other half in a blender or food processor with the tomatillos and their juice until smooth. Cut the grilled pork slices into cubes.

Grind the roasted cumin and coriander seeds and oregano in a clean coffee or spice grinder.

Heat the oil in a medium-sized pot over high heat. When hot, add the onions and sauté until browned.

Turn the heat down to medium and add the pork cubes, the puréed chiles and tomatillos, the simmered beans, the chopped chiles, the roasted ground spices and the cilantro. Simmer until the pork is tender about 20-30 minutes. Serve with warmed tortillas for dunking.

Notes

Use pork loin for a leaner dish. If using pork shoulder, trim off the excess fat. For a big crew, I'll double or triple the recipe.

Variations

I'll sometimes add half a head of chopped cabbage to turn this into a one-dish dinner.

HAM AND EGG FRIED RICE

Chopsticks are traditional, but feel free to use a fork if you're really hungry!

And you thought ham and eggs were only for breakfast. This recipe turns those great flavors into a great, quick, and comforting dinner.

The Gist

Ham chunks are sautéed with bamboo shoots, water chestnuts, and a green leafy vegetable. Cooked brown rice, green onions, green peas, and scrambled eggs go in at the end.

Ingredients

3 cups dry, uncooked brown rice

6 cups water

2 tsp. salt

6 eggs

2 Tb. oil or bacon fat

3 cups chopped ham

6 cups chopped green leafy vegetable, such as chinese greens, bok choy, collard greens, or spinach

2 cans sliced water chestnuts, drained

2 cans sliced bamboo shoots, drained

1 bunch green onions, minced

2 cups frozen peas

Method

Combine the rice, water, and salt in a sauce pan. Bring to a boil, then turn down to a simmer and cook until all the water is absorbed (about 20 minutes).

While the rice is cooking, chop the ham, green leafy vegetable, and mince the green onions. Take the frozen peas out to start thawing.

Scramble the eggs together, then cook in a skillet with a little butter or bacon fat until just set. Remove to a bowl and chop any big pieces with a fork.

When the rice is about done, heat the oil or bacon fat in a large skillet over high heat. Add the ham chunks and toss until hot. Add the water chestnuts, bamboo shoots, and chopped leafy greens and toss until the greens are just wilted.

Shut the heat off. Add the hot rice, green onions, and green peas and toss thoroughly. Add the scrambled eggs and toss together. Serve hot.

Variations

Any stir-fry-able vegetable would work in this dish, though I tend to like leafy greens for the color. A more traditional (and still very nutritious) choice would be bean sprouts. Chopped cabbage would also work well.

For a more complex flavor, sear half of the ham in the bacon fat over high heat before you add the rice and everything else. The combination of seared and steamed ham cubes is very tasty.

Notes

Traditionally, of course, the rice is stir fried for fried rice and the salt is added to the stir fry. I've found, though, that it takes a fair amount of oil to prevent the rice from sticking. Stir frying the ham and vegetables, then adding the rice at the end, gets you the great seared flavor with much less oil. I also find that adding the salt to the rice when steaming it produces a nice contrast between the salty ham and rice and the non-salty eggs and vegetables.

I like using long grain brown rice for this recipe because it cooks up a little drier and less sticky than short grain, but short grain brown rice would work just as well.

YUCATAN-STYLE PORK CHOPS (OR ROAST)

Yucatan-style pork chops served with Mexican rice. Garnish of whole jalapeño peppers is only for the very brave!

This recipe was inspired by a flavor combination I saw for a pork roast. Works great on pork chops, too!

The Gist

Pork chops are marinated in minced fresh garlic, orange juice concentrate, puréed chiles Chipotle en adobe, and salt. Then grilled.

Ingredients

8 pork chops

1/4 cup minced fresh garlic

1/2 cup orange juice concentrate

1/4 cup puréed chiles Chipotle en adobe

1 Tb. salt

> Chile Chipotle en adobe comes in cans in the Mexican section of your grocery store. When you open the can, you'll find whole, smoked jalapeño chiles in sauce. I purée the chiles and sauce in the blender, then keep extra in a jar in the fridge for instant, smoky heat. Very tasty!

Method

Combine all the ingredients except the pork chops to make the marinade. Toss the pork chops thoroughly in the marinade. If time allows, marinate overnight in the fridge for best flavor. Otherwise, marinate for whatever time you have, then grill the chops on a very hot grill. 2-3 minutes per side will probably do it.

Variations

This marinade also works very well on a whole pork loin. Cut the loin into two pieces to make it easier to handle, and do marinade for 1 to 3 days so the flavor has a chance to penetrate. I'll still do the loin on a hot barbecue, with flips ever 5-10 minutes and moving it around to avoid flare-ups. Total cooking time will be around 30 minutes, depending on your grill. Let it rest at least 20 minutes before carving. The roasts can also stay in a warm oven for an hour or more until you're ready to serve.

I'll sometimes also add fresh bay leaves to the marinade. They lend a wonderfully aromatic smell and flavor to it.

A whole pork loin done this way makes for a very fancy and easy dinner.

MY CASSOULET

As easy as "pork and beans," but way too good to call it that!

A traditional french cassoulet can be a very involved affair. As Julia Child states in Mastering the Art of French Cooking, "the concoction of a good cassoulet is a fairly long process. You can prepare it in one day, but two or even three days of leisurely on-an-off cooking are much easier."

Yikes!

After making the full-on version a few times, I created an expedited version to capture the key flavors. Just two steps to start earlier, then the rest is a straight shot through. Plus I add some cabbage to up the vegetable content and dilute the fat. Hope you like it!

The Gist

Marinated pork slices and sausages are browned in the fat from crisped bacon, then leeks, garlic, parsley, thyme, and bay leaves are sautéed in it. Broth, a bottle of white wine, and soaked white beans go in an all simmer away until done. Chopped fresh cabbage goes in at the end.

Ingredients

1 lb. bacon

4 lbs. sliced pork shoulder or pork chops

2 lbs. aromatic pork sausage

2 Tb. freshly ground black pepper

1 Tb. granulated garlic

2 tsp. salt

2 lbs. dry Great Northern Beans

2 Tb. chicken stock base

1 tsp. beef stock base

3 leeks, cleaned and sliced

6 cloves garlic, minced

1 head cabbage, chopped roughly

1 bunch parsely, chopped

4 Tb. fresh thyme, chopped finely

3 fresh bay leaves

big pinch of cloves

1 750ml bottle white wine

Method

Two start-ahead steps. First, rinse the beans well and cover with hot water at least a few inches higher than the beans (they will swell as they soak). Then, mix together the salt, pepper, and granulated garlic, sprinkle over the sliced pork and rub in well.

Let the beans soak and the pork marinate at least an hour.

When you're ready to construct, chop all the vegetables. Cut the bacon into pieces and sauté until crisp. Remove the bacon pieces and use the hot bacon fat to sear the sliced pork and sausages. Remove them to a bowl once seared.

Sauté the leeks, fresh garlic, parsley, thyme, and bay leaves in the remaining bacon fat until the leeks are well wilted. Drain the beans and add them to the pot with the chicken and beef stock bases. Pour in the bottle of white wine and, if necessary, add just enough water to cover the beans. Simmer for about 30 minutes, or until the beans are getting tender.

Add the seared pork slices and simmer for 30 minutes. Add the seared sausages and simmer for another 15-20. The beans and pork should be just about tender enough to eat. Add the cabbage and cook until the cabbage is the way you like it (still crisp or cooked until soft).

Serve in big bowls with a crusty whole wheat bread for dunking in the broth. Enjoy!

Notes

I like a garlic and basil sausage in this, but you can try different varieties, even italian sausage. Julia mentions polish sausage as an option(!). I suppose you could try chorizo, too. Just depends whatever sort of flavor you'd like to throw in there!

Traditionally, cassoulet is also made with a shoulder of mutton or lamb, but I'm not a big fan of either in stews. If you like, you could substitute skinless chicken pieces for the pork slices, or even add them in.

CARNITAS BURRITO BAKE

Ay caramba! Mucho alimento para muchas personas.

One of the reasons I'll make and freeze extra southwestern black beans and mexican rice is to make this recipe. Add some extra Yucatan-style pork chops and this dish makes a very fast and delicious new life for leftovers. This is also a great party dish to feed a crowd.

The Gist

Mexican rice, southwestern black beans, and roast pork mixed with roasted chiles are layered between whole wheat tortillas, then topped with black olives, green onions, chile sauce, and cheddar cheese. Delish!

Ingredients

4 cups Mexican rice (see Recipe)

4 cups southwestern black beans (see Recipe)

4-6 Yucatan-style pork chops, boned and chopped (see Recipe) or 4 cups shredded roast pork

8 Pasilla chiles (either raw or roasted and peeled), seeded and chopped

2 cups grated Monterey Jack cheese

2 packages whole wheat tortillas

1 24-oz. can red chile sauce

2 cans black olives, slided

2 bunches green onion, chopped

2 cups sharp cheddar cheese, grated

lard or bacon grease

> I find the easiest way to roast fresh chiles is on the barbecue. Heat your grill to very hot, then roast the chiles on it till a little blackened, turning frequently. Place the roasted chiles in a bowl, cover with alumnium foil, and let them sit and steam for about 30 minutes. The chiles will then be very easy to peel.

Method

Start your oven preheating to 350°F.

Use the lard or bacon grease to grease a large casserole dish or lasagne pan. Spread a layer of the red chile sauce on the bottom, then put down a layer of tortillas. If you're using a dish with straight sides, cut some of the tortillas in half to do the edges. Spread the Mexican rice on top of the tortillas, then add another layer of tortillas.

Mix the pork and chiles together, then spread these on the tortillas. Sprinkle the grated Monterey Jack cheese over the pork and chiles, then add another layer of tortillas. Spread the southwestern black beans in a layer, then top with a final layer of tortillas.

Spread more of the red chile sauce over the top layer of tortillas (as much as you like!). Sprinkle the sliced black olives and chopped green onions over this, then top with the grated cheddar cheese.

Cover with aluminum foil and bake at 350°F for an hour.

Notes

This recipe is basically like a lasagne, but with whole wheat tortillas substituting for the noodles. It gives you all the great flavors of a burrito without the trouble of individually wrapping them. Plus it's easy to make in quantity for a party.

Variations

Since this is basically a burrito done in layers, feel free to substitute any sort of burrito fixings you like. Fresh salsa and guacamole would be great served on the side as accompaniments.

BAKIN' HAM

This meal takes a little time to bake, but bakes in one roasting pan for a complete dinner. Perfect for a fancy and easy Easter dinner.

The Gist

A very light glazing of ham juice, pineapple juice, cayenne pepper, dry ginger, dry mustard, fresh ground black pepper, and ginger is basted over a roasting ham, then over the ham, yams, sweet potatoes, red onions, and pineapple cubes—all in the same pan!

Such a beautiful and impressive holiday dinner you'll hardly believe it's so good for you!

Ingredients

1 ham (your choice of size)

1 tsp. cayenne pepper

2 tsp. ground ginger

2 tsp. dry mustard

2 tsp. fresh ground black pepper

2 Tb. brown sugar

1-2 garnet yams per person

1-2 sweet potatoes per person

2 red onions, quartered

1 can of pineapple chunks (juice saved)

As you saw in my recipe for Extra Crisp Bacon, I'll drain off the excess fat from frying bacon and save it in a jar in the fridge for further frying adventures. Excess fat from a ham can be rendered down and saved in the same jar. It's just as yummy!

Method

Start your oven preheating to 350ºF. Total roasting time will be about 2-1/2 hours, so this is the perfect dinner to start just before you watch a movie.

Drain any juice from the ham into a small bowl. Add the juice from the canned pineapple. Add the cayenne pepper, ginger, dry mustard, black pepper, and brown sugar. Stir thoroughly.

Set the ham in a roasting pot big enough to hold it and the vegetables. Start with just the ham, and pour the glaze mix over it. Cover the roasting pan and bake the ham for an hour, basting 2 or 3 times along the way.

While the ham is baking, wash the yams and sweet potatoes and cut each into 2 or 3 pieces. Peel and quarter the red onions.

After the ham has baked for an hour, remove the roasting pan from the oven. Arrange the yams and sweet potatoes around it. Tuck the onion quarters evenly around, and sprinkle the pineapple chunks on top. Baste the glazing juice thoroughly over everything.

Return the pan to the oven and bake covered for another hour, basting ever 20 minutes or so along the way. Uncover the pan and roast for 30 more minutes (this will thicken the glaze). Baste especially thoroughly the last 30 minutes to help the evaporation along.

Remove from the oven and either serve immediately, or let rest before carving the ham. Everything will stay hot for several hours until you're ready to eat, especially if you leave it (covered) in a turned off oven.

Notes

Hams these days come vastly better trimmed than a decade ago. Remember the thick layer of skin and fat on the outside of hams? It's hard to find these days. Still, I will generally trim any excess fat off the outside of a ham before roasting it.

LAMB

Lamb has a distinct flavor which puts some people off. All the same, a properly prepared lamb can be delicious, and I like it in curries, for example. For this book, I'm including my lamb recipe which even non-lamb-likers will love!

MEDITERRANEAN ROAST LEG OF LAMB

The Gist

A boneless leg of lamb is marinated in salt, fresh ground black pepper, garlic, rosemary, and Zinfandel port then barbecued.

Ingredients

1 boneless leg of lamb

1/2 cup chopped fresh rosemary

1/2 cup chopped fresh garlic

1/2 cup Zinfandel port (or other Port or Madeira wine)

2 Tb. salt

2 Tb. fresh ground black pepper

Wonderful to tempt even the biggest lamb skeptic!

Method

Remove the fabric covering holding the lamb together and cut off any excess fat. You may also want to separate it into two pieces to make it easier to grill and to help the marination.

Combine the rosemary, garlic, port, salt, and pepper and mix thoroughly. Set the lamb in a container or bowl and pour the marinade over it. Turn to evenly distribute the marinade.

Set the lamb in the fridge and marinate for 2 or more days, turning daily. (If you're short of time, just marinate for the the afternoon at room temperature.) On the day you're cooking it, remove from the fridge to let it come to room temperature.

Heat your grill to very hot. Set the lamb on it and turn after 5 minutes, then every ten minutes until the desired degree of doneness. Medium rare will happen in about 25 minutes, depending on how hot your grill is.

Remove the lamb from the grill and let stand at least 20 minutes before carving.

FISHIES

Fish can be a great and regular part of your diet—just forget the deep fried fish! You've likely heard how they're packed with heart health omega-3 fatty acids (whatever those are!). Hopefully, governments can get their fishery policies in order before fish becomes too expensive to eat!

Following are just a few of my favorite ways to have fish. They'll make fish lovers even of folks who think they don't like fish! A key—as with turkeys—is not to overcook your fish. Overcook any fish and it becomes a dry mass of fibers. Yuck! Give me my fish on the moist, slightly translucent, and extremely succulent side, please!

Very fresh fish. And they aim to stay that way.

FAR EAST GRILLED AHI

$25 in a restaurant. $9 made at home—and you can have seconds!

Soy sauce and horseradish combine to give a sashimi-like snap to seared ahi tuna.

The Gist

Ahi steaks are marinated for an hour or two in double black soy sauce, horseradish, salt, and pepper before being seared on a very hot barbecue.

Ingredients

4 fresh ahi steaks, at least 1-inch thick (even thicker is just fine)

4 Tbs. double black soy sauce (regular soy sauce would also work)

1-2 tsp. japanese horseradish (regular is fine in a pinch)

2 tsp. fresh ground black pepper

1 tsp. salt

4 Tbs. olive oil

> When choosing your ahi at the store, look for the ones with the deepest red color and the least amount of white tendons in them. Sushi-grade ahi would be just great, but it is expensive.

Method

Combine the soy sauce, horseradish, pepper and salt and mix thoroughly. Place this marinade in a shallow dish big enough to hold all four steaks. Coat the fish thoroughly in the marinade, being sure to get the sides, too. Marinate for 1-2 hours on the countertop.

Heat a barbecue to very hot. Just before putting the fish on, add the olive and flip the fish in it. This helps the fish not to stick. Grill for 1-2 minutes per side.

Notes

Ahi steaks are one of the few fishes which will actually hold together well on a grill and even take a flip without falling apart. For most grilled fish, a rack or grill to hold the fish is highly recommended.

I prefer my ahi just seared on the outside so it is still essentially raw in the middle. If this is a little too much for you, feel free to cook it longer. Do take it off while it is still at least pink in the middle because well-done ahi gets quite dry. One would hate to have to get out the tartar sauce!

SHANGHAI TANG GRILLED HALIBUT

The charred skin on the bottom (right) is delicious and kept it from sticking!

In the manner of the famous Hong Kong store, here's an east-meets-west version of fresh halibut that melts the palates and hearts of even your biggest fish skeptics. Who needs deep fried?

The Gist

Fresh halibut is marinated in minced cilantro, grated lemon rind and fresh ginger, pepper, double black soy sauce, and sesame oil, then grilled.

Ingredients

2 Tb. grated fresh ginger

rind of 1 lemon, grated

2 Tb. minced fresh cilantro

3 Tb. double black soy sauce

1 Tb. sesame oil

1/2 tsp. salt

1 tsp. fresh ground black pepper

1 large halibut steak (approximately 2 pounds) or several smaller fillets

> Do check the ingredients when buying sesame oil. Good varieties are 100% sesame oil. Cheaper, less flavorful brands are mostly a different oil and just a little sesame oil. 100% sesame oil is often expensive in regular grocery stores, but very inexpensive in asian grocery stores in half-gallon metal jugs.

Methods

If possible, buy halibut steaks with the skin still on. This helps hold the fish together on the grill and keeps it from sticking.

Mix the ginger, lemon rind, cilantro, soy sauce, sesame oil, salt and pepper together thoroughly. Rub gently on all sides of the halibut, evenly distributing the spices. Let marinate at room temperature for 1-2 hours.

Heat a grill very hot and place the fish on it skin side down. Close the cover and let cook for 3-4 minutes only. This keeps the fish moist and tender. The flakes of the fish should just barely starting to separate, and still and little translucent in the center.

> Double black soy sauce is also available in asian markets. It is more concentrated and less watery than regular soy sauce. It's perfect when you want intense soy flavor without a lot of liquid, as in this marinade.

Remove and serve immediately, or let set until ready to serve. This fish is excellent hot off the grill, or served at room temperature. Please don't keep it warmed over! The fish will dry out and lose its delicate, moist texture.

Notes

The halibut can cook in any shallow baking or broiler pan if cooked under the broiler. Grill skin-side-up for 3-4 minutes under a very hot broiler.

If your halibut does not have skin on it (or you're using halibut steaks), set them on a rack lightly oiled with sesame oil, then set the rack on the grill. You'll lose some of the grill marks, but your fish will hold together.

Alternatively, if you're brave, you can try brushing your grill with sesame oil immediately before placing the steaks on them. With a good spatula and a little dexterity, you'll still be able to get the fish off. Still no flipping or it will fall apart almost for sure.

A TUNA SANDWICH...

...can be a truly great thing. Most are swimming in way too much mayonnaise. Here's how I make a quick meal of one (or two!).

The Gist

Make an easy tuna salad with drained, canned tuna, equal parts mayonnaise and yogurt, minced red onion and celery. Have on whole wheat bread with lettuce and tomato. Eat along with a can of corn for a complete meal.

> I buy tuna in water because it's less oily and has far fewer calories than in oil. These is an easy way to cut out a lot of calories.

Ingredients

2 cans tuna in water, drained (white or chunk light)

1 tbs. mayonnaise

1 tbs. yoghurt

2 tbs. minced red onion

2 tbs. minced celery

4 slices whole wheat bread

> I almost always use half mayonnaise and half yoghurt when a recipe calls for mayonnaise. To me, there's no loss of flavor or creaminess, but there are far fewer calories.

4 slices tomato

4 pieces lettuce

1 can of corn

**Hard to imagine a less expensive and
more delicious lunch!**

Method

Combine the tuna, mayonnaise, yoghurt, onion, and celery and mix thoroughly. Distribute onto the 4 slices of bread. Put 2 slices of bread together with the lettuce and tomato in between. Enjoy with the can of corn on the side.

Notes

I prefer chunk light tuna to white because it seems to have more flavor and is less dry. I suspect it has a slightly higher fat content than white, though I haven't checked the labels to be sure. Thankfully, my cat likes it too, so I can keep some around for both of us!

> Canned corn is great to keep around when you'd like some more vegetables with your meal. I open and eat it at room temperature right out of the can. No dishes or pans!

Spreading some tuna salad on each slice keeps the sandwich moist and eliminates the need for extra mayonnaise on the other slice of bread.

This produces a very tasty tuna salad with far fewer calories than the usual variety. I eat it regularly and without hesitation.

Variations

Tuna Mexicana: skip the celery and instead add a small can of drained, mild green chiles. Black olives would also be good.

Thai Tuna: combine the tuna with 1 tbs. olive oil, 1 tsp. thai fish sauce, 1/2 tsp. lime juice, a small can of mild green chiles, and 2 finely minced kafir lime leaves (I get them off my tree.) Exotic and very tasty.

THAI SHRIMP AND MUSHROOM CURRY

Here I've served the curry over brown rice and fresh steamed green beans with a tomato garnish for a beautiful one-plate dinner. Who needs to go out?

This recipe is very simple to make with store-bought Thai red curry paste, and gets an extra flavor punch if you use homemade curry paste (see Recipe).

The Gist

Heat a little red curry paste in a large sauté pan, add fresh shiitake mushrooms, coconut milk, shrimp, fresh lime leaves, and some sliced fresh red chiles. Serve over rice. You're done!

Ingredients

2 Tbs. red Thai curry paste (store bought or see Recipe)

2 -13 oz. cans coconut milk

2 lbs. raw shrimp, shelled and deveined

1 lb. fresh shiitake mushrooms, halved

1 tsp. sugar

3 Tb. thai fish sauce

1 cup fresh purple or regular basil leaves

3 fresh red chile peppers, seeded and sliced

6-10 kaffir lime leaves

> Many stores now carry lemon grass and thai fish sauce, but the kaffir lime leaves are hard to come by. Their flavor is unique, so if you can't find them, simply omit them. Only you will know!

2 stalks lemon grass, sliced crosswise about 1/8-inch thick

Method

Heat the curry paste in a large sauté pan over medium heat. After it sizzles for a minute or two add the coconut milk, sugar, fish sauce and mushrooms and bring to a simmer. Simmer for a minute or two. Add the shrimp, give a stir, then shut the heat off. Just before serving, stir in the basil and lime leaves and the chile and lemon grass slices. Serve over brown rice.

Notes

Many grocer stores now stock Thai curry paste in jars. There are differences between the red, yellow, and green curries, but any would work with this recipe.

Try my recipe for homemade Thai curry paste for a more intense and fresher flavor than from any jar.

CHINESE SALT AND PEPPER SHRIMP

Some chinese restaurants will ask if you'd like the shrimp with the shell or without—but the best ones only offer it with the shell on because the shell has a lot of the flavor. I eat the whole shrimp, but feel free to skip the tails if you like. I figure all that shell is good for your nails!

The Gist

Whole shrimp are marinated in salt and pepper, then tossed in an egg white and corn starch mix, then deep fried. Minced green onion, garlic, and red pepper flakes go on at the end.

Ingredients

2 lb. whole shrimp in the shell

2 tsp. salt

2 tsp. fresh ground black pepper

2 egg whites

2 Tb. corn starch

peanut oil for frying

4 Tb. minced green onion

2 Tb. minced fresh garlic

2 tsp. red pepper flakes

Method

Rinse and thoroughly drain the shrimp. Mix together the salt and pepper, then sprinkle over the shrimp. Toss thoroughly. Let marinate for an hour at room temperature, or longer in the fridge. Bring back to room temperature before frying.

Lightly beat the egg whites. Sprinkle the corn starch over them, then beat to combine.

Start your peanut oil heating. While it's heating, mince the onion and garlic, then combine with the red pepper flakes.

Drain any extra liquid from the shrimp, then pour the egg white and corn starch mix over them. Toss together.

When the oil is very hot, give the shrimp one more toss, then use a large slotted spoon to pick some up and lower them into the oil. Only add as much as your pan and oil can accommodate while still sizzling strongly (you may need to do two or three batches). Fry the shrimp until the coating starts to brown and the shrimp are bright pink (just a minute or two).

Remove the shrimp to a bowl lined with paper towels. Keep warm in a warm oven while you free the remaining shrimp. Be sure to heat the oil back to very hot in between batches and to scoop out extra bits of shrimp with your slotted spoon so they don't burn in the oil.

When complete, top with the minced onion, garlic, and red pepper and serve.

Notes

I love to use the whole shrimp and eat the whole thing—head and all. The intense flavor of the shell and the crunch of the shrimp inside is one of life's true pleasures. Still, heads-off shrimp in the shell would still be good if you're a little shy. I haven't ever tried shelled shrimp this way, but there's no reason they wouldn't be good, too!

RAGIN' CAJUN SEAFOOD GUMBO

A little homestyle Creole for you!

This Cajun classic is done-over with more vegetables, less fat, and brown rice to make it a delicious and healthy one-dish dinner.

The Gist

Bell peppers, onions, and celery are sautéed in a roux of oil and flour. Seafood stock and andouille sausage go in, then a seasoning mix, then shrimp, oysters, and crab meat to finish.

Ingredients

5 green bell peppers, chopped

5 red bell peppers, chopped

4 large yellow onions, chopped

1 bunch celery, chopped

4 cloves minced garlic

1/2 cup vegetable oil

1/2 cup flour

6 cups seafood stock

1 pound andouille sausage (or other spicy, smoked sausage) cut into slices

1 pound raw, shelled shrimp

1 pound crab meat (real or imitation)

2 jars fresh, raw oysters

For the seasoning mix:

2 bay leaves

2 tsp. salt

1 tsp. ground white pepper

1 tsp. ground black pepper

1/2 tsp. cayenne pepper

1 Tbs. fresh chopped thyme (2 tsp. dried)

1 Tbs. fresh chopped oregano (2 tsp. dried)

Basic brown rice (see recipe)

> Leftover water from boiling lobsters is great for this recipe. If that doesn't happen to be sitting in your freezer, check your grocery store for bottled clam juice or use japanese dashi powder to make stock.

> Crab meat generally comes already cooked. You can extract it yourself from the crab (whole or king crab legs), or buy it in cans. It is expensive. Imitation crab meat is much cheaper and tastes decent with all the spices in this recipe.

Method

Take the seafood out of the fridge to start warming up. Chop the peppers, celery, and onions and set in a bowl. Chop the garlic. Chop the fresh herbs (if using) and combine them with the rest of the spice mixture in a separate bowl.

Heat the vegetable oil in a large pot over high heat until it starts to smoke (be careful of hot spatters throughout this process!). Gradually whisk in the flour and cook the mixture until dark brown (this just takes a minute or two). Add the vegetables and stir thoroughly so nothing burns on the bottom. Sauté for a few minutes then add the garlic and seasoning mix and sauté for a few more minutes.

Add the stock and sausage. Heat the mixture to a simmer and cook for about ten minutes. Add the raw shrimp and oysters, heat for another minute or two, then shut the heat off. Add the crab meat and serve over brown rice.

Notes

Some people prefer their gumbo thicker than this recipe makes it. If that includes you, After you bring the stock mixture to a boil whisk in a thin paste of flour, corn starch, and water until you achieve the desired thickness. You can also thicken further with cajun filé powder for a thicker and richer flavor.

A bottle of Tabasco or other hot sauce is fine on the table if folks like more heat.

Variations

Feel free to substitute your favorite seafood for any of the types suggested. Scallops work well instead of oysters. Lobster meat could substitute for crab. You could also add clams or mussels in the shell. You could even use pieces of fish.

Here are my suggestions for when to add different types of seafood so they are done but not overdone:

- For clams or mussels in the shell, add them to the boiling stock and simmer just until the shells open.

- For raw fish, shrimp, or oysters, add to the boiling liquid (when the shellfish would be about done), heat for just a minute, then shut the heat off.

- For any cooked fish (including crab or lobster), add right after you turn the heat off.

BLACK BEAN STEAMED SALMON

Here I served the salmon with Sage Lentils and Linguine (see Recipe), but it's also great over plain noodles or rice and perhaps a steamed vegetable on the side.

This dish started off as a chinese-style steamed salmon, but I drastically pumped up the seasonings—and people ate it all. So here you go.

The Gist

Salmon is steamed with a spice mixture on top of minced bacon, garlic, ginger, and green onion, plus some rice wine, sesame oil, red pepper flakes, and chinese black bean sauce.

Ingredients

4 salmon steaks or fillets, preferably with skin on

2 Tb. chinese black bean sauce

2 Tb. dry rice wine or sherry

2 Tb. sesame oil

4 Tb. minced bacon

3 Tb. minced fresh garlic

3 Tb. minced fresh ginger

4 Tb. minced green onion

2 tsp. red pepper flakes

> Although tiny french lentils are great in this recipe, they are pricey. Regular lentils will work just as well.

Method

Combine all ingredients except the salmon and mix thoroughly. Set the salmon in a shallow dish which will fit in your steamer and evenly distribute the marinade ingredients over the top.

Heat the water in your steamer to boiling. Put the salmon dish in it and cover. Steam for 8-10 minutes. The salmon will be done at this point, but not overdone and dry as one typically gets. Serve over rice or noodles.

Notes

If your salmon steaks are thick, they might take a minute or two less. If thin, they'll be done a minute or two sooner.

If you're not planning on serving right away, undercook the salmon by 2-3 minutes, shut the heat off, and leave the salmon in the hot steamer. The remaining heat will be plenty to finish cooking the salmon and they can stand at ready for up to an hour.

Do save the cooking juices from salmon. They're delicious to flavor your rice or noodles with.

BROILED BLACK BEAN & BACON SALMON

The Gist

The salmon is rubbed with a little salt, pepper and brown sugar to start. Chopped bacon is crisped, then minced ginger, green onions, and black bean chili paste are sizzled in. A little rice wine goes in at the end. This is spread on the fish, which is then baked or broiled.

Ingredients

2 lbs. salmon fillets

1 Tb. salt

1 Tb brown sugar

1 tsp. fresh ground black pepper

1/2 lb. bacon, chopped

4 Tb. fresh ginger, minced

2 Tb. chinese black bean chili paste

1 bunch green onions, minced

1/4 cup rice wine

chopped fresh cilantro for garnish

Salmon for a crowd—as easy as a pan in the oven!

Method

Mix the salt, brown sugar and pepper together, then rub into the salmon. This can be done at the start, or several hours ahead of time.

Cook the bacon over medium heat until crisp. Add the ginger and black bean chili paste and let sizzle for a minute or two. Add the green onion and toss for a further bit of sizzling. Add the rice wine and reduce just a bit to burn off the alcohol.

Arrange the salmon filets in a single layer in a baking pan large enough to hold them all. Spread the bacon mix evenly over the top. Broil until desired degree of doneness, or bake in a 450°F oven for about 15 minutes. Remove from the oven, let rest for a few minutes, then sprinkle cilantro garnish over the top.

Notes

I like to broil this dish to get a little extra sizzle on the top. If the fish is thick, though, you may need to remove it from the oven, cover it with a lid or foil, and put it back in the oven with the broiler turned off for 5-10 more minutes to let the heat dissipate and finish cooking the fish. If you prefer, just baking is an easier way to cook the fish evenly.

PLANTY MANLY DISHES

One pumpkin for show and the rest for pumpkin stew. Why not?

Here are some main dishes so good neither you nor your guests will notice they're vegetarian. But, if vegetarians are coming to dinner, you're covered. They won't have to eat just the salad. I include them because I like them so much!

INSTANTO HUEVOS RANCHEROS

**Muy mucho delicioso
(Yes, my spanish is atrocious!)**

Usually, huevos rancheros requires multiple skillets and washing them afterwards. This version takes just one glass baking dish in the microwave which I then eat right out of. Great for a quick, hearty breakfast or late-night supper.

The Gist

Microwave tortillas and beans (refried or southwestern) in a covered, glass baking dish until very hot. Break raw eggs on top, cover again, and microwave just until the eggs are done. Top with chili sauce or salsa.

Ingredients

6 round corn tortillas (yellow or white)

2 cups refried or southwestern beans (see Recipe)

3 eggs

chili sauce or salsa

salt and fresh-ground black pepper

Method

Lay the tortillas in the bottom of a glass (such as Pyrex) baking dish to cover the bottom. If your dish is square (as in the photo), breaking a few in half makes it easier to cover the bottom. Spread the beans on top. Cover the dish with plastic wrap and microwave until very warm and bubbling.

Remove the dish from the microwave, uncover, and use the back of a spoon to make three circular depressions in the beans (about 2-3 inches across). Break a raw egg into each depression, cover again with plastic wrap, and microwave just until the eggs whites have all turned white. You'll need to watch if for this step (1-2 minutes at most) so the yolks don't become hard-cooked (unless you like your eggs this way!).

Remove the dish from the microwave and top with chili sauce or salsa and a little fresh ground black pepper. Eat it right from the baking dish (I do!) or cut into servings and serve with a spatula.

Notes

Normally, eggs explode if you try to cook them in the microwave, then turn to rubber. This method of putting the eggs on the hot beans actually produces an egg with a tender, poached consistency. The key is watching the eggs as they cook and cooking just until the egg whites are white rather than transparent. If you continue much beyond that point, the eggs will indeed become hard-cooked and tough. Always better to err on the side of a little underdone and zap for another 30 seconds or minute if you need to.

The proportions of tortillas and beans can be easily varied to suit your tastes.

Variations

Try a little Tabasco or other hot sauce on top instead of the chili sauce or salsa. Still, add a grind of black pepper at the end for richer flavor.

For a richer dish, add some grated cheese on top of the raw eggs before the last microwaving. Sharp cheddar cheese would be a good choice.

For the meat-eating crowd, add some chopped chorizo or other hot, spicy sausage with the beans before you begin. It is mixing cuisines, but some crumbled, crisp bacon would also be delicious.

(This is making me very hungry.)

BOSTON NO-BAKE BEANS

Hotdogs are optional, frankly.

This is a Boston-style "baked" bean that is ready to go without the baking. Great when you don't have all day!

The Gist

Kidney beans are soaked, then simmered with fresh ground black pepper, garlic, mustard powder, ginger, cayenne, onions and soy sauce. Tomato paste, molasses, carrots, apples, and sausages go in at the end.

Ingredients

3 lbs. dry kidney beans

2 tsp. salt

1 Tb. fresh ground black pepper

2 tsp. granulated garlic

2 tsp. mustard powder

1 tsp. ginger (dry powder)

1/4 tsp. cayenne pepper

> Soaking the beans ahead of time, then discarding the water seems to eliminate the problem some people have with "gas" from eating beans. If you don't have time, you can go right from rinsing to simmering.

2 onions, chopped

3 Tb. soy sauce

1 6-oz. can tomato paste

1/3 cup molasses

4 carrots, diced

4 apples, cored and diced

optional: your favorite hotdogs or sausages

optional: ketchup to taste

Method

Rinse the beans thoroughly in a colander. Set them in a pot and cover by about 2-3 inches with warm water and let soak for a few hours. Then pour out the water, refill the pot with just enough water to barely cover the beans and bring to a simmer. Add the salt, pepper, garlic, mustard, ginger, cayenne, onions, and soy sauce and simmer until the beans are tender (about 30-45 minutes). There should be just enough liquid to barely cover the beans, so add a little more if the level gets low.

Add the tomato paste, molasses, carrots, apples, and sausages if you're using them. Mix thoroughly and let simmer until the carrots are tender, about 10 minutes. Taste the broth and add a little ketchup if you'd like it a little sweeter.

Serve with whole wheat bread for dunking.

Notes

Although this recipe is ready to go from the stove top, feel free to put it in a pot and bake in a 300°F oven if you like. It can go for hours like this until you're ready to eat!

PASTA CHICK-O-BEAN

With frozen italian flat beans and canned garbonzo beans (chick peas), this hearty pasta is easy and fast. Top with just cheese for your vegetarian friends or add your favorite meat to the sauce if you're feeling carnivorous.

The Gist

Fry some onions and garlic in a little olive oil, add canned tomatoes, herbs and a can of beans, then toss with some boiled paste in which you tossed the frozen vegetable at the end. That's it!

Ingredients

2 Tb. extra virgin olive oil

2 yellow onions, sliced

8 cloves garlic chopped

1 26-oz. can ground tomatoes in heavy purée

1 26-oz. can diced tomatoes in juice

2 cans cooked garbanzo beans (chick peas), drained

1 tsp. salt

2 tsp. fresh ground black pepper

1/2 tsp. crushed red pepper

your choice of fresh or dried herbs, such as: parsley, oregano, or basil

1 lb. whole wheat pasta

2 lbs. frozen italian flat beans

Unapologetic Bean Lovers of the World: Unite! This one's for you.

Method

Start a large pot of salted water heating for the pasta.

While that's heating, fry the onions and garlic in the olive oil until the onions are translucent. Add the tomatoes, garbonzo beans, salt, pepper, red pepper, and herbs and bring the mixture to a simmer.

When the pasta water is boiling, add the pasta and cook until just barely done (al denté) and still a little tough. At that point, add the frozen beans, stir for a minute, then drain.

Toss the pasta and beans with the sauce. Serve and top with grated pasta cheese mix (see Recipe). Enjoy!

Notes

With the whole wheat pasta, cheese, and two kinds of beans, this makes a hearty and protein-packed vegetarian pasta. It can be made ahead of time and kept warm in a low oven, or made way ahead of time and reheated in a low oven or microwave.

Variations

Lots of different frozen and canned vegetables work well in this recipe. For the bean, try regular kidney beans or canneloni beans (italian white kidney beans). For the second bean, regular green beans are great, as are frozen peas. I've not tried canned corn in the sauce, but don't see any reason not to try it if you're feeling adventurous!

To bring out the smoky flavor of the red pepper, fry it in the oil along with the onions and garlic.

For an interesting spicy difference, try adding a full 1 tsp. of crushed red pepper with 2 tsp. of fennel seeds in the oil with onions an garlic. Delish!

PASTA WITH TOFU TOFUBALLS

Good enough to not miss "real" meatballs. Have along with pasta and sauce for a no-carnivore meal.

The Gist

Firm tofu is mixed with bread crumbs, cheese, eggs, salt, pepper, parsley, oregano, and basil, then made into "meatballs" and fried. Serve with your favorite whole wheat pasta and sauce.

Ingredients

4 lbs. firm tofu

1/2 cup whole wheat bread crumbs

1/2 cup grated pasta cheese mix (see Recipe)

8 cloves minced garlic

3 eggs

1 tsp. salt

1 tsp. fresh ground pepper

1 tbs. dry parsley

1 tbs. dry oregano

1 tbs. dry basil

olive oil for frying

> Tofu typically comes in three varieties: silken or soft, medium, and firm or "chinese style." Be sure to get the firm one for this recipe; the softer varieties just won't hold together.

> If you can't find whole wheat bread crumbs in the store (and you probably won't be able to!), toast a crumble a few slices of whole wheat bread.

Method

If you have time, put 2 pounds of the tofu in the freezer, freeze it solid, let it thaw and then squeeze out the excess water. This helps the balls to hold together. You can also use the tofu right from the package, but the mix may take more bread crumbs and eggs to hold together.

Add the remaining ingredients and mix thoroughly.

Heat some olive oil in a pan over medium heat. Form the mix into balls, dropping each one into the oil as you make it (they tend to fall apart if you handle them twice).

Fry the balls with the cover off to cook off excess moisture. When the bottoms are browned, flip the balls with a spatula.

Serve the balls with your favorite whole wheat pasta, sauce, and the grated pasta cheese mix on the side.

Notes

Tofu has gotten a bad rap in my opinion, probably because most people have tried it plain. It is rather plain and a little tart by itself. Think of it as something like flour: it gets made into other things, as in this recipe. Your guests probably won't even recognize it, and certainly won't think you were too cheap to buy hamburg! And the vegetarians in the crowd will love you for it.

Variations

Fresh herb tofuballs: use fresh herbs instead of the dried. You may want to increase the amounts, especially of the parsley. Use the frozen and thawed tofu or more bread crumbs and eggs so the mixture holds together.

Tofu cutlets parmesan: make the mix into cutlets instead of meatballs. This requires a somewhat drier and more cohesive mix, so you may need to increase the eggs and bread crumbs. Fry the cutlets in olive oil. After you flipped them, place a slice of provolone cheese on top, a spoon of sauce, and sprinkle with the grated pasta cheese mix. Delicious!

MA PO TOFU

A traditional Szechuan dish that's easy enough to make it a regular in your house! I love serving it on a bed of steamed vegetables and brown rice to make a complete meal.

The Gist

Garlic and chinese chili paste are sizzled in a little oil, then tofu is braised in chicken broth, soy sauce, sherry, and little sugar. Sliced water chestnuts, bamboo shoots, green onions, sesame oil, fresh ground black pepper and a little thickening finish it.

Ingredients

2 Tb. vegetable oil

2 lbs. extra firm, "chinese syle" tofu, cubed

8 cloves fresh garlic, minced

1 Tb. chinese hot chili paste (more to taste)

optional: 1/2 lb. ground pork

2 cups rich vegetable stock *or*

       2 cups chicken broth

1/3 cup soy sauce

2 Tb. sherry or rice wine

2 tsp. sugar

> Many grocery stores now carry a full range of tofu, ranging from silky or soft varieties (perfect for desserts), to the extra-firm or "chinese" style. Make sure you get the firmest variety your store carries for this dish.

2 cans sliced water chestnuts, drained

2 cans sliced bamboo shoots, drained

2 Tb. flour

2 Tb. corn starch

2 bunch green onions, chopped

2 Tb. sesame oil

fresh ground black pepper

steamed green (your choice)

brown rice

A great way to utterly explode all those myths about "bland" tofu!

Method

Start the brown rice first. (Two parts water to one part brown rice, simmered until the water is absorbed will do it!) Drain and cube the tofu. Mix together the water, chicken stock base, soy sauce, sherry, and sugar. Open and drain the water chestnuts and bamboo shoots. Wash and chop the green onions. Mix together the flour and corn starch with just enough water to make a thin paste. Have your choice of green in a pot ready to steam.

Heat the oil in a large sauté pan. When hot, add the minced garlic and chili paste (and ground pork, if you're using that) and sizzle and stir for a minute. Add the tofu and broth mix. Bring to a simmer, then add the water chestnuts and bamboo shoots.

While that's coming to a simmer, turn on the pot with your greens in it and heat just until hot, then turn off the burner.

When the tofu is simmering again, mix in the flour and cornstarch paste with a fork so it blends in evenly. Heat until just simmering, then turn off the heat. Stir in the green onions and sesame oil, then top with a generous portion of fresh ground black pepper.

Serve over a bed of steamed greens and brown rice.

Notes

This dish is traditionally made with the ground pork, but it makes a very delicious vegetarian dish if you omit the pork and use a rich vegetable broth instead of the chicken broth. A potato, onion, and celery stock would do nicely. If you have them available, a few dried shiitake mushrooms would be a great addition.

For the steamed green, I'll often use collard greens. Kale, swiss chard, or spinach would also work well.

SOUTHWESTERN PUMPKIN CHILE STEW

Worth getting an extra pumpkin at Halloween just for this stew!

This stew has such a wonderful and full flavor, people will never notice there's no meat. Well worth the trouble to peel and cube a pumpkin or winter squash.

The Gist

Cumin seeds, Mexican oregano, sesame seeds and almonds are toasted and ground. Onions are browned in olive oil, then in goes garlic, New Mexico chile powder, pumpkin, mushrooms, tomatoes, cauliflower, hominy, and green peas.

Ingredients

4 tsp. cumin seeds

4 tsp. Mexican oregano

1/2 cup sesame seeds

1 cup almonds

4 Tb. extra virgin olive oil

2 yellow onions, chopped

8 cloves garlic, minced

2 Tb. New Mexico chile powder

6 cups fresh pumpkin or winter squash, peeled, seeded, and cubed

1 lb. fresh mushrooms, sliced

1 26-oz. can diced tomatoes in juice

1 26-oz. can ground tomatoes in heavy purée

2 tsp. salt

1 head cauliflower, cut into florets

2 small cans yellow hominy (reserve liquid)

2 cups fresh or frozen peas

1 bunch fresh cilantro, minced (save some for garnish)

optional: crème fraîche for garnish (or sour creme)

> No two ways around it: peeling a raw pumpkin is hard work. Save this recipe for a day when you're up to it. Also, unfortunately, your day-after-Halloween carved pumpkin won't work. It goes rapidly downhill after carving, as you know!

Method

In a small skillet, roast the cumin seeds until toasted and fragrant. Shut off the heat, add the oregano, and set aside to cool. Grind in a spice grinder or small (clean!) coffee mill when cool.

Similarly, use the skillet to toast the sesame seeds, then the almonds, then set aside to cool. Grind to a fine meal in a meat grinder or food processor.

Heat the olive oil and onions in a large pot and cook over high heat until the onions are well browned. Turn the heat down to medium, then add the garlic, ground cumin and oregano, and chile powder. Stir for a minute or two, then add the pumpkin, mushrooms, tomatoes, and salt. If there is not enough liquid to cover the pumpkin, add the reserved liquid from the hominy cans. Cook until the pumpkin is almost tender.

Add the ground nuts, cauliflower, and hominy. Simmer for a few minutes until the cauliflower is tender. Check for seasoning and add more salt or chili powder if desired.

Add the peas and cilantro. Stir, then shut off the heat. Serve with a garnish of cilantro and, if desired, crème fraîche.

Notes

This is a very full-flavored stew which stands on its own as an entrée. For a fancier dinner, start with a green salad and serve with a hearty whole wheat bread for dunking.

SPICY INDIAN GARBONZO & GREEN BEANS

**So delicious this will win over even your biggest Indian food skeptics.
Very healthy and low in fat, too!**

This delicious combination makes a great entrée or a very substantial side dish. Wonderful with whole wheat pitas or Indian nan bread.

The Gist

Browned onions and garlic are tossed with garbonzo beans, tomatoes, and a typically rich Indian spice mix. Green beans at the end add crunch and color.

Ingredients

First spice mix

2 Tb. ground coriander

4 tsp. ground cumin

1/2 tsp. cayenne pepper

2 tsp. turmeric

Second spice mix

4 tsp. cumin seeds, roasted then ground

2 Tb. ground amchoor powder

4 tsp. paprika

> This recipe calls for two spices (the amchoor powder and the garam masala) which you're likely only to find in an Indian grocery store. Thankfully, there are many of these around. It's also a great place to buy your coriander, cumin, paprika, cayenne, and garbonzo beans!

2 tsp. garam masala

1 tsp. salt

Everything else

5 Tb. butter

4 onions, minced

16 cloves fresh garlic, minced

1 26-oz. can diced tomatoes in juice

8 cups cooked garbonzo beans

2 Tb. lemon juice

2 jalapeño peppers, seeded and minced

1 Tb. minced fresh garlic

2 lbs. green beans, washed and cut in 1-inch lengths

> You can use canned garbonzo beans, but I think the flavor of cooked dried ones is much better. Soak the dried beans overnight, drain the water and rinse them, then cover with water and cook. They'll be done in about an hour.

Method

Start by making your two spice mixtures. Note that, for the second, you'll need to roast the cumin seeds in a small pan on your stove until slightly smoky, let them cool, then grind them. Mince the onions and garlic (keep them separate), and have your jalapeños, garlic, and green beans ready to go.

Heat the butter in a large pot and add the onions. Cook over high heat until well browned, stirring frequently. Add the garlic and toss for another minute or two. Turn the heat down to medium high, then add the first spice mixture and cook for a minute. Add the tomatoes and cook another minute. Add the garbonzo beans and mix well.

Add the second spice mixture, lemon juice, jalapeños, and garlic. Mix well, turn the heat to low, cover, and let cook about 10 minutes. Shut the burner off and mix in the green beans. Let sit for at least a minute (it can go longer), then serve.

Notes

I like to add the green beans right at the end so they're still bright green and crisp when you serve. The rest of the dish can be made up a day ahead. When you're ready to serve, heat it up and add the green beans.

CRUSTED BROCCOLI SOUFFLÉ

And you thought it wouldn't actually hold together. Heh, heh, heh.

A very dramatic and all-in-one entrée. Add a tossed salad and you have a complete meal.

The Gist

A classic broccoli soufflé (eggs, butter, flour, milk, cheese, broccoli) is baked in a spring form pan lined with slices of whole wheat bread.

Ingredients

8 eggs, separated

6 tbs. butter

6 tbs. unbleached white flour

2 cups hot milk

1 tsp. salt

1/4 tsp. white pepper

pinch of cayenne pepper

pinch of nutmeg

big pinch of cream of tartar

1-1/2 cups grated swiss or pasta mix cheese

4 cups broccoli florets

butter to rub pan

whole wheat bread slices

> Eggs are much easier to separate if they are fresh and brought to room temperature first. Separating them with the shells is not as hard as you might think. If you want to play it very safe, break each egg one at a time into a small bowl and fish the yolk out with a slotted spoon.

Method

Start your oven heating to 375°F.

Separate the eggs and have the yolks and whites ready to go in separate bowls.

Rub the sides and bottom of a 14-inch spring form pan with butter. Stand up slices of whole wheat bread around the sides to make a ring. For now, lean them against the side so they don't fall over. You can stand them up straight once there is batter in the pan.

> Egg whites are very easy to beat to stiff peaks if the egg whites are at room temperature, the bowl and beater are dry (no water!), and you add a little cream of tartar. The cream of tartar helps the whites beat the same way a copper bowl would (the old fashioned way!).

Put the milk in a glass jar in the microwave to heat up. You will need it steaming hot.

Heat the butter and flour in a sauce pan and whisk together until they are thoroughly hot and bubbling. While whisking vigorously, slowly beat in the hot milk a little at a time. When the milk is all added, keeping whisking as you beat in the egg yolks one at a time. Keep whisking as you bring the mixture to a simmer. It should be very thick. Turn off the heat and beat in the salt, white pepper, cayenne, and nutmeg.

Whip the cream of tartar and egg whites together in a dry bowl until it forms stiff peaks.

Stir the cheese into the egg yolk mix. Fold about one-quarter of the egg whites into the egg yolk and cheese mix. Dump the broccoli florets on top of the whipped egg white, then pour the egg yolk mix in. Carefully fold the mixture together until just barely blended.

Pour about a 2-inch deep layer of the final batter into the spring form pan, then stand up the bread slices so they're straight. The batter will now hold the bread in place. Add the remaining batter, but no higher than 1-inch below the tops of the bread slices. The bread slices will hold the batter in place as it rises. If you have extra batter, cook it in a separate dish.

Place the soufflé in the middle of your oven. Don't open the door for the first 20 minutes. Cook until the top is golden brown and puffed, about 30-40 minutes. Depending on your oven, it may need to go longer.

Remove the soufflé to a large serving dish and carefully remove the side of the pan. Serve each person a generous helping of soufflé with a slice of the now-toasted bread.

Notes

If you don't have a spring form pan, a high-sided pan will work just fine.

SIDES TO THE FRONT

Pity the violence done to so many side dishes: goopy, dreary, and floating in butter. These are a breath of fresh flavor, including a garlic mashed potatoes that, once made for my family, is now and often and urgent request. Plus many others so good I've found it necessary to keep an abundant store of plastic containers for take home!

EVERYDAY BROWN RICE

Good to make in extra quantities so you have some leftover to microwave or make fried rice. I make my own and bring it to chinese restaurants with me.

The Gist

Bring 1 part brown rice and 2 parts water to a boil, then cook on very low heat until all the water is absorbed.

Ingredients

3 cups brown rice

6 cups water

Method

Combine the rice and water in a saucepan. Bring to a boil over high heat, then turn the heat down to simmer and cook until all the water is absorbed (about 20 minutes).

Please don't stir the rice at all. This will make it gummy and stick together.

Brown rice is so simple and easy to make that I always make extra to have on hand. It's microwave-ready in a jiffy.

Notes

This recipe makes enough rice for 6-8 average rice eaters and is completely scalable. Feel free to make a half-recipe or double recipe if that's what you need.

Brown rice has more protein, nutrients, and fiber than regular rice and is better for you. I make my own and bring it to chinese restaurants with me. Leftovers are easily heated in the microwave. The flavor is nuttier than white rice. Folks raised on white rice may object to the flavor of brown rice, but I find white rice bland by comparison.

There are several varieties of brown rice: short grain, long grain, and basmati. They are almost interchangeable, so try them all and see which ones you like. I tend to use short grain with sweeter dishes (such as chinese food), and long grain with savory ones (such as chicken soup).

> The two most common varieties of brown rice are long and short grain. I use either, depending on what mood I'm in. Brown basmati rice is also excellent. For a little excitement try red or black rice (really!).

When making a brothy ricey something, you can either cook the rice separately as above, or cook it in the broth to thicken the broth at the same time.

You can also substitute a broth for the cooking water with excellent results. For example, I'll cook brown rice with chicken or seafood stock to go with cajun food.

For the truly adventurous, there are even varieties of black rice you can try! They are very fully flavored so need to go along intensely flavored food, but they are also very dramatic and sure to impress.

OVEN STEAK FRIES

I do hope there's some ketchup nearby!

French fries are so good it's no wonder they're America's favorite vegetable—to the horror of nutritionists and our waistlines! This version makes a wonderfully crisp fry with a moist and tender center. And it's easy to do at home!

The Gist

Thick-cut potatoes get soaked in warm water and salt, drained, and roasted in the oven on a cookie sheet rubbed with a little oil. A flip halfway through browns both sides.

Ingredients

4 large russet potatoes

2 Tb salt

warm water to cover

1-2 Tb vegetable oil

> I like russet potatoes for fries, golden potatoes for mashed, and red potatoes for potato salad. Russets seem to be best for fries but, otherwise, choose your favorite!

Method

Slice the potatoes lengthwise to create meaty-sized fries (how big is up to you!). Place them in a bowl, sprinkle the salt over them, and add enough warm water to cover. Let them soak at least 10 minutes, but they can stay longer if you like.

Preheat your oven to 450°F. Drain the potatoes in a colander, then transfer them to a bowl and toss with a few paper towels to remove excess water.

Rub a thin layer of oil on the bottom of a non-stick cookie sheet (you may need two so the potatoes aren't crowded). Place the fries in a single layer on the sheet flat side down. If the the oil has beaded up on your cookie sheet, move the fries around a little so they get a thin coating of oil on the bottom.

Bake for 20 minutes or so (until the bottoms are browned), then flip the fries over and return to the oven. This gives the white top side a chance to brown.

Remove and serve immediately, or shut the oven off and keep warm in the oven until ready to serve.

Sweet potato fries: my, oh my.

Notes

Every source I've seen seems to agree that russet potatoes make the best fries, so who am I to argue? I have done redskin potatoes, though. They have a different texture but are still good. Whatever the type of potato, I always leave the skins on for extra nutrition and fiber.

The key to crisping up the potatoes is soaking them in water for a bit to remove some of the starch from the surface layer. I add salt at the same time to get the potatoes evenly and thoroughly salted.

These are best served right out of the oven because, like all fries, they lose their crispness as they sit. The cooking time is good for getting the rest of dinner together. You could even do an oven roast at the same time, make a salad, and call it a day.

Variations

This also works to make great fries with sweet potatoes or yams.

GARLIC MASHED POTATOES

Exceptional, and with just enough butter and sour cream to richen the flavor. With the already rich and buttery flavor of yukon gold potatoes, not much is needed. Cooking makes the garlic flavor rich and gentle.

The Gist

Cook 4 lbs. of yukon gold potatoes with 1 cup of garlic until tender, pressure cooker method preferred. Remove the excess water. Add salt, white pepper, butter, and sour cream, then whip with a hand mixer. Stir in chopped fresh parsley at the end.

Ingredients

4 lbs. yukon gold potatoes

1 cup whole fresh garlic cloves (peeled)

4 Tb. butter

1/4-cup of sour cream

1 tsp. salt

2 tsp. ground white pepper

1 bunch fresh parsley, chopped fine

**Ready to go with almost anything.
Extra cloves of steamed garlic is no extra charge!**

Method

Scrub the potatoes and remove any bad spots. Leave the peels on. This increases the nutrients and the fiber. Once you've tried this, you'll wonder why you ever peeled potatoes.

Place the potatoes on a rack in a pressure cooker and add the garlic on top. Process per your cooker's directions. Usually, this means 1 cup of water in the bottom and 15 minutes at 15 pounds for whole potatoes. When finished, let the pressure come down by itself (this is a good way to keep them warm for an hour or more), then remove the rack and any water left in the bottom.

Add the butter, sour cream, salt and pepper. Mash them a little with the hand mixer to break up the potatoes, then whip away. The longer you go, the fluffier they'll be (3-5 minutes does the trick). Lastly, mix in the chopped parsley with a suitable implement, such as a serving spoon.

I like to buy the containers of whole, fresh, peeled garlic cloves and keep them in the freezer until needed. I find the flavor as good as fresh, but without the peeling. Then, just take out what you need and thaw for 30 seconds in the microwave.

Once mashed, the potatoes will stay warm for about 30 minutes on the stove top. Place them in a warm oven to keep them warm longer. Don't put them on a hot burner because the potatoes on the bottom will burn.

Variations

If you don't have a pressure cooker (or don't want to bother), steam the potatoes and garlic in a tightly covered pot with about 1/2-inch of water on the bottom. They will take about 30 minutes to steam, and then can stay warm that way until you're ready to mash them.

Notes

My preferred method for cooking potatoes for mashed potatoes is either steaming or in a pressure cooker because it's faster and you lose less flavor to the broth, especially when cooked with garlic cloves as in this recipe. It's worth having a pressure cooker for mashed potatoes even if you don't use it for anything else—though it does have a host of other uses. I have two: one small for potatoes, and one quite large to handle anything from a whole turkey to canning quart jars. Of course, you can just boil the potatoes and save the potato-garlic broth for soup stock (it's great for that), but I seldom find myself that ambitious any more.

> I have a small electric coffee grinder which I use just for grinding pepper. It easily grinds as much as you need to either a coarse or fine texture. This lets me get whole white peppercorns and have fresh ground white pepper, too.

> If you can't find the whole peeled garlic cloves in containers, you can still place bagged, fresh garlic heads in the freezer, then take them out when you need them and microwave 30 seconds to thaw. The garlic is then much, much easier to peel than when it's fresh.

I prefer yukon gold potatoes for mashed potatoes, red skin potatoes for potato salad, and russet potatoes for baking or for french fries. You can use russets in this recipe, but they won't have quite the creamy consistency of yukon golds.

Likewise, you can use ground black pepper instead of white pepper, and I have done that on occasion when I found myself out of white pepper. The flavor won't be as good, but only you will know the difference!

TRUE GRITS (A.K.A. POLENTA)

Whatever happened to good ol' fashioned grits? Truth is they're still around: they just got all gussied up as polenta and corseted with the myth they require constant stirring. Not so with a decent pot and low setting on your burner, making this a really easy and elegant side dish. Leftovers are also great sliced and broiled.

The Gist

Boil water and salt, whisk in the polenta and cook till thick. Add the butter and cheese at the end.

Ingredients

5 cups water

1 tsp. salt

1-1/2 cups polenta (course cornmeal)

1 Tb. butter

1/3 cup grated parmesan-romano cheese mix

> Make sure you get coarse ground cornmeal for this (probably labeled polenta). With regular cornmeal, you'll end up with porridge!

Method

Bring the water and salt to boil in a sauce pan. Add the polenta in a slow steam while whisking constantly so no lumps form. Once the mixture is thickened, turn your burner down to its lowest setting and simmer till thick and the corn is soft, about 30 minutes, stirring every few minutes along the way. Add the butter and cheese and serve.

Corny, but so good!

Notes

Most recipes I've seen specify stirring the polenta constantly while cooking, but I haven't found this necessary. I'll just whisk until the mixture thickens, then turn the burner down to the lowest setting and stir every few minutes. A good, even conducting pot and low simmer setting help.

Also, in all fairness to grits lovers, I suspect that grits are generally from white corn, while polenta is from yellow corn. It's all corn to me!

Variations

Polenta is so easy to make I always make extra—either to reheat, or to make Grilled Polenta or Polenta Gratin (next two Recipes). Just be sure to pack the leftovers while they're still warm and sauce into a container which makes a good shape for slicing (rectangular is my usual choice).

GRILLED POLENTA

So fancy and so easy to do when you have a container of leftover polenta in the fridge. The crisp exterior and warm, creamy interior is almost to die for (almost!).

The Gist

Slice some chilled leftover polenta and grill it. That's it!

Ingredients

Leftover polenta from the previous Recipe, packed into a container and chilled.

Method

If you have the leftover polenta in the fridge, just flip it out of its container onto a cutting board and slice it about 1/2-inch thick. If you want to make it up fresh, pour the hot polenta into a metal loaf pan and let it cool and harden completely before slicing.

Heat your grill very hot. Place the polenta slices on it and grill for 3-5 minutes per side. Serve hot.

Grilling the polenta produces a wonderful, crispy crust with a creamy textured interior. Good enough to snack on by itself!

Notes

You can grill your polenta ahead of time and keep it warm in the oven. Place it in a single layer in a pan so the top and sides stay nice and crunchy.

If your grill gets really hot (as mine does!), you won't need to worry about the polenta slices sticking. If you'd like to be extra sure (or make them extra crisp), brush both sides with a little extra virgin olive oil before grilling.

POLENTA GRATIN

This substantial side dish can double as an entrée for a light dinner. Who said only pasta came in sauce!

The Gist

Make a tomato sauce with sautéed onions and garlic, salt, pepper, basil, and parsley. Bake with slices of polenta layered with your choice of cheese.

Impressive side dish or dinner on its own? Your choice!

Ingredients

3 Tb. extra virgin olive oil

1 yellow onion, chopped

6 cloves garlic, minced

2 Tb. dried or fresh basil

2 Tb. dried or fresh parsley

1 28-oz. can ground tomatoes in heavy purée

1 tsp. salt

2 tsp. fresh ground black pepper

8-10 slices of cooled polenta, 1/2-inch thick

8-10 slices your choice of cheese (such as cheddar, mozzarella, etc.)

Method

Heat the olive oil in a sauce pan over medium heat. Add the onions and garlic and sauté until the onions are softened. Add the basil and parsley and stir for a minute or two (this helps bring out the fragrance in the herbs). Add the canned tomatoes, salt, and pepper and bring to a simmer.

Slice the cheese and polenta (if not already sliced). Butter a high-sided baking dish. Pour 3/4 of the sauce into the bottom of the dish. Place the polenta and cheese slices in the dish in alternating layers. Pour the remaining sauce down the middle of the top.

Bake uncovered in a 350ºF oven until the sauce is bubbling thoroughly, about 30-45 minutes. Serve.

Notes

This dish can be assembled well ahead of time and then go into the oven when dinner is getting close. It also can be baked in advance and kept warm (probably covered) in the oven.

Variations

I used cheddar cheese for the photo, but other cheeses also work well. You might try mozzarella or provolone. For an extra punch, sprinkle crumbled bleu cheese over the top before baking.

ROASTED GARLIC BUTTER

Not a side dish in itself, I use this butter to make croutons or garlic toast.

The Gist

Roast garlic cloves in a little olive oil, then mix in the blender with butter, extra virgin olive oil, butter, and peppercorns.

Ingredients

1/2 cup fresh garlic cloves (peeled)

2 Tbs. extra virgin olive oil

1/2 cup extra virgin olive oil

1/2 cup butter, cut into pats

1 Tb. peppercorns

Method

Mix the garlic cloves and 2 Tbs. of olive oil together, then spread them on a sheet of aluminum foil. Bake them in a 350ºF oven or toaster oven until the cloves are brown and roasted (about 20 minutes).

While the garlic is roasting, pour the 1/2 cup of extra virgin olive oil into your blender container. Add the 1/2 cup of butter cut into pats and the peppercorns.

When the garlic is done, remove it from the oven and let it cool for a minute or two. Then add the garlic, the oil from roasting, and any of the brown bits you feel inclined to scrape. Blend on low speed until smooth. The garlic butter may be used immediately, or placed in a container in the fridge. It will keep in the fridge for quite some time.

Notes

The butter will be quite liquid when warm, but will harden into a thick (but still spreadable) paste in the fridge. Butter bread before toasting to make garlic toast, and cut the bread into little cubes if you would like to make croutons. These croutons are great on any salad, superb on caesar salad, and far superior to any store-bought variety.

ROASTED GARLIC TOAST

These are great served as an accompaniment to pasta, for dipping in soups and stews, and cut up into croutons. Or just eat them as snacks!

The Gist

Spread some garlic butter on one side of a piece of whole wheat bread and toast in the toaster or toaster oven.

Ingredients

Roasted garlic butter (see recipe)

whole wheat bread

Method

Spread some garlic butter on one side of pieces of whole wheat bread and toast in your toaster or toaster oven until golden brown.

So good and so easy!

Variations

Sprinkle a little of the grated parmesan-romano cheese mix on the bread before toasting to make roasted garlic cheese bread. Because the cheese would fall off in the toaster, these need to be toasted in a toaster oven or your regular oven.

For this recipe, it's important to get a suitable whole wheat bread. It should be sturdy and not too sweet. Some are just too soft and sweet for my taste. Save them for french toast!

Notes

When toasting in a toaster oven or your regular oven (preheated to 450ºF), place the slices of bread right on the racks. A pan or foil underneath prevents the bottoms from toasting.

Leftovers can go in plastic bags in the fridge and eaten right out of the bag. They will still be crisp because of the oil. Or given them a brief reheat in the toaster oven or oven if you'd like them warm. The microwave would make these tough and not crisp.

FRIJOLES

So good and so simple to make. Just takes a little time. Perfect to make on a Saturday afternoon or in the evening while watching a movie. Much better than what comes out of a can!

The Gist

Simmer pinto beans with garlic, ground cumin, and Mexican oregano until they reach the consistency you like.

Ingredients

2 lbs. dry pinto beans

6 cloves garlic, lightly mashed

1 tsp. salt

1 tsp. ground cumin

1 tsp. Mexican oregano (or regular oregano)

Quick! Pass the tortillas and salsa!

Method

> Pinto beans are available in large, really cheap bags in the mexican foods section of your store. You'd be surprised how quickly you can use them up!

Rinse the beans thoroughly in a colander, then pour into a pot and cover by several inches with warm water (the beans will swell up as they absorb water). Let set for 30-60 minutes, then rinse again in a colander.

Return the beans to the pot and add just enough water to cover them by about 1/2 inch. Add the lightly mashed cloves of garlic and bring to a boil. Turn the heat down and add the salt, cumin, and oregano. Simmer for 2-3 hours, or until the beans are as thick as you like. Stir occasionally, being sure to scrape the bottom for any sticking beans. Add water as necessary to keep all the beans covered in liquid. If you like your beans really thick, at the end of cooking mash them in the pot with a potato masher.

Serve with anything you like beans with, especially Mexican food.

Notes

The beans will get progressively thicker as they cook, and get really thick if you mash them at the end. Classical refried bean recipes (Frijoles Refrito) call for spooning the beans into a fry pan, mashing them, and cooking them in the fry pan until really thick. I found you can skip this step and still have suitably thickened beans if you soak them first, add just enough water to cook them, and give them a little mashing at the end.

Variations

For fuller flavor, roast whole cumin seeds in a small fry pan (instead of the ground cumin), and add the oregano when the seeds are nice and toasty. Let them cool slightly, then grind them in a clean coffee or spice grinder. This step takes just a minute or two, and you have plenty of time for it while the beans are cooking.

For an extra hearty consistency, mix in some chunks of jack cheese at the very end and stir to dissolve. Pepper jack cheese is particularly good.

MEXICAN RICE

This rice takes some time in the initial stages, but then finishes cooking by itself. It is so much better than what you usually get in Mexican restaurants, and leftovers freeze quite well.

The Gist

Long-grain brown rice is soaked in hot water, drained, toasted in oil, then cooked with puréed tomatoes, white onion, and garlic, plus chicken broth. Frozen peas and carrots go on top as it finishes.

Ingredients

3 cups long-grain brown rice

3 Tb. peanut oil

2 cups tomato purée

1/2 white onion, chopped

4 cloves garlic

4 cups salted chicken broth or water plus stock base

1 lb. frozen peas and carrots

Method

Place the brown rice in a bowl and cover with hot tap water. Let stand for 15 minutes, then drain in a fine-mesh strainer. Shake to remove excess water and let drain thoroughly.

Purée the tomato purée, white onions, and garlic together in a blender or food processor.

Heat the peanut oil in a medium pot over high heat. When quite hot, turn your fan on high and lean away as you dump in the rice so you don't get spattered. You may get a cloud of hot steam initially. Toss the rice to coat the grains evenly in oil, then toast, stirring constantly, until the grains are browned and smell toasty.

With the heat still on high (or medium high if your stove is really hot), lean away again as you dump in the tomato purée. Stir as the mixture bubbles until the mixture is thick and a lot of the moisture is gone. Add the chicken broth and stir the mixture thoroughly, then cover, turn the heat down to simmer, and cook about 20 minutes. When the rice is almost done, add the frozen vegetables on top and cook until the vegetables are heated through.

Shut the heat off, stir the vegetables into the rice, then serve (or keep warm on a very low burner or in a low oven.

Mexican rice served with Yucatan-style pork chops. Muy bueno!

Variations

For an express version of this recipe, omit the soaking and toasting steps. Just stir the raw rice, purée mixture, and broth together in a pan, bring to a boil, and simmer until done. Still add the frozen vegetables when the rice is almost done. The flavor and texture won't be quite the same, but it will still be delicious!

Notes

The soaking and pan-toasting steps give an amazing texture and rich flavor to the rice. I've tried eliminating steps, but it isn't the same. Do feel free to go with the express variation described above if time is at a premium.

SOUTHWESTERN BLACK BEANS

These beans are great by themselves as a side dish, and great made into Black Bean & Chicken Enchilada Bake (see Recipe). They're easy to make, but take some time for chopping and cooking, so I usually make extra and keep a container in the freezer ready to go.

So tasty you'd hardly know they're good for you!

The Gist

Black beans are simmered with all the spices and tomatoes until thick and done.

Ingredients

2 lbs. dried black beans

3 tsp. cumin seeds

3 tsp. coriander seeds

3 tsp. Mexican oregano

1 yellow onion, minced

8 cloves garlic, minced

6 fresh jalapeño chiles

1 bunch cilantro, minced

2 bay leaves

1 tsp. dried thyme or 2 tsp. fresh thyme, minced

1 Tb. fresh ground black pepepr

1 26-oz. can ground tomatoes in heavy puréé

3 tsp. salt

Method

Rinse the black beans thoroughly in a colander and pick out any small stones. Place in a pot with enough water to cover by about 1-inch and start these heating to a simmer.

In a small skillet, roast the cumin and coriander seeds over medium heat until fragrant and toasted, then shut off the heat and add the oregano. Give a stir, then let cool.

Mince the onion and garlic. With the chiles, I like to remove the seeds from four of them, leave the seeds in the other two, and then mince them. If you're show about the amount of heat you'd like in your beans, remove the seeds from all of them.

Grind the cumin, coriander, and oregano in a spice grinder or coffee mill. Add these to the beans, along with the onion, garlic, jalapeños, cilantro, bay leaves, thyme, pepper, tomatoes and salt (that should be everything). Simmer until the mixture is thickened and the beans are soft, adding a little water along the way if needed to keep all beans submerged. To make them thicker, simmer with the cover off.

Serve as a side dish or as part of another great creation (like my Black Bean Chicken Enchilada bake, see Recipe).

Notes

I'll usually make double this amount and keep a container ready to go in the freezer. They're great whenever you'd like a spicy, hearty, and healthy side dish.

For the "bunch" of cilantro, I use an entire bunch as it comes from the store. This makes a cup or more of minced cilantro. Seems like a lot, but it tastes great to me!

HERBIE DUMPLINGS

So fast and easy to make, these dumplings will become a regular in your kitchen. These dumplings furnish the second "herbie" in Double Herbie Chicken Stew with Dumplings.

The Gist

Flour, baking powder, baking soda, salt, butter, and dried herbs are buzzed together in a food processor, then mixed with just enough milk to form a batter.

Ingredients

3 cups whole wheat flour

3 tsp. baking powder

1 tsp. baking soda

1 tsp. salt

1 Tb. dried parsley

1 Tb. dried rosemary

1 stick of butter, cut into pats

milk to form a batter

Here's an herbie dumpling sitting on chicken stew—just a natural match!

Method

Place the flour, baking powder, baking soda, salt, parsley, and rosemary in a food processor and buzz together until well blended, about 30 seconds. Add the pats of butter and buzz for another 30 seconds. The butter should be thoroughly dispersed and the mixture flaky.

Pour the mixture into a bowl. A little at a time, add just enough cold milk so dollops of batter will hold together. Not too much milk (please!) or the dumplings will dissolve in the broth. Drop the mixture in dollops onto a simmering soup, stew, or broth and cook covered until done, about 15-20 minutes.

Variations

Feel free to substitute or add just about any herb you'd like to try. Sage would be great with turkey soup, for example.

For fresh herbs, buzz all the dry ingredients first, then the fresh herbs, then the butter last.

A few tablespoons of finely minced onion is very good added at the end with the milk.

HERBY-VEGGY BREAD STUFFING

Fresh herbs and vegetables make all the difference. Chop and taste!

The Gist

Celery, onions, and fresh herbs get chopped and sautéed in butter until just tender. Add concentrated chicken and beef stock base. Add pepper and more salt if needed, then toss with cubes of whole wheat bread.

Ingredients

1 head of celery

4-5 yellow onions

2 lbs. mushrooms

1 thumb-sized piece of fresh ginger

1 bunch fresh sage

1 bunch fresh rosemary

1 bunch fresh oregano

1 bunch fresh parsley

1 bunch fresh thyme

1 stick of butter

2 Tbs. concentrated chicken stock base

1 Tbs. concentrated beef stock base

1 loaf whole wheat bread

salt and pepper

Optional: raw shrimp or oysters (or both!)

> The whole wheat bread for the stuffing should be sturdy and not too sweet. Too soft and the stuffing becomes a gooey mass; too sweet and the flavor is strange. Best to scout out varieties ahead of time. Likewise, whole wheat sourdough, though good for many other uses, would not work here.

Method

Peel and chop the onions. Separate, wash and chop the celery. Wash and finely mince the ginger. Wash and mince the herbs. Wash and slice the mushrooms (I often buy containers of washed and sliced mushrooms to save time.) Cube the bread.

Melt the butter in a large sauté pan. When it's warm, add the chopped onions and celery and sauté for a few minutes over high heat. Add the herbs and cook for another minute or two. Then add the mushrooms and continue to cook just until the mushrooms begin to give off their juice. The mixture should be highly aromatic at this point.

If you're adding the raw seafood, add it at this point, toss briefly, then shut off the heat and take the pan off of the hot burner. Too much cooking will make the shrimp or oyster tough. They don't need to be fully cooked: just warmed a little.

Dissolve the chicken and beef stock bases in a little warm water, then add them to the stuff and toss. I use a paste-like concentrate. If you're using reduced stock, add about a half a cup each. Add freshly ground pepper (about 2 tablespoons worth), and check for salt. With most stock bases, the mixture will already be highly salty.

Use a serrated bread knife to cut the loaf of whole wheat bread into roughly 1-inch cubes. Place the cubes in a large mixing bowl, then pour the sautéed mixture over it and toss together gently.

Your stuffing is now ready to go in the bird. Any extra stuffing can go into a covered baking dish and cook along with the turkey. It will cook in about 45 minutes.

Here's the version with the optional hot italian sausages. Delicious—and almost a meal in itself! Plus it's higher in nutrition and fiber and lower in fat than most other stuffings. Extra keeps well in the freezer.

Notes

I use a mixture of 2 parts chicken stock base to 1 part beef stock base because, combined, they have a very turkey-like flavor. This gets more turkey flavor into the stuffing, rather than just chicken.

The quantities of herbs are approximate. Feel free to add more or less of particular ones if you like. I often double the sage, and sometimes omit the parsley or rosemary. With a few tries, you'll find the combination you like. The only mistake you can make is not to use enough herbs. The sauté mixture has to be rather strongly flavored so mixing in the bread doesn't make it bland.

Some folks will peel the ginger, but I don't bother. Just check it for any moldy spots and make sure to mince it finely.

I find the seafood a luxurious addition. Be sure only to warm it at the outset and not cook it. If it's already cooked at the beginning, it will overcook and become tough in the bird.

Variations

I'll sometimes use italian sausage instead of the seafood. For sausage, cut it into chunks and sauté it first with a little extra virgin olive oil until browned, the proceed with the onions and celery and the rest of everything. Cut the amount of butter in half.

WHOLE GRAIN CORNBREAD

Enough for a mess of almost anything: a mess of folks or a mess of stuffing!

This bread can be made either as a bread or into muffins. I usually add the sugar (the Southern version) if I'm making Spicy Cajun Cornbread Dressing (next Recipe) to go along with an Orange-Ginger Hickory Smoked Turkey.

The Gist

Whole wheat pastry flour, corn meal, corn flour, salt, baking powder, some milk, eggs, and butter. Simple and classic.

Ingredients

1-1/3 cups whole wheat pastry flour

2/3 cup whole grain corn meal

1/2 cup whole grain corn flour

5 tsp. baking powder

1/2 tsp. salt

3 Tb. butter

1-1/3 cups milk

1 egg

> Whole wheat pastry flour has been around for years in specialty stores, but now King Arthur markets it in general grocery stores as whole "white" flour. It's lighter in texture than regular whole wheat flour, and is great for any kind of cakes, pies, and the like.

> Be sure to use whole grain corn flour to get all the nutritional punch. Conventional varieties are degermed, enriched. etc.

Method

Combine all the dry ingredients in a food processor. Blend for about 30 seconds to mix thoroughly. Add the butter cut into pats, then blend for another 30 seconds until the butter is thoroughly combined with the dry mixture. Scrape the mixture into a bowl.

In a separate bowl, whisk together the milk and egg, then pour it into the butter-flour mixture. Stir just until thoroughly blended.

Pour into a buttered loaf pan and cook in a 350° oven until browned (approximately an hour). Remove to a rack to cool.

Variations

Southern Cornbread: add 1/3 cup of sugar. Southerners love their cornbread sweet, so it's almost impossible to add too much!

Cheesy Cornbread: add 1/2 tsp. cayenne and 2 cups of your favorite grated cheese. Southerners would use cheddar, and probably the sugar, too!

Notes

It's very easy to make a double recipe and also make a batch of cornbread muffins to eat right away, or to make two loaves for a big batch of cornbread dressing.

SPICY CAJUN CORNBREAD DRESSING

Here's a double batch in a commercial baking pan to serve a crowd at Thanksgiving. There was very little left to take home!

This dressing-on-the-side is the perfect accompaniment to an Orange-Ginger Hickory Smoked Turkey. For a crowd, I'll make a double recipe.

The Gist

Whole grain cornbread is combined with cajun seasonings, chopped celery, onions, red bell peppers, garlic, ground giblets, milk, eggs, shrimp, and Andouille sausage for a dressing that's almost an entrée in itself.

Ingredients

1 loaf Whole Grain Cornbread (see Recipe)

1 lb. chicken or turkey giblets (or mixed)

2 Tb. chicken stock base

4 Tb. butter

1 lb. Andouille sausage, chopped

1/2 head of celery, chopped

1 yellow onion, chopped

2 red bell peppers, chopped

1 Tb. Tabasco sauce

1 13-oz. can evaporated milk

3 eggs

1 lb. raw, small shrimp, peeled and deveined (tail off!)

Seasoning Mix:

2 tsp. salt

1-1/2 tsp. fresh ground white pepper

1/2 tsp. cayenne pepper

1 tsp. fresh ground black pepper

1/2 tsp. onion powder

4 Tb. fresh chopped oregano

2 Tb. fresh chopped thyme

4 Tb. minced garlic

> White pepper is expensive in the grocery store, but white peppercorns are cheap in indian grocery stores. I buy them and grind as I need it in my "pepper" coffee mill.

Method

Make the cornbread. Place the giblets in a sauce pan with just enough water to cover and the chicken stock base. Bring to a simmer and cook until tender (about 2 hours). Let cool, then either grind the giblets or mince them in a food processor. Save the stock from cooking the giblets. (To ease the day-of agenda, both these can be done a day or two ahead.)

Chop the celery, onions, and bell peppers and have them ready in a bowl. Combine the Tabasco, evaporated milk, and eggs in a bowl and whisk them together. Combine all the seasoning ingredients in a bowl. If your shrimp is frozen, set the bag of frozen shrimp in a bowl of warm water to thaw. Crumble the corn bread into a bowl so it's also ready to go.

In a large pot, heat the butter and chopped Andouille sausage over high heat and cook until the sausage is just starting to brown. Add the bowl of chopped vegetables and cook until they are starting to wilt. Add the seasonings bowl and ground giblets and heat thoroughly. Add a cup of the reserved stock from cooking the giblets, then turn off the heat.

Mix in the bowl of crumbled corn bread. Add the raw shrimp and the egg, milk and Tabasco mix and mix thoroughly. Pour the mixture into a greased or buttered rectangular baking dish and bake in 350° oven until browned on top (about 1 hour). I will usually grease the pan with reserved bacon fat for a little extra flavor.

Notes

This dressing will be very wet when it goes into the oven, and still very moist when cooked and browned on top. That's perfectly fine, but it can go a little longer in the oven if you like it a little more set.

Extra stock from cooking the giblets can go into the gravy. I usually make Bacon Onion Giblet Gravy to go along with this dressing.

CRANBERRY-ORANGE RELISH

Such a huge improvement over canned varieties. I have leftover for breakfast with cereal and yoghurt.

The Gist

Finely chopped cranberries are tossed with chopped oranges, grated orange rind, toasted chopped walnuts, sugar, cinnamon and cloves.

Ingredients

2 bags of fresh cranberries (usually around 12 or 14 oz.)

4 oranges

1 cup walnuts

1/2 cup brown sugar

2 tsp. cinnamon

1/2 tsp. cloves

**Yummy enough to have by itself
Also great mixed with plain yoghurt and granola!**

Although fresh cranberries are often only available in stores around Thanksgiving, you can buy extra bags and freeze them. Cranberries freeze quite well, and then you can enjoy this relish any time of year. Thaw before processing.

Method

Rinse the cranberries in a colander and pick out any berries looking beyond their time (usually these are brown and mushy). Process in several batches in a food processor until finely chopped. Using short pulses with scraping down the sides once or twice seems to work best for this. Alternatively, you can grind them in a meat grinder. Place the processed berries in a large mixing bowl.

Place the walnuts on a small baking pan or sheet of aluminum foil, then put them in a toaster oven set to 350°F. They will only take 10 or 15 minutes to toast. Do keep an eye on them because they can burn quickly. Take them out to cool as soon as they smell toasty.

Grate the rind off the oranges and add this to the cranberries. Then peel the remaining white peel off the oranges and coarsely chop the oranges with a knife and cutting board. Unfortunately, either putting them in the food processor or the grinder mashes them, so hand chopping is needed. Add these to the cranberries.

Coarsely chop the walnuts, then add these to the cranberry-orange mixture. Finish with the sugar, cinnamon, and cloves. Mix it all together well, then taste for sugar. There should be just enough sugar to cut the tartness of the cranberries, but feel free to add more for your taste.

This relish can be served that day, but is best if it sits in the refrigerator for a day or two before eating.

Notes

This is an uncooked relish, rather than the traditional cooked relishes, so the day or two to marinate helps a lot with the flavor. I like the texture best when the cranberries and oranges are chopped to about the same degree of fineness, but the walnuts are only coarsely chopped and in bigger pieces. I've tried processing the walnuts in the food processor since it's already out, but you end up with a lot of walnut dust, rather than big crunchy bursts of toasted walnut flavor.

Peeling the white skin off the oranges keeps the bitterness down. The tartness of the cranberries is already enough.

I've tried this recipe with chopped fresh celery added to it, but don't like the way the vegetable flavor blends with the fruity flavors of the cranberries and the oranges. Still, it does add extra crunch, and may be to your liking.

Oh, the things I relish.

ROSEMARY POTATO ROLLS

Just *dying* to be dunked in something!

A wonderful yeasted dinner roll with a great consistency. Goes with just about anything.

The Gist

Warm water, milk, and a little sugar starts the yeast growing, then mashed potatoes, fresh rosemary, salt, olive oil, and enough whole wheat flour to make the dough finish it off.

Ingredients

1 cup water

1 cup milk

1 tsp. sugar

1 Tb. yeast

2 yellow potatoes, cooked and mashed

3 Tb. fresh rosemary, minced

1-2 tsp. salt

3 Tb. extra virgin olive oil

2 cups whole grain white flour (such as made by King Arthur)

4 cups (approximately) whole wheat flour

Method

Heat the water, milk, and sugar in the microwave until body-temperature warm (warm to the touch but not hot). Pour these into the mixing bowl of a heavy duty mixer. Add the yeast and stir to dissolve. Let the yeast start growing until the mixture is foamy.

The easiest way to make two mashed potatoes is to microwave and then mash them. Likely your microwave even has a "potato" button.

When the yeast mixture is foamy, add the whole grain white flour and mix for 2 minutes. Add the mashed potatoes, rosemary, salt, and olive oil and mix for another minute or two. Add a cup of the whole wheat flour and continue mixing. The batter should be thickening and becoming a little stringy as the gluten develops.

Continue adding the flour as you get to a bread dough consistency (about like your earlobe), switching to a dough hook along the way (or knead by hand). Continue until you have a stiff, springy dough. This is about five minutes worth of kneading in a mixer with a dough hook.

Cover the dough and set in a warm place and let rise until doubled in bulk, about 30 minutes. If you're not ready to bake at this point, you can punch it down and let it rise again.

Knead the dough briefly, then make your rolls. I usually just make balls of dough of whatever size I like. Set these in a buttered baking pan and let rise a final time, about 20 more minutes. Start your oven heating to 350°F. I set the rolls on the range top and let the heat from the oven vent keep them warm as they rise a final time.

Bake until browned and the rolls sound hollow when tapped, about 45 minutes depending on how hot your oven is. Let rest or serve immediately.

Notes

These rolls may be done before they get nicely browned on top. Just a minute under a broiler fixes that! These rolls do quite well being made in advance, then kept covered in the fridge until you're ready for them. A 15-minute reheat in a 250°F oven and they're as good as fresh-made.

"Might I offer you a roll, my dear?"

Japanese maples, papyrus, and Australian tree ferns look great in your yard, but make terrible side dishes. Oh, well.

A VEGETABLE IS A STAR

These days a glorious array of vegetables awaits you in your grocery store. Through the miracle of summer down south when it's winter up north (plus jet airplanes), most of your favorites are there to greet you year round.

Don't have a favorite vegetable? Probably because you haven't had a vegetable done right! Certainly, I've seen lots of dreary examples. Formerly crisp and tasty green things cooked to a dreary, drab much, and probably with something dreadful on top to boot. Vegetables done this way are appropriate only as punishment, in my opinion.

This chapter has some of my favorite, regular ways of doing vegetables to make them a cheery and delectable presence at every meal. Although good enough to stand on their own as a dish, a big helping of these nutritional wonders also helps to balance out other possibly fattier parts of the meal (did anyone say steak?). The recipes in this chapter will get you started on creating your own favorites to work on your side in the never ending Battle of the Bulge.

STEAMED BROCCOLI

Steaming hot and crispy green—just the way I love it!

Starring... broccoli! Bright green and tender, it's good enough to eat plain.

The Gist

Steam broccoli just until it turns bright green. Call it done.

Ingredients

2-3 heads of broccoli (or 1 bag prepared florets)

Method

Wash the broccoli and cut off the ends of the stalks. Either cut it into little trees, or leave them whole for steaming (as in the photo). This makes a dramatic presentation, and everybody gets their own!

Alternatively, if you're using a bag of prepared florets, cut one end off the bag and fill it with cold water, then pour out the water to drain.

Place approximately 1/8-inch of water in the bottom of a pot with a tight-fitting lid big enough to hold the broccoli. You may need slightly more water for a gas burner, and slightly less for an electric burner. Add the broccoli and put on the lid.

Put the pot on the burner and turn the heat on high. As soon as the water starts to steam vigorously, turn off the heat and leave the pot on the burner for a few minutes. If you're not ready to eat then, take the pot off of the hot burner and tilt the lid to let some of the steam escape. The broccoli should be bright green and tender, but still crisp. In other words, perfectly cooked. If it's started to turn olive green, it has cooked too long.

> I love the bags of prepared broccoli florets and buy them frequently. One could hardly find an easier to prepare vegetable. But, the presentation is not nearly as dramatic as the little trees. Oh, well.

Notes

In my experience, the single biggest problem people have with broccoli is overcooking it. It turns olive green and mushy and the appeal drops dramatically. The trick is to turn off the burner when the broccoli is hot but not yet cooked. The heat in the pot will then finish cooking it.

To dress the broccoli up a little for people intimidated by the site of a naked vegetable, before cooking add some thinly sliced yellow onions on top, sprinkle a little garlic powder, salt, and pepper over it, then drizzle a little extra virgin olive over it all. Still good but, if you're having something rich alongside (like mashed potatoes and gravy), I like to dunk the broccoli in either or both of those instead!

AMAZING ASPARAGUS

So good you'll wonder why you didn't do it before!

The Gist

The asparagus sits in water to crisp up, then gets blanched in boiling water and rinsed in cold water.

Ingredients

fresh asparagus

cold water

boiling water

These are good so many different ways: warm with butter, dipped in Spicy Szechuan Peanut Sauce, or even cold with a little oil and vinegar!

Method

When you get home from the store, cut the ends off of the asparagus spears and set them upright in water in some sort of suitable container. I use a straight-sided plastic container. Cut off at least 1/2-inch and more if there is any white part at the end of the stalk (the white part is very tough.)

Let them sit in the water at least 2 or 3 hours. If you want to leave them overnight, they're fine sitting on the counter covered with a plastic bag or plastic wrap. For longer, set them in the fridge (also covered).

Bring a big pot of water to boil—enough for all the asparagus to be in the water all at once. Drop the asparagus into the boiling water and use a spoon to poke them so all get thoroughly submerged.

After about a minute or two at most, shut the heat off and remove the spears to a colander with tongs. Rinse them thoroughly with cold water, then let drain.

> Thick versus thin asparagus spears seems to be one of those enduring debates. Notwithstanding the general practice of labeling of pencil-thin asparagus a "gourmet," I prefer thick —the thicker the better. They seem to me to taste better and be less stringy. Maybe it's also because I remember the thickest shoots only coming from older, well-established asparagus beds like the one my grandfather had!

They're ready to go. See the recipe for Szechuan peanut sauce for my favorite dipping sauce to go along with them.

Notes

Setting the asparagus in water (like flowers!) before cooking gives them a chance to draw in more water and become very crisp. Quick blanching and then rinsing in cold water preserves this texture and leaves the spears a beautiful bright green in color.

Asparagus cooked this way keeps quite well in the fridge for several days in a sealed container, so you could make this a day or two ahead of time and then take it out just prior to serving.

Variations

If you'd like to serve your asparagus warm, drop the spears in the boiling water, poke for about 10-15 seconds, then remove them directly to a server platter. They can sit this way for 5-10 minutes if needed before the bottom ones will start to soften up and turn a darker green (still much better than the usual overcooked variety!).

GARLIC ROASTED BRUSSELS SPROUTS

About 40 minutes in the oven creates a vegetable which may win over the biggest vegetable skeptics in your family. They'll hardly know it's good for them!

The Gist

Brussels sprouts are tossed in a little olive oil, salt, fresh ground black pepper, and chopped fresh garlic, then roasted in the oven until browned.

Ingredients

2 lbs. Brussels sprouts

2 Tb. extra virgin olive oil

1 tsp. salt

1 tsp. fresh ground black pepper

2 Tb. minced fresh garlic

Optional: dash of balsamic vinegar

Method

Start your oven heating to 450°F.

Here's the sprouts served with Pasta à la Carbonara and SuperFastEasy Grilled Chicken. Leftover sprouts are great to snack on cold like a l salad, so I often make extra.

Rinse and drain the Brussels sprouts, then place them in a large bowl. In a small bowl, mix together the olive oil, salt, pepper, and fresh garlic, then pour over the sprouts and toss thoroughly. Place the sprouts in a single layer on a large baking sheet, then bake at 450°F until browned. This will take about 40 minutes.

When you remove them from the oven, you may sprinkle a few drops of the optional balsamic vinegar over them and serve.

Notes

Sometimes I will cut the sprouts in half before roasting them. This way, more of the garlic and seasoning lodges between the leaves. Also, you can do a larger quantity several layers deep in a large roasting pan, but they will need to be tossed partway through the cooking process so the sprouts roast evenly.

HAAK (KASHMIRI-STYLE COLLARD GREENS)

Definitely not a boring vegetable, and surprisingly delicious to boot. This time I used red rice, but wild rice is great, too.

A very easy, delicious, and unusual vegetable dish. This is a great dish for people who never knew they loved collard greens!

The Gist

Collard greens seared in mustard oil and asafetida, then cooked with red pepper, seeded jalapeños, and salt.

Ingredients

4 tbs. mustard oil

1/8 tsp. asafetida

2 big bunches collard greens

6 jalapeño peppers, seeded and sliced

1 tsp. red pepper flakes (less to taste)

2 tsp. salt

1 cup cooked long grain wild rice, red rice, or even regular long grain brown rice

Method

Wash the collard greens and trim off the brown stem ends. Chop them across the stem direction and place them in a bowl.

Wash the jalapeños, cut off the stem end, then slice in half lengthwise. Use a teaspoon to clean out the seeds, then cut the pepper halves into slices. Dispose of the seeds and stem ends (the garbage disposal with lots of cold water running), then wash your hands well with dish soap to remove hot pepper residue. All the same, do be careful not to rub your eyes because there is likely still some hot pepper residue on your fingers.

> This recipe requires mustard oil and asafetida (a ground spice), which are standard items at indian grocery stores. I keep these items around for just this recipe if nothing else. If you're not inclined to seek these ingredients out, use olive oil and sprinkle in a little mustard powder with the red pepper flakes. The flavor won't quite be the same, but only you will know the difference!

Heat the mustard oil in a big pot. Turn your fan on high. When the oil is hot (almost smoking), add the asafetida and red pepper flakes, give the pan just the briefest of shakes (the red pepper will start to smoke almost instantly), then lean back as you dump in the chopped collard greens (so you don't get spattered).

Add the jalapeño slices and stir fry the green until wilted. Turn the heat off, then add the salt. Toss thoroughly, then mix in the rice and cover the pot. This dish will stay warm for a while until you're ready to serve.

Notes

This a very simple, fast, and tasty way to have collard greens. Kashmiris actually have it much hotter, but seeding the jalapeños tones down the heat. Reduce the amount of jalapeños and red pepper flakes if you prefer.

The wild rice is a non-traditional addition, but I like it for the way it adds texture and absorbs the juice from the greens.

Variations

Substitute mustard greens for the collard greens.

STIR-FRY GARLIC SPINACH

The spinach here serves as an edible bed under Easy Poach Chicken drizzled with Spicy Szechuan Oil—just waiting for a little brown rice!

Who knew spinach could taste like this? Popeye would approve. It's also great over brown rice.

The Gist

Mashed garlic cloves are seared in the oil, then stir fried with the spinach. A little salt and sugar goes in at the end.

Ingredients

2 1-lb. bags of washed spinach

2 Tb. peanut oil

1/2 cup of garlic cloves, peeled and lightly smashed

1 tsp. salt

1 tsp. sugar

Method

If you buy containers of peeled, fresh garlic cloves (my preference), you just need to smash the cloves lightly with the flat side of your knife or cleaver. Otherwise, peel them first, then smash them. They should be fairly flat (about 1/4-inch thick) so the sides will sear well.

Heat the peanut oil in a large pot over high heat until very hot. Add the garlic cloves and toss them in the oil. I like to sear the garlic until browned, but a minute or two will do if you prefer less of a roasted garlic flavor.

Add the spinach all at once and quickly toss it in the oil. When it's about halfway wilted down, shut the heat off. There will be enough heat left in the pan to finish wilting the spinach while still leaving it crunchy and bright green.

Remove the pan from the hot burner, then toss in the salt and sugar. Serve immediately or hold until you're ready to eat. This spinach is very good at room temperature.

Notes

This spinach can be made up a day or two ahead of time and kept in the fridge until you're ready. Take it out a few hours ahead of time and put it in a serving dish so it can come to room temperature. If you'd like it warm, heat for just a minute or two in the microwave so you don't overcook the spinach.

Variations

Here's a variation for the super-spinach-skeptics. Instead to the peanut oil, chop a pound of bacon and cook it in the pot until crisp. Drain off all the fat you can (there will still be enough to stir fry in) and save the fat in the fridge for another day. Proceed to sear the garlic, then stir-fry the spinach. This variation works as a main course, perhaps over brown rice with a little soy sauce on the side.

BAKED YAMS

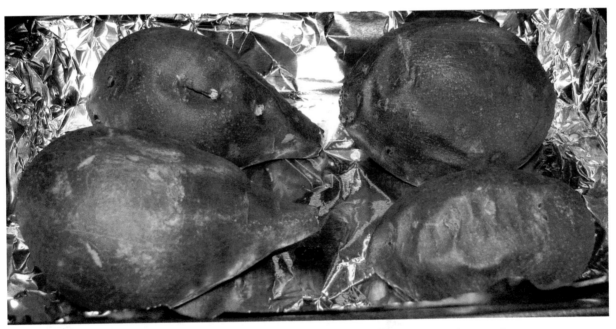

So easy and good they shouldn't be good for you—but they are!

So easy and so good. I like them with a little butter, salt, and pepper. Leftovers are great wrapped in plastic wrap and packed for lunches.

The Gist

Wash some yams, cut off any yucky parts, then bake at somewhere between 350°F and 450°F until done.

Ingredients

some yams

Method

Wash the yams, cut off any yucky parts, then place them on a sheet of aluminum foil on a baking tray. Bake them until soft and some of the juice starts to ooze out of them and caramelize on the foil (which you can discard instead of washing!). This gives you a built-in caramel sauce along with the yams.

If nothing else is in the oven (or I'm using the toaster oven), I'll cook the yams at 450°F. Turn the heat down if they start to burn (this depends on how your oven behaves.) If other things are in the oven, they can cook just fine at 350°F, but will take longer. Allow at least 1-1/2 hours so they're ready on time. After they're cooked, they'll stay warm for a good while.

Notes

Yams have gotten a bad rap because they're usually loaded with sugar, butter, marshmallows, and other nefarious critters. I like them with just a little butter, salt, and pepper. Done this way, they are a nutritional dynamo. See the yam purée recipe if straight yams are a little too unplugged for your tastes.

YAM PURÉE

An easy but fancy side dish. Almost good enough to have for dessert with ice cream!

The Gist

Yams are boiled or pressure cooked until soft, then whipped with butter, grated orange rind, ginger, cinnamon, cloves, salt and pepper.

Ingredients

4-5 large yams or sweet potatoes

grated rind of 2 oranges

4 tbs. butter

1 tsp. salt

1 tsp. fresh ground black pepper

1 tsp. ground ginger

1/2 tsp. cinnamon

1/4 tsp. cloves

1/8 tsp. cayenne pepper

A dessert or a vegetable? You be the judge...

Method

Scrub the yams and remove any bad spots. Leave the peels on. Either pressure cook or boil them until very soft (following the directions for your pressure cooker). I prefer using a pressure cooker because it's faster and you lose less flavor to the water.

Drain the yams and add the remaining ingredients. Whip the mixture with a hand mixer until a purée is formed. Some of the yam peels will collect on the beaters. You can stir them back in, or treat yourself to a snack of them as you're making dinner (my usual course of action!).

If necessary, keep the purée warm in a warm oven. It can also be prepared a day or two ahead and reheated in the oven or microwave very successfully.

Notes

Traditional yam recipes all seem to involve adding extra sugar. I just don't find it necessary and, indeed, adding it makes the result too sweet for my taste. If you must, try a little dark brown sugar or—even better—maple syrup.

There are two possible ginger variations with this recipe, depending on how spicy you like it. For the first, pressure cook about 2 tbs. of minced fresh ginger with the yams and omit the ground ginger. Unfortunately, this variation doesn't work well with boiling, but you can still try the second one.

> I prefer garnet yams for this recipe because of their more intense color and flavor, but sweet potatoes would work just as well. Because the yam is so sweet, no extra sugar is needed.

The second variation is to, again, omit the ground ginger, but add the very finely minced fresh ginger with the other ingredients before you whip them.

Cooked fresh ginger (the first variation), makes the purée spicier and gives it a more intense ginger flavor than does ground ginger. Adding uncooked ginger at the end (the second variation) makes it spicier yet.

Warning: the second variation is highly addictive!

BEETS 'N' GREENS

I first had the combination of fresh beets sautéed with their greens over a friends house and loved it. I made my own version and it's become a staple on our table.

The Gist

Fresh beets are steamed in water, butter, coriander, sugar, salt and pepper. The chopped stems and greens go in at the end.

Ingredients

1 bunch fresh beets with stems and greens (3 or 4)

2 Tb. butter

1/2 tsp. salt

1 tsp. sugar

1 tsp. fresh ground black pepper

1 tsp. ground coriander

Method

Cut the stems and greens off of the beets, then wash and roughly chop them. Set aside in a bowl.

Scrub the beets and peel them. Chop them into bite-sized pieces.

Place the beets, butter, salt, sugar, pepper, and coriander in a sauce pan. Add about 1/2-inch of water in the bottom, cover, and steam until tender (about 15 minutes).

Remove the lid and let excess water evaporate. A little juice and butter should be left. Add the chopped stems and greens and toss until the greens are wilted, 1-2 minutes. Serve.

Can't be beet!

Notes

Peeling the beets is really only necessary if the beets are large and the peels are tough. I usually just peel off any gnarly sections of peel and roots and leave the rest.

Great with golden yellow beets, too!

CHINESE RED COOKED BROCCOLI

This recipe applies traditional chinese "red cooking" technique to broccoli. Broccoli never had it so good!

Nope, it's probably not like the broccoli your mom used to make. It's delicious!

The Gist

Garlic and ginger are sautéed, then tossed with broccoli, butter, and a sauce of soy sauce, red wine, sugar, pepper, and chicken stock base. A sprinkle of dried shrimp goes in at the end.

Ingredients

2 cloves garlic, minced

2 slices fresh ginger root, minced

2 Tb. peanut oil

2 Tb. butter

2 lbs. broccoli florets

3 Tb. soy sauce

3 Tb. red wine or sherry

1 tsp. sugar

1 tsp. fresh ground black pepper

2 tsp. chicken stock base

1 Tb. dried shrimp (optional)

Method

Mix together the soy sauce, wine or sherry, sugar, pepper, chicken stock base, and dried shrimp (if you're using them).

Heat the oil in a sauté pan or wok over high heat. Add the minced garlic and ginger and toss until fragrant. Add the broccoli and toss for another 2 or 3 minutes. Add the butter and toss as it melts. Add the sauce mix and continue tossing until the broccoli are just tender (another 2 or 3 minutes). Serve hot or at room temperature.

Notes

I really like the little bits of meaty flavor the dried shrimp add, and sometimes use 2 tablespoons instead of one. Omit them for fussy eaters.

Variations

For a vegetarian version, omit the chicken stock base and shrimp. It will still be delicious, but may require a little extra sauce.

This technique is also very good with chopped white or red cabbage (or even a mixture of the two!). It's also good with carrots, but you'll have to turn the heat down and cover it for a minute or two to cook the carrots so they are tender but still crisp.

CoCo Giselle is extremely diligent about eating anything that tries to eat our vegetables. Thanks, kitty!

Fava Bean Purée All Gussied Up

Almost too pretty to eat (almost!)

This very fancy dish is a substantial first course and maybe even in lieu of a salad. Suitable for the most difficult to impress diners!

The Gist

A purée of fresh fava beans stuffs steamed baby bok choy and goes on top of sliced heirloom tomatoes. A pureé of roasted red bell peppers goes around the edges.

Ingredients

4 lbs. fresh fava beans

2 Tb. chicken stock base

2 Tb. fresh sage, minced

2 Tb. butter

1 tsp salt

1 tsp. fresh ground black pepper

8 heads baby bok choy

I can only find good heirloom tomatoes during the summer. A great time to make this. Buy extra for a designer tuna sandwich!

295

1 large heirloom tomato

roasted red bell pepper purée (see Recipe)

Method

Shell the fava beans and place them in a sauce pan. Add the chicken stock base, sage, butter, salt and pepper and just enough water to barely cover. Bring to a boil and simmer about 10 minutes. Let cook.

Purée the fava beans in a food processor, using some or all of the broth to help the process. The purée should be about the consistency of mashed potatoes.

Steam or blanch the baby bok choy so they are bright green but still crisp. Rinse in cold water, then remove the larger outer leaves.

Place a thick slice of the heirloom tomato in the center of a plate. Arrange four bok choy leaves around the edge. Place a generous dollop of the fava bean purée on the tomato and in each of the bok choy leaves. Place alternating puddles of the red bell pepper purée around the edge of the plates. Serve.

Notes

Many recipes call for removing the outer skins from the fava beans, but, after already discarding the outer pods, this leaves quite a tiny amount of fava beans. I actually don't mind the outer skins so, in the interests of not spending forever shucking fava beans, I leave them on!

Here's part of last year's oregano harvest—just in time for the fall Greek festivals!

SWEET FINISHES

After a dinner this good, you or your guests may not have room for dessert! Alert them to what's coming so they make an extra effort to save some space. Some of these recipes are good and healthy enough to have for breakfast. Others are more, ahem, "indulgent," but—after all the good stuff you've already eaten, what's the harm in a little sinfully good and indulgent dessert? The overall balance is what counts. So here's my favorites.

So simple and yet so good. Just softening the chocolate in the microwave and applying it with a spoon makes it easy to get a nice, thick layer of chocolate on the berries and eliminates the bother of melting in a double-boiler.

CHOCOLATE DREAM STRAWBERRIES

This dessert takes about 15 minutes to prepare and looks like it came from the fanciest gourmet dessert shop. Great for an easy, elegant finish to an impressive dinner.

The Gist

Melt some of your favorite semi-sweet or bittersweet chocolate in the microwave and either dip strawberries in it or apply it like frosting. That's it!

Ingredients

24 fresh strawberries, preferably large ones

12 oz. of your favorite semisweet or bittersweet chocolate

a little canola oil

parchment paper

Method

Clean the strawberries with a damp paper towel. Use a paper towel coat the inside of a glass bow with just a little canola oil (1/2 tsp.). Place the chocolate in the bowl and microwave for 1 minute. The chocolate should be just softened enough to be like thick frosting. If necessary, microwave for another 15-30 seconds (thicker makes it easier to coat the strawberries).

Either dip the strawberries in the chocolate, or use a teaspoon to apply it to the berries like frosting. Place them on parchment paper until ready to serve.

The strawberries can sit at room temperature if you're serving them that day, or refrigerate them if you're preparing a day or two ahead.

Notes

Big, ripe, summer berries are best for this, but even strawberries in the middle of the winter will work with the added sweetness from the chocolate. Fancy, long-stemmed strawberries will be prettiest, but they are rather expensive so I usually buy the largest of the regular, short-stemmed variety.

FIGS, CHEESE AND PORT

So easy to do and so impressive you'd think there's a law against it.

Easy and very gourmet. I first had this at a very fancy restaurant and have loved it ever since.

The Gist

Serve fresh figs, a good cheese, and some port for an elegant and easy dessert.

Ingredients

Fresh figs

A good cheese

Port

Method

Wash and dry the figs. Arrange them on a serving dish with the cheese. Open the bottle of port and get out some sort of little-ish glasses to serve it in. Wine glasses would do in a pinch.

> Fresh figs are not always available, but you could substitute another fruit. Fresh pineapple is available year-round and delicious if you give it a few days of ripening on the counter.

Notes

Choose any variety of good, sweet, fresh fruit to contrast with the cheese. Seedless grapes would even work.

Any variety of fancy, good cheese would do. For soft cheese, you could choose goat cheese, brie, Cambozola, etc. For hard cheeses, I would do an extra sharp cheddar, a dry Jack, Stilton, Double Gloucester, or even just a hunk of bleu cheese.

Pick any port, but do try it first to make sure you like it. A sweet sherry would also do.

The French would traditionally serve this with a good bread, as in the photo. I like whole wheat sourdough.

BERRY BERRY BERRY

This combination of fresh berries with a light sweetening and spice is so good you won't believe it's so good for you! Great by itself or to top a wide variety of desserts (such as Meyer Lemon Ricotta Cheesecake).

The Gist

Combine your favorite fresh berries with a little sugar, cinnamon, and maybe a dash of cloves. That's it!

Ingredients

1 pint fresh strawberries

1 pint fresh blueberries

1 pint fresh blackberries

1 Tb. sugar

1/2 tsp. cinnamon

1/8 tsp. cloves

Method

Rinse the berries and drain. Hull and halve the strawberries. Place in a bowl, sprinkle the sugar, cinnamon, and cloves over the top, then toss very gently. Serve.

It's verry, berry good.

Notes

Any fresh berries work great in this recipe. Raspberries or loganberries are also nice. For a color and flavor contrast, slices of fresh kiwi are also delicious and pretty.

BANANA CAKEBREAD

Admitted. We were loafing around the house today, again.

This "bread" is in between a cake and a bread in texture and richness. Sweet enough for desert with vanilla ice cream, but also good toasted for breakfast. Whole wheat pastry flour and less butter and sugar than usual punt it squarely past the "healthy" yard line.

This recipe makes 2 loaves, and can easily be doubled and extra loaves frozen.

> Bananas are less critical for this recipe than you might think. An equal amount of applesauce would work just as well, as would any puréed fruit.

The Gist

Three different mixtures (one butter, eggs, and sugar, another bananas, coffee, orange rind, and vanilla, the third dry ingredients) are combined to make the cakebread.

Ingredients

- 1 cup melted butter
- 1 cup sugar
- 1 tbs. molasses
- 4 eggs at room temperature
- 2 cups mashed bananas
- 1 cup coffee

> Adding a little molasses turns white sugar into brown sugar. Check the label and you'll see that's all it is! More or less molasses makes dark or light brown sugar.

3 tsp. vanilla extract

grated rind of one orange

4 cups whole wheat pastry flour or whole wheat white flour

1 tsp. salt

1/2 tsp. baking soda

3 tsp. baking powder

1 tsp. allspice

2 tsp. cinnamon

1 cup raisins

1 cup walnut pieces

> King Arthur now has a variety of whole wheat flour called "white whole wheat." It is a whole wheat flour, but from a different variety of wheat so it looks like white flour. It's a very good choice for desserts.

Method

Start your oven heating to 350°F. Take the eggs out to come to room temperature. Place the butter in a metal bowl and set it in the oven to melt the butter. Keep an eye on it so it doesn't burn, though 5 minutes or more in the oven is no problem.

While the butter is melting, mash the bananas, then mix them with the coffee, vanilla, and orange rind.

> Combining the dry ingredients in a bowl and then whisking them together mixes them as if sifted —without the bother of sifting!

The butter should be melted or almost so. Take the bowl out of the oven (use mitts!) so it cools a few minutes and you can handle it.

Add all the dry ingredients to a bowl (flour, baking powder, baking soda, allspice, and cinnamon), then whisk them to mix thoroughly. Add the raisins and walnuts to the flour mixture and stir with a spoon to distribute them, being sure to break up any clumps or raisins.

Add the sugar and molasses to the butter and whisk together. Add the eggs and whisk those together until smooth.

Add half the flour mixture to the butter mixture and stir until roughly combined. Add the banana mixture and stir a little more. Add the rest of the flour mixture and stir just until the batter is combined (no dry pockets of flour). Too much beating will toughen the bread.

Pour the batter into 2 buttered loaf pans and bake at 350°F until an inserted toothpick comes out clean. This takes about 1 hour and 20 minutes in my oven, but different ovens cook differently.

Notes

This recipe is great for using up bananas which have gotten riper than you like for eating. You can leave the bananas to continue ripening on the counter if you plan to make the bread within a few days, or leave them in a plastic bag in the fridge for a week or two (until you get around to it!). In the fridge, the bananas will turn black on the outside and translucent on the inside (as if cooked), but they can still be peeled and work great in the bread.

I make this recipe with regular coffee since I haven't found that minimal caffeine in the bread keeps me awake. If you're worried, please do use decaffeinated coffee.

Variations

Substitute chopped dried apricots and toasted cashews for the raisins and walnuts for a very exotic and delicious bread.

Cook the batter in muffin pans with paper liners to drastically reduce the cooking time and make a very yummy addition for school lunches.

MEYER LEMON RICOTTA CHEESECAKE

This cheesecake combines the texture of cheesecake and citrus-sweetness of Meyer Lemons with a dramatically lower fat content. What's not to love about it?

The Gist

Ricotta, eggs, buttermilk, sugar, vanilla and a dash of salt are blended together, then baked. Sweetened yoghurt is the topping

High taste and low guilt. Seconds, please!

Ingredients

4 cups ricotta cheese

4 eggs

1 cup buttermilk

1/2 cup sugar

2 tsp. vanilla extract

juice and grated rind of 2 Meyer lemons

dash salt

2 cups yoghurt

1 tsp. vanilla

4 Tb. maple syrup

Method

Preheat your oven to 350°F. Combine the eggs, buttermilk, sugar, 2 tsp. of vanilla, the Meyer lemon juice and rind, and the dash of salt in a food processor. Blend until thoroughly smooth (it may take a minute or two).

Pour the batter into a buttered spring form pan. Bake approximately 1 hour, or until lightly browned on the edges and set in the middle. Remove the cake from the oven and let cool.

Mix together the yoghurt, 1 tsp. vanilla, and the maple syrup. Spread this on top of the cooled cake. Chill the cake until ready to serve, then remove the ring from the spring form pan and serve.

Notes

If Meyer lemons are not available, just regular Eureka lemons will do. But, if you ever do come across Meyer lemons, they're worth buying if just for this recipe.

PEACH COBBLER

My version of a traditional southern peach cobbler cuts back just enough on the butter and sugar to make it healthier while still keeping a true southerner happy. Fresh, tree-ripe peaches with the peel still on are best in my opinion, but canned peaches will do in a pinch.

The Gist

Sliced fresh peaches are tossed with a little brown sugar, flour, lemon juice, and vanilla, then go on top of a biscuit dough layer and are baked.

Ingredients

8 fresh peaches, pitted and sliced

2 Tb lemon juice

2 tsp. vanilla

1/2 cup brown sugar

1/4 cup whole wheat white flour

2 tsp. cinnamon

1-1/2 cup yoghurt

3 eggs

2 cups whole wheat white flour

2 tsp. baking powder

1 tsp. baking soda

1/8 tsp. salt

1/2 cup sugar

6 Tb. butter

I'm ready to "cobble" it up! How about you?

As I have discovered, a fresh peach cobbler is only good for a day or two before the peaches turn brown. Use canned peaches to make it last longer, or give the rest to your neighbors!

Method

Butter a suitable baking dish to hold everything. I use a low, rectangular dish. Start your oven preheating to 350°F.

Wash the peaches, then slice in half around the little crease to remove the pit. Slice the halves. Sprinkle the first peach with the lemon juice, then toss gently after each peach to coat them.

When all the peaches are done, drizzle over the vanilla and toss gently. Whisk the brown sugar, flour, and cinnamon together in a bowl, sprinkle over the peaches, then toss gently.

In a bowl, beat together the yoghurt and eggs.

Measure the flour, sugar, salt, baking soda, and baking powder into a food processor (blade attachment) and process for about 15 seconds to combine. Cut the butter into pats and drop those on top of the flour mixture. Process for another minute or so to combine the butter thoroughly with the flour mixture.

Pour the flour mixture from the food processor into a large bowl. Pour the egg and yoghurt mix over the top, then combine the mix gently. Mix just until all the flour is mixed in. You should have a somewhat sticky, biscuit-like batter. Please don't over mix or the finished product will be tough.

Dump the flour mix into the baking dish and smooth it out to form a layer on the bottom. It doesn't have to be perfectly even.

Gently spoon the peaches on top of the flour batter to make a somewhat even-ish layer of apricots. If you like, you can artfully arrange the peach slices on top.

Bake at 350°F for around 45 minutes, or until a toothpick inserted in the center comes out with cake on the end instead of batter. Serve hot or at room temperature

Very good plain, or with whipped cream, or with vanilla ice cream.

Notes

Ripe, fresh apricots or nectarines would also work well. White peaches would certainly make for a very elegant dessert.

APRICOT COBBLER

This variation on a cobbler adds a topping of eggs, maple syrup, and pecans for a very different and delicious dessert.

The Gist

Quartered, fresh apricots go on top of a slightly sweet, biscuit layer. The whole thing then gets topped with a maple syrup and pecan mix, then baked.

Ingredients

8 cups fresh apricots or peaches, pitted and quartered

2 tsp. cinnamon

1 cup maple syrup

2 eggs

2 tsp. vanilla

1 cup pecan halves or pieces

1-1/2 cups whole wheat pastry flour

1/4 cup sugar

> I like to use the "grade B" maple syrup because it has more maple flavor, but the more commonly available grade A would work just fine. Please do use real maple syrup, though!

1/8 tsp. salt

1/2 tsp. baking soda

1-1/2 tsp. baking powder

1/2 tsp. ground coriander

6 tbs. butter

3/4 cups whole milk yoghurt

1 egg

Method

Butter a suitable baking dish to hold everything. I use a 14-inch spring form pan with sides about 3-inches high. Start your oven preheating to 350ºF.

Wash the apricots, then slice in half around the little crease to remove the pit. Quarter the halves. Sprinkle the teaspoon of cinnamon over them and toss gently.

In a bowl, beat together the maple syrup, 2 eggs, and vanilla. Fold in the pecans to coat.

Measure the flour, sugar, salt, baking soda, baking powder, and coriander into a food processor (blade attachment) and process for about 15 seconds to combine. Cut the butter into pats and drop those on top of the flour mixture. Process for another minute or so to combine the butter thoroughly with the flour mixture.

Beat together the yoghurt and eggs. Pour the flour mixture from the food processor into a large bowl. Pour the egg and yoghurt mix over the top, then combine the mix gently. Mix just until all the flour is mixed in. You should have a somewhat sticky, biscuit-like batter. Please don't over mix or the finished product will be tough.

Dump the flour mix into the baking dish and smooth it out to form a layer on the bottom. It doesn't have to be perfectly even.

Gently spoon the apricots on top of the flour batter to make a somewhat even-ish layer of apricots. Give the maple syrup and pecan mix one more stir, then pour this over the apricots. Even out the pecans if they ended up in clumps.

Bake at 350ºF for around 1-1/2 hours, or until a toothpick inserted in the center comes out with cake on the end instead of batter. Cool to room temp before serving (so all the juices are absorbed into the batter).

If you used a spring form pan, place the cobbler on a nice serving dish and remove the edge before serving for a very dramatic presentation.

Very good plain, or with whipped cream, or with vanilla ice cream.

Notes

Ripe, sweet, fresh peaches would also work well. If neither peaches nor apricots are in season, substitute canned peaches. Be very gently with them because they will already be cooked and somewhat soft. You could also try nectarines, but I'm not sure how that would work since nectarines are firmer and harder to pit. White peaches would certainly make for a very elegant dessert.

BERRY BERRY COBBLER

**A "moderately" healthy dessert—but oh so good!
Let's assume we had a big salad with dinner.**

Fresh raspberries, blackberries, blueberries, and a light custard on the bottom with vanilla ice cream on top make this a memorable finish to any evening.

The Gist

A mix of fresh berries goes on top of a slightly sweet, biscuit layer. The whole thing then gets baked, served in a puddle of créme anglaîse, and topped with vanilla ice cream.

Ingredients

2 cups fresh raspberries

2 cups fresh blackberries

2 cups fresh blueberries

1/4 cup brown sugar

1 tsp. cinnamon

1/4 tsp. cloves

1-1/2 cups whole wheat pastry flour

1/4 cup sugar

1/8 tsp. salt

1/2 tsp. baking soda

1-1/2 tsp. baking powder

1/2 tsp. ground coriander

6 tbs. butter

3/4 cups whole milk yoghurt

1 egg

créme anglaîse (See Recipe)

vanilla ice cream

Method

Rinse the berries in cold water and drain thoroughly. Gently toss them with the brown sugar, cinnamon, and cloves. Set aside.

Measure the flour, sugar, salt, baking soda, baking powder, and coriander into a food processor (blade attachment) and process for about 15 seconds to combine. Cut the butter into pats and drop those on top of the flour mixture. Process for another minute or so to combine the butter thoroughly with the flour mixture.

Beat together the yoghurt and eggs. Pour the flour mixture from the food processor into a large bowl. Pour the egg and yoghurt mix over the top, then combine the mix gently. Mix just until all the flour is mixed in. You should have a somewhat sticky, biscuit-like batter. Please don't overmix or the finished product will be tough.

Dump the flour mix into the baking dish and smooth it out to form a layer on the bottom. It doesn't have to be perfectly even.

Gently spoon the berry mixture on top of the flour batter to make a somewhat even-ish layer of fruit.

Bake at 350ºF for around 1-1/2 hours, or until a toothpick inserted in the center comes out with cake on the end instead of batter. Cool to room temp before serving (so all the juices are absorbed into the batter).

If you used a spring form pan, place the cobbler on a nice serving dish and remove the edge before serving for a very dramatic presentation.

To serve the cobbler, make a small puddle of the créme anglaîse on a plate. Carefully plop a serving of cobbler on the puddle. Top with good quality vanilla ice cream. Enjoy before all the ice cream melts!

Notes

This dessert is best made with fresh berries which, thankfully, are pretty available year-round in the store. Frozen berries—although very good in other uses—are too watery for this dessert.

CRÉME ANGLAÎSE

A very good, light custard sauce to go with all sorts of things. It's the base in the Berry Berry Cobbler.

The Gist

Eggs are beaten with sugar, then hot milk is whisked in and the mixture heated until thickened. A flavoring like vanilla goes in at the end.

Ingredients

1/4 cup sugar

4 egg yolks

1-3/4 cup milk

1 Tb. vanilla

Method

Beat the sugar and egg yolks together in a sauce pan until they are light yellow in color and thoroughly combined. Pour the milk into a suitable container (like a glass-handled mixing cup) and microwave until hot (somewhere around 2-3 minutes).

Slowly pour the hot milk into the egg and sugar mix while whisking constantly. Heat over low heat while whisking until thickened, but be sure to stop well short of a simmer or the eggs will cook and separate. Take off the heat and whisk in the vanilla.

Serve warm or cold. If you're chilling it, let it cool a bit first, then put a piece of parchment paper or plastic wrap on top so a skin doesn't form.

Notes

Other potential flavorings include orange, coffee, rum, or even chocolate! A few squares of your favorite chocolate at the end would do it. Mix any of these in while the crème is still warm so they dissolve.

YUMMY YAMMY PECAN PIE

Here's a healthier take on a classic pecan pie. I made this once for Thanksgiving and it has been requested for every year since then. Who's to argue with success?

The Gist

The crust is a butter, sugar, egg, salt flour pastry. The filling is roasted yams, brown sugar, corn syrup, eggs, cream, butter, vanilla, salt, cinnamon, allspice, and nutmeg. A sugar, corn syrup, egg, butter, vanilla, cinnamon, and pecan mixture is poured on top of the filling for baking. And, yes, pastries are next to impossible to make from just a short summary like this! But you get the idea.

Ingredients

Pastry Ingredients

2 cups whole wheat pastry flour

4 tbs. sugar

1/2 tsp. salt

6 tbs. butter

1 egg

4 tbs. milk

Filling Ingredients

6 garnet yams

2 tbs. butter

1/2 cup brown sugar

1 egg

2 tbs. milk

2 tbs. vanilla extract

1/2 tsp. salt

1/2 tsp. cinnamon

1/4 tsp. allspice

1/4 tsp. nutmeg

Topping Ingredients

1-1/2 cups sugar

1-1/2 cups dark corn syrup

4 eggs

3 tbs. melted butter

4 tsp. vanilla extract

1/8 tsp. salt

1/8 tsp. cinnamon

1-1/2 cups pecans

> Double-check how much vanilla extract you have left before making this recipe! It uses a surprising amount. I've started it and had to go out for more vanilla. Such a bother.

Get your piece fast! They won't last!

Method

First off, start an oven or toaster oven preheating to 325°F. While the oven is heating, wash the yams and cut off any bad spots. Place the yams on a baking sheet (maybe lined with aluminum foil) and place them in the oven to bake. Bake the yams until they are very soft and the juice has started to ooze out of them and form little pools of caramelized syrup. This process will take an hour or more, depending on how large the yams are.

To make the pastry crust, combine the flour, sugar and salt in a food processor and whiz together until thoroughly mixed (about 10-15 seconds). Cut the butter into tablespoon sized pats and distribute over the top of the flour mixture. Process together until the butter is completely distributed through the flour and the mixture starts to look flaky (about 30-40 seconds).

Beat together the egg and milk. While the blender is running, pour this mixture slowly into the pour spout. By the time you've added it all, the dough should be starting to form chunks. Do not over process or the crust will be tough. This whole process should take 20-30 seconds. If your flour is very dry, you may need to add a few more drops of milk to get the dough to come together.

Rub the insides of a 12-inch spring form pan (or high-sided tart pan) with some more butter. Dump the dough mixture from the food processor container into the pan and use your fingers to press the dough onto the bottoms and sides to make a roughly even-thickness crust. Precision is not critical.

If the yams are done, proceed to make the filling. Otherwise, skip ahead to make the topping, then circle back for the filling.

To make the filling, mash the yams together with the butter and brown sugar. The yams should still be warm enough to melt the butter. If not, melt the butter in the microwave, then mash it in. Beat the remaining ingredients together, then whip into the yam-butter-sugar mixture with a hand mixer. It all should be very thoroughly mixed. Snack on the pieces of yam peel which got caught on the mixer blades (yummy!).

Spoon enough of the filling into the crust to fill it about 2/3 of the way up. If you have any extra, place it in a separate baking dish to cook separately.

To make the topping, beat together all the ingredients *except the pecans* until thoroughly mixed and all the sugar is dissolved. Stir in the pecans with a mixing spoon.

Spoon enough of the topping over the filling to come within about 1/4-inch of the top. If you have extra filling in a separate dish, be sure to spoon some over that, too.

Bake the pie in a preheated 325°F oven until the pie is set and a knife inserted in the center comes out clean. This will take about 2 hours for the big pie and less for the extra filling, if any. Let cool before serving, and serve at room temperature with either vanilla ice cream or whipped cream. The recipe for whipped cream follows.

Notes

This pie takes some to make, but is well worth the trouble. I've given pies to people in the neighborhood and run into issues about how much is *not* left before the other spouse gets home! I make them large to minimize contention.

The recipe calls for whole wheat pastry flour. New varieties of whole wheat white flour work just as well. Standard whole wheat bread flour is a little too hearty for use in pastries. If you're going to do it, you might as well do it right. You still get a lot of fiber and nutrition from the yams.

Variations

This recipe is also very good with using cooked pumpkin (either canned or fresh) instead of the yams. It might need a touch more sugar because the pumpkin is not as sweet as the yams.

VERY WHIPPED CREAM

A few ingredients take whipped cream to a whole new level. Forget the can!

The Gist

The cream gets whipped with vanilla extract, brandy, Grand Marnier, and a little sour cream.

Ingredients

2 cups heavy cream

1 tbs. vanilla extract

1 tbs. brandy

1 tbs. Grand Marnier

1/2 cup sugar

1/4 cup sour cream

Method

Place a metal mixing bowl and set of beaters in the freezer. Leave for at least 30 minutes so they're very cold. Make sure the cream is in the refrigerator and cold.

Remove the bowl from the freezer and pour in the cream. Add all the remaining ingredients to the cream and beat at least until soft peaks form. How long this takes depends on your mixer, probably 3-5 minutes.

If you're brave, you can keep mixing until stiff peaks form, but stop before the mixture starts to turn grainy—the sign of impending butter. I've actually never had whipped cream change to butter on me, but it happens to some people. Go figure.

Keep the whipped cream refrigerated until serving time. If this has been a few hours, give it a quick whisking to combine the liquid on the bottom with the foam on the top.

Leftovers are very good on top of your morning coffee.

Notes

For this recipe, make sure you start with heavy whipping cream that has nothing else in it; no stabilizers, no flavoring, nada. These days, I've seen a proliferation of "Bavarian style" whipping cream in store which is packed full of inferior flavorings. Yuck. You may have to search around for the real thing.

For a more "créme fraîche" sort of flavor, you can increase the amount of sour cream. Because the sour cream typically already has stabilizers in it, it should still whip up just fine.

FOREVER YOURS

Here's the end of a busy afternoon. If this doesn't leave you with at least as much satisfaction as surprising your spouse with flowers, it's hopeless!

You've just spotted a crate of deliciously tree-ripened pears at the local farmers market: the kind that only show up at the peak of the summer. You'd like to buy the whole crate, but what to do with them? Your family can only eat so many. You just wish for a way to keep that flavor so you can enjoy them the whole year round.

There is a simple way to do this: canning! That's right; remember the whole bit with the glass jars and a pressure cooker? Maybe your mom used to do it. Maybe you've just seen it on Martha Stewart. Maybe you've never seen it. If so, you're in for a real treat.

Canning is the best way to save the flavors of summer for the whole year round. Fresh fruit from the store almost never compares. Usually, fruit for the store is picked unripe so it survives the handling and shipping. The flavor is never the same. And all the commercial jams and jellies are so full of sugar one can hardly taste the fruit at all.

These recipes present a new approach to canning fruit: one that dispenses will all the pectin and fruit juice bother and with most of the sugar. The result is a jar bursting with fruit flavor, just sweet enough and perfect for toast or with ice cream. And nothing makes a more impressive, tasty, and economical Christmas present than a jar of jam you canned yourself last summer. Those jars are my yearly gifts to friends and families.

The secret is my own way of canning fruit. Most recipes call for lots of apple or white grape juice, boxes of pectin, and pounds of sugar to yield a jelled product. You end up mostly canning sugar and fruit juice but not so much fruit. And all you taste is sugar.

Instead, I simmer down just the cut fruit with a little lemon juice and just enough sugar to cut the tartness. The product is almost all fruit and just full of flavor. As you'll see in these recipes, adding just one or two additional flavorings turns out a little jar of magic far superior to anything I've ever had from a store.

The second secret is using a pressure cooker to process the jars instead of the standard boiling water bath called for with fruit. Certainly, a boiling water bath works just fine. But it's heavy to handle and takes a long time to boil. I used to spend hours just boiling jars.

Using a pressure cooker, I can process the jars for just 15 minutes at 5 pounds of pressure and then turn the heat off. It takes about ten minutes to come up to pressure, then another ten or fifteen for the pressure to come down. Then you're ready for the next batch.

The pressure cooker is a tremendous time saver and effectively sterilizes the jars. You can then store the jars at room temperature. I've never had a jar spoil, though the color and flavor do suffer after about three years. Just be sure to give them away or eat them before then!

The first recipe presents basic fruit canning directions. Specific recipes then follow.

BASIC FRUIT CANNING INSTRUCTIONS

These apply to any fruit. Check out the following recipes for some favorite flavor combinations of mine. Then try your own!

The Gist

Fresh fruit is cored, cut, tossed with a little lemon juice, then slowly simmered down and brought to a boil. Pack in hot, washed jars and process in a pressure cooker for 15 minutes at 5 pounds of pressure. Extra flavorings are optional but delicious.

> A few special implements help a lot. A set of canning jar tongs is key for removing the hot jars when done. A canning funnel also helps a lot for filling jars. A bigger pressure cooker is not necessary, but will do more jars at one time.

Ingredients

5-10 lbs. of fresh fruit to start with, more if you like

a bottle of lemon juice

sugar to taste

1 box of pint canning jars

> Bottled lemon juice is fine for canning. Fresh also works, of course, but you won't notice the flavor difference and it's more work if you're juicing lemons, too!

Method

Core and cut the fruit into chunks. Big pieces, halves, quarters, etc., are all fine. As you cut the fruit, drizzle a little lemon juice over it and gently toss. This helps white fruits not to turn brown, and the extra ascorbic acid helps to preserve all fruit.

Place the fruit in a large pot and start it over low heat. It will take a while to heat up and the liquid to come out of the fruit. As it heats, sprinkle about a cup of sugar over it and stir.

Continue stirring the fruit occasionally as it heats so the bottom doesn't stick and burn. As the liquid comes out, you can turn the heat up to medium. Taste and add more sugar as you like. The fruit is done when the whole mixture comes to a simmer. There should be some thick liquid and big chunks of fruit. Feel free to cook longer, but I like the fruit chunks.

While the fruit is heating, wash the jars and lids in hot, soapy, water. Rinse them thoroughly. Place the lids in a bowl of hot water. Fill the jars with hot water and place them on your counter.

Place a half inch of water and the rack the cooker came with in the bottom of the pressure cooker. Start it on simmer to start heating it up.

One at a time, fill the jars, leaving 1/4-inch space on the top. Wipe the edge of the jar with a damp paper towel in case any fruit got on it (it will seal better). Screw the lid on just a little tight. Not super tight! Some air will come out during the canning process, which creates the vacuum in the jar.

My apple and pear doohickey.

Place the jars in the warming pressure cooker. When it's full, put the lid on and turn the heat up to high. Make sure the valve on the pressure cooker is open. Wait until there's a strong jet of steam coming out of the valve, then close it (different cookers have different ways of opening and closing a valve). Bring the pressure up to 5 pounds, then turn the heat down to medium high. Regulate the heat to maintain the pressure at 5 pounds for 15 minutes, then turn the heat off. Wait until the pressure comes down to zero by itself. If your pressure cooker doesn't have a gauge, this will take 10-15 minutes.

Test the valve to make sure it doesn't hiss at you when you start to open it (to confirm the pressure is down). Open the valve, then remove the cover. Use the tongs to remove the jars and set them on your counter to cool. As they cool, the dome lids will suck down with an audible "pop!". This confirms that the jars are sealed.

If any jars don't seal (this rarely happens), take off the lid, make sure the edge is clean and not chipped, then screw on a new, washed lid and reprocess in the pressure cooker.

Once cooled, the jars will keep at room temperature for years. For best flavor, enjoy them within the first year or two.

The really nice pressure cookers have machined aluminum edges which fit precisely together and avoid the need for a rubber gasket. These are really great because the gaskets eventually wear out. I have two (one small for food and one large for canning) which I bought at a local restaurant supply store. They're more expensive than the home models, but they are great tools and I highly recommend them.

Notes

It's good to start with small batches of fruit the first time through while you get the hang of it and so the process doesn't take too long. I do more when my fruit trees are ready and it's time to pick them. Two shopping bags full of fresh plums, for example, take me about six hours to pick and turn into about 3-dozen pints of jam.

Most canning recipes also call for peeling the fruit. This removes a lot of the fruit, the vitamins in the peel and just under it, and a lot of the fiber. I simply wash the fruit and leave the peel on for most fruit, such as pears, plums, peaches, and apricots. Apples I used to peel, then discovered the peel, left on, mostly dissolves and produces a wonderfully thick applesauce! Nothing like a little experimentation.

Stone fruits (plums, apricots, peaches) of course need to be pitted. Apples and pears need to be cored.

Most jam I like to can in 1-pint jars. That seems to be about the right amount for most people. Half-pint jars are pretty, but you spend a lot of time washing, filling, and canning the jars. Apple sauce I'll do in quart jars because I make it in such large quantities. What else would you do with 5 bushels of apples?

Some folks are afraid to use pressure cookers for fear they will "blow up." However, all modern pressure cookers have a safety valve which would release before that happened. Some cooker contents would then spurt all over your stove, but that would be about it. In all the years I've used various pressure cookers, I've never had a safety valve release, despite using them for all sorts of things. They are, for instance, also great for cooking potatoes for mashed potatoes: faster, and you lose less flavor than in boiling water.

PEAR AND MEYER LEMON JAM

Try this for a unique and flavorful combination. Good on toast, ice cream, pancakes, and so on.

The Gist

Pears are cooked with sliced Meyer lemons, a little lemon juice, ground coriander, and sugar to taste and processed according to the basic recipe.

Ingredients

10 lbs. fresh, ripe pears

2-4 Meyer lemons

lemon juice

1 tsp. ground coriander

sugar to taste

1 box pint canning jars

Method

Core and cut up the pears. Toss them with a little lemon juice as you do so, then place them in a big pot and begin cooking them over low heat. Cut the ends off of the lemons, then cut in half lengthwise, then cut into slices about 1/8-inch thick. Discard the seeds. Use 4 lemons if you'd like a more lemony flavor, or 2 lemons for less.

Add to the pears, add the ground coriander and 1 cup of sugar, then give the whole mixture a good tossing.

As the mixture starts to cook down, taste the liquid and add more sugar if you like. You can also add a little more coriander if you'd like the jam a little spicier.

When the mixture reaches a hot simmer, process it according to the basic recipe.

The pears lack either the tree or a partridge. Otherwise, we are ready for Christmas.

Meyer lemons are fruitier and sweeter than the standard Eureka lemons found in most grocery stores. They are perfect for desserts and such. If you can't find them, use half as much Eureka lemon because they are so tart.

Notes

I like just a little coriander with this combination because it gives a subtle undertone of spice without standing out. Cinnamon, nutmeg, or cloves would be different but also good.

PLUM-BLUEBERRY JAM

Adding blueberries pumps up the color and flavor for a very special jam.

The Gist

Plums are pitted and sliced, then combined with blueberries, lemon juice, and sugar to taste, then processed according to the basic recipe.

Ingredients

10 lbs. fresh, ripe plums

2-3 lbs. blueberries, fresh or frozen

lemon juice

sugar to taste

1 box pint canning jars

Method

Slice the plums in half lengthwise around the groove in the fruit to reveal the pit, then remove it. Quarter the plums. Toss them with a little lemon juice as you pit and slice them.

Start the plums heating over low heat. Wash the blueberries if fresh, then add them. Add a cup of sugar to start with.

As the mixture heats and the juice starts to come out, taste the juice and add more sugar if desired. Once the juice starts to come out, you can turn the heat up to medium to accelerate the process.

Bring the mixture to a robust simmer. Pack and process in jars according to the master recipe.

A plum dandy jar of jam.

Ripe plums in season are key because most store-bought plums are rather bland. Any variety, though, will do. I've used Santa Rosa plums and Sugar Plums with great success.

Notes

I usually make this jam without additional spice to accentuate the flavor of the plums and blueberries. If you would like some extra spice, I would try either cinnamon or ground ginger.

If fresh blueberries are available and sweet, they will hold their texture better than frozen. Otherwise, frozen blueberries will work just as well.

EASY APPLESAUCE

For my taste, store-bought applesauce is long on sugar and short on flavor. The homemade variety is great, but a lot of work. This version cuts back on the work and the waste by leaving the peels on. I've found that, for most varieties of apples, the peels almost entirely dissolve during the cooking process, making the applesauce wonderfully thick and tasty—and preserving all the vitamins and minerals typically right under the skin in fruits and vegetables. Plus keeping all the fiber. What's not to like about it?

The Gist

Core and slice apples, toss with lemon juice, then simmer slowly with sugar to taste, vanilla, and cinnamon until thick and saucy. Process in quart jars for 20 minutes at 5 pounds of pressure.

Ingredients

10 lbs. apples

lemon juice

sugar to taste

2 Tbs. vanilla extract

2 tsp. cinnamon

1/2 tsp. allspice

Method

Wash, core, and slice the apples. I have a little doohickey that cores and slices the apples in one step, and works for pears, too. Toss the apple slices with a little lemon juice as you do them.

As you get batches of the apples sliced and tossed with lemon juice, dump then in a large pot and start them on low heat with a little water in the bottom (around a 1/4-inch). As the apples start to fall apart, turn the heat up to medium. Be sure to stir the

A truly saucy sauce.

mixture frequently and scrape the bottom of the pan well so it doesn't burn. Add a little sugar, which seems to help the process along.

As the mixture comes to a simmer, add sugar to taste, the vanilla, and the cinnamon. Give it a final tasting and add more sugar, vanilla, or spices if you like.

Bring the mixture to a hot, robust, simmer, and pack in hot, washed quart jars. Leave about 3/8-inch of space on the top of each jar. Process jars in a pressure cooker at 5 pounds of pressure for 20 minutes.

Variations

Feel free to try different spices to suit your taste. I sometimes do a little cloves or nutmeg instead of the allspice. You could also try ground ginger instead of the cinnamon.

Notes

This recipe produces a wonderfully thick and flavorful applesauce without and thickening agents at all. There will be little, soft, residual pieces of peel left in it. If this really bothers you, do go ahead and peel the apples first. The result will still be worlds better than what you buy in the store, though it will take more apples to make a given amount of sauce.

I usually do applesauce in quart jars because I have so many apples at once when my trees are ready, but there's no reason you couldn't pack it in pint jars instead. You would then only need around 15 minutes of processing time at 5 pounds of pressure.

The vanilla gives the applesauce a rich, buttery flavor, though it's still fat free!

**My Santa Rosa plum tree makes truly delicious plums—great for eatin'!
But what to do with several hundred??**